Global Perspectives Series

The Story of the Church in South Africa

GLOBAL LIBRARY

The Story of the Church in South Africa

Kevin Roy

GLOBAL LIBRARY

© 2017 by Kevin Roy

Published 2017 by Langham Global Library
An imprint of Langham Creative Projects

Langham Partnership
PO Box 296, Carlisle, Cumbria CA3 9WZ, UK
www.langham.org

ISBNs:
978-1-78368-248-5 Print
978-1-78368-250-8 Mobi
978-1-78368-249-2 ePub
978-1-78368-251-5 PDF

First published as *Zion City RSA* in Cape Town 2000 by the South African Baptist Historical Society, assisted by the Department of Church History, University of Pretoria.

Kevin Roy has asserted his right under the Copyright, Designs and Patents Act, 1988 to be identified as the Author of this work.

All rights reserved. No part of this publication may be reproduced, stored in a retrieval system or transmitted, in any form or by any means, electronic, mechanical, photocopying, recording or otherwise, without the prior written permission of the publisher or the Copyright Licensing Agency.

British Library Cataloguing in Publication Data
A catalogue record for this book is available from the British Library

ISBN: 978-1-78368-248-5

Cover & Book Design: projectluz.com

Langham Partnership actively supports theological dialogue and an author's right to publish but does not necessarily endorse the views and opinions set forth, and works referenced within this publication or guarantee its technical and grammatical correctness. Langham Partnership does not accept any responsibility or liability to persons or property as a consequence of the reading, use or interpretation of its published content.

Dr Kevin Roy's history of the South African church is my go-to text every time! For over a decade now, I recommend it in every new member's class and to every one of our pastoral interns. When I lectured at seminary, it was a required text. It's not simply the best, it is the only option! If you want a concise, readable, well-written account, Dr Roy's text is in a league of its own. Here you can feast on an exciting, colourful, informative, and sobering account of how Christ has built his church in southern Africa against all odds – in the face of war, persecution, heresy, division, and discouragements of every kind. Yet the gospel's advance is unstoppable! Kevin has been a dear friend, example, and encourager to me for some fifteen years now, and I am delighted that Langham is giving this book a new lease on life. It has been one of Africa's best-kept secrets for too long.

Rev Tim Cantrell, PhD
Pastor of Antioch Bible Church
President, Shepherds' Seminary,
Johannesburg, South Africa

South Africa is a country of great diversity. The varieties of our natural terrain, local tribes and foreign involvement have all helped to form our unique and multifaceted identity. The church of Jesus Christ in this land has also been stamped with this distinctive plurality. In this book Dr Roy serves us well by telling the story of the church in South Africa in a way that captures something of this complex and diverse history. Its strength is found in the way he firmly situates the church in the political context of its day, and also in the obvious broad and non-sectarian love he has for the body of Christ. It is certainly a candid and surprisingly comprehensive book on the South African church, and one I can heartily recommend.

Paul Hartwig, PhD
Lecturer in Church History and Systematic Theology,
Cape Town Baptist Seminary, South Africa

Kevin Roy has written a clear and accessible account of South Africa's Christian history that is both well informed and judiciously balanced. Constructed around the personal stories of a number of flawed but faithful Christian witnesses, it never fails to inspire.

Rev Alan Spence, PhD
Minister, United Reformed Church, Deal, UK
Former Moderator, Uniting Presbyterian Church of South Africa

Many books have been written on the history of the church in South Africa. But the difficulty is in finding one which is unbiased in its presentation of the facts, one which represents the whole Christian community with a breath of fresh air that dispels the stench of our past partisanship. As a black South African with a strong AIC background, I have not only found Dr Roy's book to be a captivating account of the events, but a very sensitive, refreshing and trustworthy account on what needs to be known concerning the history of the church in our Rainbow Nation.

Sipho J. Mfusi
Missionary to the Zulus and *AmaZioni*

CONTENTS

    Foreword ix
    Preface xi
    List of Abbreviations xv

1   An Overview 1
        The Dutch Period   1
        The British Period   2
        The Modern Period   3

2   The Dutch Period 7
        Van Riebeeck and the Dutch Settlers   8
        The Indigenous People of the Cape   10
        Slaves and the First Minister   12
        Arrival of the French Huguenots   13
        George Schmidt and the Moravians   14
        Lutheran Beginnings   20
        Helperus Ritzema van Lier   21
        Michiel Christiaan Vos   24
        The Re-establishment of the Moravian Mission   25
        Some Closing Reflections on the Dutch Period   28

3   The Start of the British Period 31
        The London Missionary Society (LMS)   33
        Dr Johannes Theodorus van der Kemp   33
        Ntsikana – The Morning Star of the Xhosa Church   38
        John Philip   41
        Churches of British Origin   44
        The Journey So Far   70

4   "Ethiopia Shall Stretch Out Her Hands" 71
        Robert Moffat   71
        David Livingstone   76
        The Great Trek   79
        Daniel Lindley   82
        The Formation of Two New Afrikaans Reformed Churches   85
        Andrew Murray   87
        Revival   92
        Charles Pamla   96

	Doctrinal Conflict in the Dutch Reformed Church	98
	Bishop Colenso	99
	Ethiopianism	102
	Lutherans	108
	Reflections on the British Period	110
5	A South African Pentecost	113
	The Second Anglo-Boer War (1899–1902)	114
	Prisoner-of-War Camp Revivals	116
	Zion and Pentecostal Beginnings	117
	The Apostolic Faith Mission (AFM)	120
	The Full Gospel Church of God	123
	Assemblies of God (AG)	127
	Nicholas Bhengu	128
	Further Pentecostal Movements and Churches	130
	The African Instituted (or Independent) Churches	131
6	The Growing Church Struggle	147
	The Ecumenical Movement	147
	The Rise of Apartheid	149
	The Development of the Christian Council of South Africa (CCSA) and the Growing Rift between Afrikaans and English Churches	150
	The Federal Mission Council (FMC) of the DRC and Its Efforts to Devise a Just Racial Policy	154
	Sharpeville and Cottesloe	160
	Albert Luthuli	164
	Z. K. Matthews	166
	Beyers Naudé	169
	A Non-Political Interlude	174
7	Towards a New South Africa	187
	The Struggle Intensifies	187
	The Newer Charismatic Churches	202
	The Collapse of Apartheid	209
	The New South Africa	214
8	The Last Twenty Years: A Brief Postscript.	217
	The Truth and Reconciliation Commission	220
	Looking Ahead	221
	Bibliography	223
	Index	227

Foreword

South Africa has one of the most colourful, variegated, and bewildering arrays of Christian churches in the world. One of the disadvantages of this complexity is that many Christians live in isolation from one another, and the limited knowledge they have of their fellow believers is often informed more by prejudice than truth.

Anything that can overcome this isolation and help people to be better informed is all to the good. For this reason, the present publication is to be heartily welcomed, providing, as it does, a sympathetic and informative introduction to the story of Christianity in South Africa.

Of course, history can be a slippery thing. Exactly what is told and how it is told depends, largely, on the perspective of the writer. As a Baptist minister and a lecturer at a Baptist Theological College in Cape Town, Dr Kevin Roy writes from within that part of the Christian community sometimes described as conservative and evangelical. His work therefore provides us with a valuable perspective from within that community. Yet his approach is refreshingly free of any sectarian spirit and provides a warm, sympathetic and accurate picture of the whole Christian community, from Calvinistic to Charismatic, from Catholic to *AmaZioni*. Indeed, this book could be described as representing an ecumenical evangelical perspective in the best sense of those words. The reading of this history can only promote the spirit of reconciliation and mutual understanding so vitally necessary in our beloved country. I can heartily commend it to students of theology and all those who wish to enhance their understanding and knowledge of the unique story of the church in South Africa.

Professor J. W. Hofmeyr
Department of Church History
University of Pretoria

Preface

The Lord has established Zion, and in her his afflicted people will find refuge. (Isaiah 14:32)

For much of the twentieth century, South Africa was a symbol of racial conflict and oppression. To write the story of the church in South Africa is to enter into a minefield strewn with conflicting interpretations, powerful emotions and deep prejudices. And who is free of these emotions and prejudices? But an honest awareness of our limitations and inherited prejudices can help us to transcend these in seeking to paint the wider picture. For the last forty-five years – one of the most eventful periods of South Africa's history – the author has been part, albeit a very small part, of the story that follows. This has made the writing of these pages often a deeply emotional and sometimes painful experience. All I can hope is that this has not unduly distorted the account, but has instead given it a measure of authenticity.

Some of the guiding principles in the writing of this book have been as follows:
- I have tried to cover the whole spectrum of Christianity, from Calvinistic to Charismatic, from Roman Catholic to African Independent – all who profess the Christian faith in some way or other. My approach has been sympathetic, but without attempting to conceal the faults and frailties of those involved. If the gospel is indeed the power of God for the salvation of everyone who believes (Rom 1:16), then the bearers of this good news, however weak or imperfect their service, have made a valuable contribution to the spiritual and social welfare of South Africa and all its peoples.
- Wherever possible I have tried to let the characters speak in their own words, so that readers can have a more direct basis on which to make their own evaluations.
- My aim has been to write this history in such a way that readers who are adherents of the various churches and movements described acknowledge the record to be a fair and honest account of who they are and what they believe.

- Where there have been conflicting perspectives on certain persons, events and movements my policy has been to present them all. Readers can make their own judgment.

In writing this book, I have drawn heavily on two books on the history of Christianity in South Africa. Both are multi-author works, the one edited by J. W. Hofmeyr and G. J. Pillay, and the other by R. Elphick and R. Davenport. I can highly recommend them to anyone wanting to read further in South African church history. This book does not attempt to compete with those publications. Nor could it, for the author does not have the scholarly ability or resources of those writers. My intention has rather been to complement those excellent volumes by giving more detailed attention to persons and events only briefly mentioned in them.

As I have worked on this text I have become increasingly aware of its defects, chiefly in the area of omissions and imbalances. One major imbalance is the relatively little space given to the Roman Catholic Church in relation to its size and influence in South Africa. Perhaps its leaders were able to avoid those more peculiar characteristics that ensure inclusion in popular histories! Many other comments and suggestions have been made by those who have read this text: What about the Adventists, KwaSizabantu, the Bible Societies, the development of theological education, church architecture, the role of the church in education, developments in worship and music? Alas, all these and many other important aspects of the story of the church have been neglected. My apologies to those who feel that what has been omitted is more important than some of the things included.

One of the most sensitive and difficult issues I have struggled with in the writing of this book is that of terminology, especially the names of various ethnic/social groups. Certain names that were in common use at one time are today regarded as pejorative and insulting (e.g. Hottentot, Kaffir). These are strictly avoided, except in quotations. But the whole area of identification of groups is problematic. The traditional division of South Africans into "whites, coloureds, blacks and Indians" has no scientific basis and has been frowned upon as apartheid usage. But the existence of distinct groups is a social reality, and in post-apartheid South Africa there is a more relaxed use of these terms, seeing that they no longer form the basis of a legalized system of discrimination. I have used these terms according to current official usage, but I apologize in advance for any discomfort felt by readers concerning my use of terminology. Any suggestions for improvement will gladly be received.

I am deeply indebted to many people for their help in the writing of this book. I must especially mention Dr Frederick Hale, who gave generously of his time to read through the manuscript and made many valuable suggestions concerning grammar, style and content. Without his assistance, the final product would have been a lot worse, and if I had implemented more of his suggestions, the results would have been much better. I must also thank my students at the Baptist Theological College, Cape Town. Their enthusiastic discussions during lectures helped to shape this book. Professor J. W. Hofmeyr of the University of Pretoria was the first to teach me South African church history and inspired my ongoing interest in the subject. I am especially grateful to the Department of Church History at the University of Pretoria for financial assistance with this publication. Finally I thank my longsuffering wife and children for their patience and support during the writing of this book.

God bless you all. *Nkosi sikelel'i Afrika.*

Kevin Roy
January 2000, updated 2016

List of Abbreviations

ABM	American Board (of Commissioners for Foreign) Mission(s)
AEB	Africa Evangelistic Band
AFM	Apostolic Faith Mission
AG	Assemblies of God
AIC	African Instituted (or Independent) Church
AMEC	African Methodist Episcopal Church
ANC	African National Congress
BMS	Berlin Missionary Society
CCCZ	Christian Catholic Church in Zion
CCSA	Christian Council in South Africa
CESA	Church of England in South Africa
CI	Christian Institute
CPSA	Church of the Province of South Africa
DEIC	Dutch East India Company
DRC	Dutch Reformed Church
FMC	Federal Mission Council
FGC	Full Gospel Church
GK	Gereformeerde Kerk
GMC	General Mission Council
GMS	Glasgow Missionary Society
HMS	Hermannsburg Missionary Society
IFCC	International Fellowship of Christian Churches
LMS	London Missionary Society
NGK	Nederduitse Gereformeerde Kerk
NHK	Nederduitsch Hervormde Kerk
NMS	Norwegian Missionary Society
NP	National Party
PAC	Pan Africanist Congress
RMS	Rhenish Missionary Society
SA	South Africa

SADF	South African Defence Force
SACC	South African Council of Churches
SAR	South African Republic
WCC	World Council of Churches
ZAC	Zion Apostolic Church
ZAFM	Zion Apostolic Faith Mission
ZCC	Zion Christian Church

1

An Overview

These days you can buy beautifully produced coffee-table books with titles such as *France from the Air* or *Botswana from the Air*. They consist entirely of satellite images or photographs taken from an aircraft flying over the most interesting parts of the country. We shall begin our story of the beginnings and growth of the Christian community in South Africa with just such an overview, a flyover covering 360 years in a few minutes before we land in Cape Town again and start the journey afresh by ox wagon.

The Dutch Period

Roman Catholic naval explorers and missionaries from Portugal were the first people professing the Christian faith to make contact with South African soil. But no continuing church issued out of these early contacts. Then in 1652 about ninety employees of the Dutch East India Company landed at the Cape of Good Hope with the purpose of establishing a refreshment station where the company's ships could be supplied with fresh food and water on their way to the East. From that time, and from those small beginnings, there has been an unbroken and continually expanding Christian presence in the regions that were to become South Africa.

Not that any church growth records were broken in these early years. Over the next century and a half, the Dutch Reformed Church (the only church permitted in the Cape) increased from one congregation to seven. We shall call this first 150 years the Dutch period, as church and society in the Cape were under the jurisdiction of Dutch authorities. While initial growth was slow, important foundations were laid. The faith spread from the Dutch-speaking community to a few of the indigenous Khoikhoi people, to some of the slaves who had been imported to the Cape, and to most of those of mixed parentage who were to become what is called the coloured community. The family of Reformed churches that have their roots in this early period is the largest of the denominational families in South Africa today, numbering some four and a half million souls, divided between four major bodies and a number of smaller ones.

Towards the latter part of this first period, the Moravian and Lutheran churches laid their first foundations, not without some resistance from the Dutch civil and ecclesiastical authorities.

The British Period

The Dutch period came to an end towards the end of the eighteenth century when the British took control of the Cape during the Napoleonic wars. Over the following century the British extended their control from the Cape to cover the whole area that is now known as South Africa. We shall call this the British period (c. 1800–1910). Significant immigration throughout this period resulted in the planting of virtually all the denominations existing in Britain at that time – Anglicans, Methodists, Roman Catholics, Presbyterians, Congregationalists and Baptists, together with some smaller bodies.

The late eighteenth and early nineteenth century saw a tremendous upsurge of missionary interest in European and American Protestantism. It is not surprising, then, that during the nineteenth century many missionary societies entered South Africa with the aim of gathering converts from the indigenous African peoples. These included the London Missionary Society, the Moravians, the Wesleyan Missionary Society, the American Board of Commissioners for Foreign Missions and various Lutheran and Reformed missionary societies. Missionaries from Britain, America, Germany, France, Switzerland, Norway, Sweden and other parts of the world converged on South Africa to build there the walls of Zion as best they could according to their abilities and insights. Catholic missionaries from many lands also came to South Africa to extend their church. All took advantage of the fairly liberal policy of the British administration governing such activities.

It was during this period that diamonds were discovered in Kimberley and gold in Johannesburg. This stimulated rapid economic growth and large-scale population redistribution. During this period the British colonial authorities fought major wars against the Xhosa peoples in the Eastern Cape, the Zulus in Natal, and the Boers in their northern republics. The triumph of British arms in these conflicts led to the incorporation of all these territories within the Union of South Africa in 1910, a year that marks the birth of the modern state of South Africa within its present borders.

As a result of immigration and missionary work during the nineteenth century, the church saw significant growth, both in numbers and in the complexity of its make up. In addition to the original Dutch Reformed Church (which had been virtually the sole representative of Christianity for more than a century) there were now also Anglicans, Methodists, Congregationalists, Presbyterians, Baptists, Lutherans, Roman Catholics, as well as smaller groups such as Quakers and the Salvation Army. Further divisions, resulted in two Anglican churches, three Dutch Reformed churches and several Lutheran churches, and so on, which complicated the ecclesiastical scene even more. But that was not all. Conflict and tensions between the indigenous African people and the politically and economically dominant white people inevitably affected church relations. The closing decades of the nineteenth century saw groups of African Christians separating from mission-established and controlled churches to form African-initiated churches wholly controlled by Africans. This small trickle was to become a mighty flood in the twentieth century.

The Modern Period

The third and last period in our story consists basically of the twentieth century. In future tellings of this story, the 1994 elections which marked the transition from white minority rule (bringing to a close more than three centuries of white ascendancy) to black majority rule will be an obvious dividing line.

This period was characterized by extraordinary growth and diversification in the church. It was time when four significant factors had a profound impact on the development of modern South African Christianity:

1. The Pentecostal movement and ongoing charismatic movements;
2. The rapid growth of African Instituted Churches;
3. The ecumenical movement that affected most mainline churches;
4. The growing struggle for equal social, political and human rights for all people, which culminated in the victory of the African National Congress led by Nelson Mandela in the 1994 elections.

Of the more than fifty million inhabitants of South Africa, about 70 percent profess adherence to the Christian faith and claim some sort of connection, however tenuous, to particular churches. In addition to the traditional mainline churches, which still represent a very significant proportion of South African Christianity, there is a whole new generation of churches, movements, fellowships, and groupings that had no existence prior to the twentieth century. These include:

1. The classical Pentecostal churches (e.g. Apostolic Faith Mission, Full Gospel Church, Assemblies of God, Pentecostal Protestant Church) which grew out of the Pentecostal movement at the beginning of the century.

2. Thousands of AICs, each separately organized but bearing certain family characteristics and often with impressive names (e.g. The Zion Christian Church, The Christian Catholic Apostolic African Church in Zion of South Africa, The Ethiopian African Church of Zion in South Africa).

3. New Charismatic groupings (e.g. International Fellowship of Christian Churches, Vineyard, His People, New Covenant Fellowship, Christian Ministries Network) which have emerged out of charismatic renewal movements in more recent decades.

A newcomer to the South African Christian scene is likely to be overwhelmed by the confusing array and complex history of thousands of separate and widely different denominations. Yet each church has its own fascinating history and imbedded in each are thousands of little stories – wonderful, sad, heartwarming, tragic, inspiring tales of men and women who have laboured, with sacrifice and devotion, to the best of their insights and abilities, to build the walls of Jerusalem in South Africa. This book will attempt to tell some of these stories.

The development of Christianity in South Africa has not only been characterized by growing complexity but also by changing complexion. In the nineteenth century black people begin to enrol in the churches in significant numbers. In the twentieth century the number of black Christians surpassed the number of white Christians, and today the church as a whole is predominantly black. Yet the stories of black Christians are hardly known. White culture, with its European roots, was more attuned to keeping records, documents, and letters – all of which yield the very stuff from which historians compose their histories. Very little of this kind of source material exists in the case of the thousands of black preachers, prophets, church founders and leaders who played a profoundly significant role in the development of the church. This book will endeavour, as far as possible, not to neglect the stories of black pioneers and builders who rejoiced in the coming of Zion to South Africa.

2

The Dutch Period

In a prominent place in central Cape Town stands a large statue of the Portuguese sailor Bartholomew Diaz, the first European to round the Cape of Good Hope. On his return journey in 1488 he erected a cross at False Island and was thus probably the first Christian to set foot on South African soil. About ten years later his compatriot, Vasco da Gama, also rounded the Cape and went on to discover the sea route to India. It was he who gave the name *Terra do Natal* (in honour of the birth of Christ) to a part of the east coast of southern Africa that he sailed past on Christmas Day. The name endures to this day in the province of KwaZulu-Natal.

By 1505 the Portuguese had erected a fort at Sofala, about 32 kilometres south of Beira, and soon after that Catholic missionaries were active in that area. Outstanding among these was a Jesuit, Gonzalo da Silveira, who was martyred for his faith in 1561. By 1667 there were a number of Roman Catholic communities in the area now known as Zimbabwe. It is possible that these missionary efforts had some influence south of the Limpopo River in the area that was to become South Africa. But the fruits of these early Catholic missionary efforts were fragile and many did not endure, especially in the interior of Africa.

The first enduring community of people professing the Christian faith on South African soil was the group of some ninety employees of the Dutch East India Company (DEIC) who landed at the Cape of Good Hope in 1652. Their purpose was to establish a refreshment station to supply fresh food and water to company ships on their way to Java and Sumatra. Who were these people? What were their beliefs and convictions? What other peoples did they encounter at the southern tip of Africa, and how did they relate to them?

Van Riebeeck and the Dutch Settlers

When Jan van Riebeeck sailed for the Cape of Good Hope, Holland was in the midst of a golden age. The Dutch had won independence from Spanish after a long and bitter conflict called the Eighty Years' War. Part of the motivation for that struggle was the determination of the Dutch to maintain their Reformed faith as outlined in the Belgic Confession of Faith and the Heidelberg Catechism. That faith had been defined even more sharply by the Synod of Dort (1618–1619) at which the challenge of Arminianism was firmly rejected. The young republic that emerged in the seventeenth century seemed to be bursting with energy and originality. In art, science, industry, architecture, navigation and commerce, the Dutch excelled and, in some cases, led the world. Close parallels can be drawn between the sturdy Calvinism of the seventeenth-century Dutch and the faith of the New England Puritans, Scottish Presbyterians and Swiss Protestants. Common to all of these were strong convictions concerning human depravity and inability apart from the grace of God, and the divine predestination of the elect to salvation and glory in Christ according to the sovereign will and power of God. Societies where such convictions held sway were often characterized by a high degree of order, stability and prosperity – along with, in the eyes of critics, inflexibility in certain moral and spiritual matters.

This, then, was the social and religious context of the first Dutch settlers who made their home in the shadow of Table Mountain. Not that the motive for their coming was religious. Nor were they chosen for their religious convictions. Indeed, many of those early soldiers and sailors were crude and dissolute in their habits. Their motives were purely commercial. They were employees of the DEIC, sent solely to establish a refreshment station for the benefit of Dutch ships. Furthermore, the DEIC was anxious that the scope of the settlement at the Cape should not be extended, lest further expense be incurred by the company.

Religion, politics and commerce in the seventeenth century were, however, far more closely intertwined than is the case today. Governments then considered it their duty to both control and support religious activities. The charter of the DEIC required that the spiritual needs of its employees be catered for through the provision of suitable ministers, who were also required to promote the true Christian faith among any non-Christian peoples the company made contact with. Van Riebeeck's awareness of his religious responsibilities is reflected in the prayer he offered up on the occasion of his landing at the Cape:

> O merciful, gracious God and heavenly Father, by whose divine Majesty we have been called to manage the affairs of the United Dutch East India Company here in the Cabo de Boa Esperance [Cape of Good Hope], as we are gathered in your holy name, we ask for guidance to do justice . . . so also that these wild and savage people might be converted to the true Reformed Christian Faith (if possible) to the praise and glory of your holy name and the well-being of our rulers, . . . So we pray to you, most merciful Father, that you will grace our present company with your Fatherly wisdom, and enlighten our hearts so that all evil passions, misunderstandings and such like faults will be kept far from us. Purify our hearts from all base affections that we may be may guided in such a way that our decisions will redound to the praise and glory of your most holy name, so that we might fulfil our necessary duties in the service of our earthly Lords and Masters without any consideration of personal gain or profit. This we pray and ask in the name of your dear Son our Redeemer and Saviour, Jesus Christ, who also taught us to pray – Our Father who art in heaven . . .[1]

Van Riebeeck's determination to take his spiritual responsibilities as governor in the Cape seriously can also be seen in his insistence on attendance at church services and in the penalties prescribed for absenteeism. At the first offence, the offender had to forego six days' wine rations, on the second a month's salary, and for a third offence the punishment was to work for a whole year in chains, without payment.[2] These rather harsh measures, strange to modern ears, reflect the reality of the seventeenth century, in which penalties for the non-observance of required religious practices were the norm. It was precisely during this time that John Bunyan, author of *Pilgrim's Progress*, spent twelve years in Bedford gaol for failing to conform to religious practices required by law in England.

For the first ten years there was no ordained minister of the church in the Cape. The spiritual needs of the settlers were met by the provision of a "sick-

---

1. Hofmeyr, Millard and Froneman, *History of the Church*, 6 [author's translation].
2. Hofmeyr, *Church History: Study Guide*, 12.

comforter," a lay person set aside for full-time ministry but not allowed to administer the sacraments or preach his own sermons. At services he would read an approved published sermon. Complaints were made that the first sick-comforter, William Wylant, was exceeding his authority by sometimes preaching his own sermons. Wylant responded by explaining that because of his poor eyesight he had to learn the sermons by heart so that the service might run smoothly.[3] He undertook in future to follow his instructions. This incident illustrates the fear of heretical preaching and the strict control of religious activities that characterized seventeenth-century government at the Cape.

Needless to say, no services of any other denomination were permitted. From time to time ships carrying Catholic priests would stop at the Cape. They were received respectfully but were forbidden to celebrate Mass on shore. Some of the residents at the Cape were Lutherans, but even they were not permitted to form a church or hold services until late in the eighteenth century.

The Indigenous People of the Cape

When the Dutch arrived in 1652 they encountered a people calling themselves the Khoikhoi. Various Khoikhoi tribes inhabited the whole of the Cape coastline from the Great Fish River in the east to the Orange River in the west. They were a pastoral people who kept sheep and cattle. The Dutch called them "Hottentots," doubtless an allusion to the many click sounds found in the Khoikhoi language. The harsher semi-desert areas of the interior were inhabited by the San, or Bushmen, a hunter-gatherer people closely related to the Khoikhoi.

The Khoikhoi had many contacts with Portuguese, Dutch, English, French, and other seafarers for more than a century before to the Dutch settlement in the Cape. They had traded sheep and cattle in exchange for iron, bronze and other materials. So when van Riebeeck's group landed in the Cape, there was no initial conflict or any seeming cause for concern. Indeed, the DEIC had no designs to make the Cape a launching pad for further European settlement in the interior. Strict instructions were given to van Riebeeck to prevent any such expansion and to maintain good relations with

---

3. Ibid., 13.

the indigenous people. The DEIC had no desire to become involved in the expense and trouble of maintaining a colony.

Very soon, however, van Riebeeck found that he could not obtain adequate supplies of fresh meat by trading with the Khoikhoi. He became convinced that the establishment of European-managed farms was necessary for the success of the company's operations in the Cape. In 1675 the DEIC acceded to van Riebeeck's request to grant land to some of his people, who became known as "free burghers." Once this process was started, there were demands for more and more land, provoking resistance and reaction from the Khoikhoi, who found themselves being displaced from their traditional lands. Major conflict had already broken out in 1659 when a Khoikhoi leader by the name of Doman led an attempt to expel the Dutch. But the Khoikhoi could not prevail against the weapons of the Dutch. As the original refreshment station evolved into a colony, and the trekboers (frontier farmers) penetrated farther into the interior, further wars and conflicts broke out. The Khoikhoi found themselves increasingly reduced to the status of labourers on European farms.

In 1713 a smallpox epidemic hit the Cape when a parcel of dirty linen from a visiting ship was sent ashore for washing. There had been an outbreak of smallpox on the ship, but those infected had recovered. Their linen, however, was still infected. The disease first broke out among the slaves, killing about a third of them. It then spread to the white community, one quarter of whom succumbed to the disease. All traffic and business came to a standstill as panic seized the town. The Khoikhoi were the last to be hit by the disease, with the worst results. Unlike the European and slave immigrants, they were strangers to this disease and had virtually no resistance to it. The effect was devastating; in some places scarcely one in ten survived. In the south-western Cape the Khoikhoi population was decimated. Those who survived lost their old clan names and became known collectively as "Hottentots."

While relations between the Dutch and the Khoikhoi were largely characterized by prejudice, hostility and suspicion, there were also instances of more positive interaction. Some of the early sick-comforters laboured to impart the Christian faith to certain Khoikhoi people. In 1662 a Khoikhoi woman, Eva, was baptized. She later married the assistant surgeon of the settlement. The first school in the Cape, established in 1663, included four slaves and a Khoikhoi child among its predominantly Dutch pupils.[4] All

---

4. Hinchliff, *Church in South Africa*, 5.

baptized believers, whether slaves, Khoikhoi or Dutch, initially worshipped together in the same church.

But despite these positive points, the interaction between Dutch and the Khoikhoi was largely a tragic tale of hostility, suspicion, prejudice and oppression. From the Dutch side, the "Hottentots" were good-for-nothing, lazy, dirty, thieving vagabonds and savages. From the Khoikhoi side, the Dutch were oppressive, cruel, and ruthless land-grabbers. What impact, if any, did the Christian message have on this sad situation? It is surely true that if all who professed the Christian faith were truly governed by the Spirit of Christ, things would have been very different. Yet the history of all "Christian" societies has shown that while the heroic faith and love of individuals has had a great and wide influence for good, society as a whole, even "Christian society," is more often governed by greed, selfishness and prejudice. Our story will abound with these contrasting elements, the tragedy of sin abounding, the triumph of grace over sin. For the cynic, the story consists only of hypocrisy, cant and humbug. For the believer, it is a story of light shining in darkness, the spirit struggling against the flesh, grace in the midst of sin and evil.

Slaves and the First Minister

Slaves began to be imported in 1658 to relieve the labour shortage at the Cape. This introduced a third element into the population, and by 1807, when the importation of slaves was forbidden, there were about 29,000 slaves in the Cape, compared to 26,000 whites and about 18,000 Khoikhoi. It was from these three groups that the present "coloured" community in the Cape emerged.

The slaves were imported from many parts of South and Southeastern Asia (especially India and Indonesia), as well as from Madagascar and elsewhere in Africa. Some of the Christian masters of these slaves[5] wished to impart the Christian faith to them and have their children baptized as Christians. Only a minister could baptize, which brings us to the arrival in August 1665 of the first ordained minister, Johan van Arckel. One of the first questions he had to face was the legitimacy of baptizing the children of slaves. The great Synod of Dort had discussed this question and directed that the infants of slaves should

---

5. It must be remembered that slavery was a normal part of society in the seventeenth century. Many Christians owned slaves – just like the Christian Philemon to whom Paul wrote a letter some 2000 years ago.

not be baptized, even if they had been adopted into Christian families. They were to wait until they were of an age to be instructed in the elements of the Christian faith. Notwithstanding the decision of Dort, however, a different practice had developed in the Dutch possessions overseas with the approval of church and state authorities, namely, that infant slaves born to heathen parents might receive baptism if their masters pledged to bring them up in the true faith. Following this latter directive, van Arckel baptized a number of slave infants. Van Arckel only remained in the Cape for five months, and in 1666 his successor, Philippus Baldeus, caused a stir when he refused to baptize the infant of a slave. His decision was overruled by both the secular and church authorities in the Cape who affirmed that slave children could receive baptism on the good faith of the children's master or mistress.

The close control of church affairs meant that the secular authorities were obliged to occupy themselves with many theological and ecclesiastical issues and questions. Could Lutherans receive Holy Communion in the Reformed Church? (Yes, provided they could give an adequate confession of faith.) Could the infants of Roman Catholics be baptized in the church? (Yes, provided persons of the Reformed faith could be found to sponsor them.) Could Lutherans and Roman Catholics have their own services and ministers? (Definitely not.) Could slave children whose parents had been baptized by the Portuguese receive baptism? (Yes, if sponsored by a company official.)

Still more questions arose with the arrival in the Cape of a group of French Huguenots.

Arrival of the French Huguenots

Like many other countries in sixteenth-century Europe, France had been troubled by a series of religious wars between Catholics and Protestants. These conflicts came to an end with the Edict of Nantes (1598) which granted some measure of freedom to the Huguenots, as French Protestants were called. Nearly a century later this edict was revoked by the "Sun King," Louis XIV, as part of a programme to exalt the absolute power of the monarchy within a strong and unified state. Protestantism became illegal. Hundreds of thousands of Huguenots left in a mass exodus.

The Directors of the DEIC invited some of these to settle in the Cape, and so it was that between 1688 and 1700 some 150 French-speaking Huguenots came to the Cape, settling in the area of Drakenstein (now Paarl), Franschoek and Stellenbosch. The Cape wines enjoyed around the world today owe their origin in part to the skill and industry of the early Huguenot settlers.

Although the Reformed faith of the Huguenots was essentially the same as that of the Dutch, the authorities were concerned that linguistic differences would lead to a division in the community. They thus adopted a policy of restricting the use of French so that the Huguenots would be assimilated into the Dutch-speaking community as soon as possible. Schoolmasters teaching the French children had to be fluent in Dutch so that the children could learn it. The second minister of the Huguenots, arriving in 1702, was required to preach only in Dutch, and a request that he be allowed to preach in French once a fortnight for the sake of those not able to follow a Dutch sermon was refused. Occasional services in French were, however, held up to 1726, by which time the French community had been absorbed into the Dutch-speaking community and the use of French had died out. The descendants of the Huguenots can be found today in the thousands of South African families bearing French surnames.

The impact of the Huguenots on the religious life of the Cape Colony was considerable. Unlike the Dutch settlers whose motive for coming to the Cape was primarily commercial, the Huguenots left their native land and came to the Cape so that they might maintain their faith.

George Schmidt and the Moravians

Despite the sincere efforts made by some of the sick-comforters and ministers to impart the Christian faith to the indigenous Khoikhoi people of the Cape, little success was achieved. A letter written to the Classis (Presbytery) of Amsterdam in 1678 mentioned that only one Hottentot had been received into church membership (a reference to Eva). A few reasons can be suggested for those meagre results:

1. The few sick-comforters and ministers were hard pressed to meet the spiritual needs of the colonists. Opportunities to reach out to the Khoikhoi were limited.

2. Protestant enthusiasm for missions to non-Christian peoples was at a low ebb during the seventeenth and eighteenth centuries. Only towards the end of the eighteenth century did the Protestant churches in general awaken to their responsibility to extend the gospel throughout the world.

3. Levels of spiritual life in the Cape were probably not high during this period, and the attitudes of the colonists to the indigenous people were marked by prejudice.

One exception to the general lack of Protestant interest in missions in the eighteenth century was a small community in Germany known as the Herrnhuters, or Moravians. Their roots can be traced back to the great proto-Reformer of Prague, Jan Hus, who suffered martyrdom in the fifteenth century. One of the fruits of his testimony was a group of devout Christians known as the Bohemian Brethren or *Unitas Fratrum*. They were scattered during the Thirty Years' War, that terrible religious war that wrought such devastation in Germany and surrounding countries in the seventeenth century.

Remnants of the group were invited by Count Zinzendorf to settle on his estates in Saxony in 1722. There the *Unitas Fratrum* was reborn and Herrnhut, the village where they lived, became a community of deeply spiritual Christians imbued with an extraordinary vision to spread the gospel throughout the world. From that tiny community, missionaries were sent to the Virgin Islands, Greenland, North America, South Africa, Australia and Tibet. The proportion of missionaries to home communicants has been estimated as 1:60 compared with 1:5000 in the rest of Protestantism. Moravian influence was a major factor in the evangelical awakening in England, for John Wesley owed his conversion largely to the influence of the Moravian Peter Boehler.

The Moravians of Herrnhut were part of the wider movement of pietism, which exercised a profound influence on the Lutheran and Reformed churches in the eighteenth century. The origin of pietism is generally traced to a German Lutheran pastor, Philip Spener, and in particular to the publication of his book *Pia Desideria* (1675) in which he urged the importance of Bible study, prayer, personal experience of Christ and the new birth through faith in him, good works and mission. A disciple of Spener, Hermann August Francke, became a professor and pastor at the newly established University of Halle. So great was Francke's influence that Halle became a major centre of pietism in Europe.

Zinzendorf, a godson of Francke, attended the boarding school there, embracing with enthusiasm the ideals of personal commitment to Christ as Saviour and zeal for missions. When Zinzendorf later invited religious refugees to settle on his estate in Saxony, the Moravian Brethren at Herrnhut, under his leadership, became the second major centre of pietism after Halle.

When the king of Denmark, Frederik IV, desired to procure missionaries for his colonial possessions in India, it was to Francke that he turned for help, resulting in the establishment of the Danish-Halle mission. Its pioneering missionaries, Ziegenbalg and Plütschau, were students from Halle. On their way to India, they stopped over at the Cape of Good Hope and took note of the spiritual need of the Khoikhoi people there. Zinzendorf met Ziegenbalg and Plütschau at Halle and may well have heard of them speak of the needs of the Khoikhoi. It was to him that two members of the Reformed Church in Amsterdam appealed, asking him to send one of the brethren to the Cape for the sole purpose of reaching out to the Khoikhoi with the gospel. The man chosen for this task was George Schmidt.

Born in Moravia in 1709, Schmidt joined the community at Herrnhut in 1725. He travelled to Austria to minister to persecuted Protestants, but was imprisoned there, together with a companion who died as a result of the ill-treatment he suffered. Schmidt was released at the end of six years after being forced to sign a revocation of his faith. After doing some further work in Roman Catholic parts of Europe, Schmidt was chosen to go to South Africa. The fact that he was sent alone was partly so that he could atone for his lapse in Austria.

Before going, Schmidt was examined in the faith by a commission of Reformed ministers in Amsterdam, who gave him their approval. So it was with the approval and recommendation of the church and DEIC authorities in Amsterdam that Schmidt came to the Cape. The local clergy, however, were less than enthusiastic about this arrival from a community regarded by many of them as a strange sect that probably held to unorthodox doctrines. In an interview with some of the ministers at the Cape, he was asked if he intended to administer baptism to the Hottentots, to which he replied that he had not come to baptize but to preach the gospel.

On 27 November 1737 Schmidt wrote a very respectful letter to the Council of Seventeen (as the governing body of the DEIC was known):

> Your most honourable and noble Lords!
>
> As the Lord has hitherto helped me and protected me under the wings of his majesty, I take the freedom to write briefly to my Lords to express my deep gratitude for the gracious help I have received from my Lords. May the Lord crown your work with mercy.
>
> I arrived at the Cape on July 9 and waited until September 4, when I obtained an opportunity to go into the interior. I travelled to the Sonderend River. There, with God's help, I built a hut, and began cultivating some vegetables for food.

On October 27 I made a beginning with the Hottentots, to teach them to read. I am teaching 4 men, 2 women, and 4 children, who come daily, sometimes twice daily. On Sundays I teach them about the Saviour. So far has the Lord helped me. To him be praise and honour. Amen.

May your favour remain with me, most noble and honourable Lords as I live in humble respect under the banner of the Crucified.[6]

Shortly after this, on 23 December 1737, Schmidt wrote a much longer letter to Zinzendorf, recounting in detail events of his journey to the Cape and after his arrival. This letter contained some of Schmidt's more frank observations on life and conditions in the Cape. His opinion of the sailors, the employees of the DEIC and even the clergy was not high:

Dearly beloved and honourable Sir,

You know what a terrible condition the whole world is in. So also I found it on the ship. In the beginning there were many trials. All that I could hear or see was vanity, foul speech, drunkenness, godlessness . . . although the captain was a good man . . . Humbly and gently I spoke to them and asked if they did not regard such things as sin, and if they didn't know what was written in the Bible about how a true Christian must believe and that the name Christian is not enough without a testimony – . . . I spoke often to the captain . . . who agreed with everything . . . concerning the Hottentots he could not believe I would have much success with them, and if I did, it would surely be a sign that the end of the world is near.

. . . I spoke with a Swiss soldier, showing him the way of salvation . . . Becoming convinced . . . he began praying in secret asking the Saviour to open his eyes . . . I spoke to the dominie [clergyman] who gambled and so on with the officers, asking him if his conscience didn't bother him. . . .

[Schmidt was able to persuade four of the ship's company who began meeting together for religious exercises. Further on in his letter he gives a fascinating description of the Cape and the interior, and the six weeks he spent with the captain of the ship]

---

6. Hofmeyr, Millard and Froneman, *History of the Church*, 39 [author's translation].

... I wanted to work, but obtained no employment as everything is done by slaves here. They are badly treated by many nominal Christians. Godlessness is great in the land. A demon of drink dominates, and most people are given to drunkenness. I also visited the ministers – blind leaders whose god is their belly. They believe in the conversion of the Hottentots even less than the devil does. If *he* didn't believe in it he would not have troubled me so. But the Lord is with me, and what can the poor spirit do more than what the Lord permits. Many mock me, but I care not. They don't know what they are doing. If I can only accomplish the purpose of my precious Saviour, I will be satisfied. I love not my life. ...

On September 12 we came to the Sonderend River. ... On the 13th we visited the Hottentots. Among all the Hottentots in the surrounding area, there is only one who has a house. The others dwell in straw or reed shelters, and move from place to place, wherever they find grazing for their sheep and cattle. Some own about 500 cattle, others have less. They must also supply the Company with young beasts, in return for some tobacco and drink. Their food is milk, meat and certain roots. They wear a sheepskin, with something over their private parts. Otherwise they are naked. They can also make shoes. The one who owns a house has also a wife and children ... his name is Africo ...

[Schmidt then describes how he built a house, and began cultivating the ground]

... November 1, in the evening Africo, with whom I first began, asked me if those who wanted to learn from me must abandon the superstitions of the Hottentots. Certainly, I replied, it was surely clear that they could not believe such deceptions, but must turn away from them. Yes, he said, it is false, and I began to speak to him of the first man Adam, his temptation and fall, and of Jesus, the promised Saviour, who purchased salvation for all people. ... Now I am teaching 4 men, 2 women, and 4 children. They come everyday to learn, sometimes twice daily. The first already know their letters. They are not always together, but they come again. Before and after the lesson I pray with them. On Sundays I read to them something about the Saviour, and explain the meaning to them.

December 15. An infant of Africo died, and he came to me and asked how he must bury it. He now wants my advice in everything, caring not for the ceremonies of the Hottentots. I went with him and helped him to dig a grave. We buried the child without ceremony.[7]

A few years after sending this report, Schmidt gathered a group of Khoikhoi together at Baviaanskloof (Baboon Ravine, later renamed Genadendal). He felt that those in this group were ready for baptism. After consulting with Zinzendorf about the matter, he received the following act of ordination by mail:

To brother George Schmidt

My Brother!

Why don't you baptize the Hottentot children who die in infancy? He who came with water and blood also died for them. I ordain you as a minister of our church, to administer baptism and the Lord's Supper, in the name of the Father and of the Son and of the Holy Spirit. Amen. (As an apostle of the Lamb you are anyway my superior in this life.) Again, dear brother, I rejoice over you, and since your last report, I have no anxiety concerning you. You are so happy, living in such peace and quiet with all your neighbours. May the Lord Jesus give you souls. In the meantime, ask the Lamb for helpers. We will do whatever we can for you. I am very happy with you. But you concentrate too much on the outward and too little on the inward of the Hottentots. What do pray with them? Pour out your heart before the Lamb. . . . tell the Hottentots, and their children, the story of the Son of God. If they feel something, pray with them, if nothing, pray for them. If their convictions increase, baptize them, there where you shot a hippo. May the Lamb be with you forever. I am also going away, the carriage leaves immediately for Briel.

Rotterdam, 27 August 1741

Your Z[8]

---

7. Ibid., 29–34 [author's translation].
8. Ibid., 35 [author's translation].

The "peace and quiet with all your neighbours" referred to by Zinzendorf was about to be rudely disturbed. When Schmidt proceeded to baptize five of his followers, the news was greeted with displeasure by the Reformed clergy in Cape Town who felt that Schmidt was not a properly ordained minister and that the baptisms were therefore most irregular. They requested that Schmidt be recalled and replaced by two sick-comforters to continue the work among the Khoikhoi.

It must be remembered, when we consider the reaction of the three Reformed clergymen, that this was the early eighteenth century when all religious activities were carefully controlled by the state and the legally established church and any deviations from proscribed procedures were viewed with horror. Still, it is to be regretted that the narrow spirit of the clergy resulted in the evangelization of the Khoikhoi being put back nearly fifty years.

Schmidt, deeply disappointed at the response of the authorities in the Cape, decided to go to the Netherlands in 1744 with a view to obtaining wider powers to pursue his work. He never returned. Ironically, the decision of the Amsterdam Classis, in responding to the three Cape clergy, was that it was not necessary for Schmidt to be recalled.

While these events (or rather, non-events) were unfolding in the Cape, the Protestant churches in Britain and North America were being deeply stirred by powerful movements of spiritual renewal associated with the likes of John Wesley and George Whitefield in England and Jonathan Edwards in America. The Moravians were deeply involved in these evangelical awakenings. However, this spirit does not seem to have reached the Cape before the arrival in 1786 of the young Dutch minister Helperus Ritzema van Lier. But before taking up his story, let us consider the fortunes and travails of the Lutherans at the Cape.

Lutheran Beginnings

The early Dutch settlers at the Cape included some German Lutherans. They were permitted by a special arrangement to receive communion in the Reformed church – on condition that they held a correct doctrine of justification. A number of them, however, wished to have their own services and their own Lutheran minister. In 1742 a petition to this end was drawn up. This was the first shot in a struggle lasting nearly forty years and waged in a succession of petitions, letters, and memoranda crossing the oceans between the Cape, Amsterdam and Batavia (today's Jakarta in Java). The repeated efforts of the Lutherans to obtain their own church were consistently blocked by representatives of the Reformed church who, while professing no animosity against the Lutherans, argued that the multiplication of churches in the Cape would only lead to confusion, complications and friction. In all these actions, as with the Moravians and the Huguenots, we see the Cape colonists striving to maintain the ideal of a united community, speaking one language and professing one religion. They could little have dreamt just how complex and varied the Christian community of South Africa would later become in language, culture, and confessional tradition.

The efforts of the Lutherans eventually paid off. In 1774 a Lutheran businessman, Martin Melck, erected a remarkably church-like "warehouse" in Cape Town, and in 1778 permission finally came from Amsterdam for the Lutherans to have their own church. They lost no time in calling a minister, Andreas Kolver, who arrived at the Cape in 1780.

It was not long before the friction and complications predicted by the Reformed church did indeed arise. Regulations governing church relations stipulated that in cases where parents belonged to different churches, boys were to be baptized in the father's church and girls in the mother's. All the children could be baptized in the Reformed church if the parents so wished. Kolver was not prepared to adhere to these regulations, and soon complaints were being heard that he was baptizing girls whose mothers were Reformed. The authorities ordered Kolver to conform to the regulations, but strife over the baptism of children continued. When the Council of Seventeen (the governing body in Amsterdam responsible for the Cape) decided in 1786 that all children on reaching the age of eighteen could join the church of their choice, irrespective of which church they had been baptized in, the Reformed felt sorely aggrieved. The Lutherans had an unfair advantage, they argued, in that children would be more inclined to learn Luther's Small Catechism than the lengthier Heidelberg Catechism of the Reformed. These conflicts persisted until the first British occupation, when the Lutherans concluded that they were no longer subject to laws made by the previous government.

Helperus Ritzema van Lier

It would be an injustice to the early history of the church in the Cape to omit the story of one its brightest morning stars, Helperus Ritzema van Lier. He can truly be described as the Jonathan Edwards of the early Cape Colony.

Born in Holland in 1764, van Lier gave evidence of extraordinary intellectual powers at an early age. As a young boy, he could repeat verbatim long speeches or sermons to which he had listened.[9] By the time he left school at the age of fifteen, he had mastered French, Latin and Greek. Following the wishes of his parents, he took up the study of theology, completing his Master's and Doctor's degrees before he turned eighteen. Yet all the time, by his own confession, his soul was in darkness, in bondage to lust, pride, unbelief and self-righteousness. It was a series of calamities, particularly the death of a young lady with whom he was in love, that brought van Lier to his knees and to a personal experience of the grace of God in the gospel of Christ. It was about this time that he first made acquaintance, through correspondence, with the great English evangelical leader, John Newton. An intimate friendship developed between the two men. As Newton knew no Dutch and van Lier no English, they corresponded in Latin! A series of letters written in 1789 by van Lier to Newton were translated by the renowned poet and hymn writer, William Cowper, also a close friend of Newton, and published under the title, *The Power of Grace Illustrated. In Six Letters from a Minister of the Reformed Church to John Newton.*[10]

An invitation to the Cape brought van Lier to southern Africa. In 1786 he was inducted as a minister of the Cape Town Dutch Reformed congregation, his first sermon being preached from the text "For I resolved to know nothing while I was with you except Jesus Christ and him crucified" (1 Cor 2:2).

The spiritual condition of the slaves and the Khoikhoi became a source of great concern to van Lier. He laboured to arouse among the Christians a sense of responsibility to reach out to these people with the gospel. In a sermon preached in 1789, for example, he urged the following:

> Of set purpose does Jesus use the expression *to all creatures* – in order to teach us that the Gospel must be brought to everyone who can bear the name of man – to the most ungodly heathen and the most barbaric nations, to the simplest and the most ignorant. No exception may be made. Jesus has anticipated all excuses. His Gospel must be proclaimed to every human being, however savage, ignorant, degraded or sinful he be. No one can be too ignorant or too sinful for the Gospel to be offered to him; no one is so virtuous as not to need the Gospel. No man,

---

9. Du Plessis, *History of Christian Missions*, 61.
10. Gerdener, *Bouers van Weleer*, 7.

whatever profession of virtue or innocence he may make, can do without the Gospel; to no man, however guilty and depraved he be, may the Gospel be refused.[11]

The work of van Lier was deeply influential in awakening among the Christians of the Cape Colony a new spirit of concern for the slaves and the Khoikhoi, thus preparing the way for the revival of the Moravian mission as well as the arrival of the other missionaries in the closing decade of the eighteenth century.

While engaged in his pastoral labours in the Cape, van Lier found time to write on both religious and scientific themes. The Hague Society for the Defence of Christianity awarded him a gold medal in 1790 for his work on the importance of religion for the common man. He was also awarded a gold medal by the Academy of Siena for a scientific treatise on the various kinds of air.

But the extension of the gospel to those who knew not Christ was the cause closest to van Lier's heart. When the Dutch Reformed Synods in Holland requested the DEIC to establish a society or seminary for the propagation of the gospel in its Indian and African possessions, he wrote to his uncle, a professor of theology in Rotterdam, as follows:

> I feel myself impressed to write to you again concerning the proposed Society and Seminary for the Propagation of the Christian Religion among Heathen and Mohammedans. I am in great hopes that this Society will eventually be established. The great importance of the glory of God, of the extension of the Kingdom of Jesus, and of the salvation of so many thousands, who now are still afar off and aliens from the commonwealth of Israel, but who may be brought nigh by the blood and the Spirit of our Saviour, must impart to you new courage and strength, and must make endurable the many cares and disappointments which are inseparable from an enterprise such as this.
>
> So soon as you have decided to inaugurate this new Society, I should rejoice to be your correspondent in these parts, and shall attempt to raise a considerable sum and forward it to the Society.[12]

---

11. Du Plessis, *History of Christian Missions*, 63.
12. Ibid., 63.

But van Lier did not live to see the realization of this scheme. Within three years of writing the above letter, he died, surrounded by his wife, four children, his sister and two ministerial colleagues. He was only twenty-eight.

Michiel Christiaan Vos

Van Lier's early death was a great loss to the church at the Cape. But his spirit of concern for the slaves and the Khoikhoi people lived on, and was indeed extended and increased by the labours of Michiel Christiaan Vos, whose ministry in the Cape began in 1794, the year after van Lier died.

Born in the Cape in 1759, Vos was a sickly child, often close to death. Spiritual life in the Cape churches was then at a low level, according to Vos's later testimony. After a time of spiritual searching and struggle in prayer, the light of the gospel began to shine in his heart, bringing him peace and assurance. He was then about seventeen years old. Immediately he developed a deep concern for the welfare of the slaves. "The more I thought on the condition of the slaves, the stronger grew my desire to become a minister in this land," he recalled.[13]

But there were grave financial obstacles in the way of his studying theology in Holland, without which he could not become a minister. His doctor also warned him that such a journey would result in him finding his grave halfway to Europe, to which he replied, "Even if some little place halfway to Europe is destined to become my grave, still all your arguments will not deter me from proceeding thereto."[14]

When Vos completed his studies in Holland, there was no post available in the Cape, so he remained nine more years in Holland where he served three churches with great acceptance and blessing. At last, in 1794 Vos was able to return to the Cape as minister of the church at Roodezand (now Tulbagh). In his inaugural sermon, which he preached from Mark 16:15 ("Go into all the world and preach the good news to all creation"), he announced his intention to preach to the slaves and the Khoikhoi also and urged his hearers to cooperate by bringing their slaves and employees to special classes he would be holding for their instruction. There was inevitably some opposition to these new measures, but his persuasive sincerity was able to overcome the prejudices and doubts of many. Soon a simple catechism that Vos had

---

13. Ibid., 67.
14. Gerdener, *Bouers van Weleer*, 13.

prepared for the instruction of slaves and Khoikhoi was in circulation among the farmers. His parish was so extensive that some of his flock lived up to ten days' journey from the church. Yet Vos devised a plan enabling him to visit all of them every two years. He not only wholeheartedly supported the Moravian missionaries who came in 1792 to revive Schmidt's work among the Khoikhoi in Baviaanskloof, but also wrote a letter to Holland asking for help in missionary work, which played a role in the arrival of four missionaries sent by the London Missionary Society (LMS) to the Cape in 1799.

After nine years of ministry in Tulbagh, Vos left for Europe, largely at the insistence of his wife who was not happy with her lot in the Cape. While in London, Vos was invited to go to Ceylon. Initially declining this call on the grounds of his wife's health, he eventually felt compelled by the need of the Protestants in Ceylon to respond affirmatively. Vos planned to go alone, his wife remaining in Europe, but when her health improved, she decided to accompany him. She died a month after their arrival.

Vos was to spend five years in Ceylon, returning to the Cape in 1809. During the last seven years of his ministry he served the church at Caledon. He was sometimes so weak that he had to be carried to the church, where he would preach while sitting in a chair in front of the pulpit. Vos was a late example of the spirit of pietism, with its emphasis on spiritual experience, holy living, good works and mission. Wherever he preached, in Holland, South Africa, England or Ceylon, his labours bore abundant fruit. Certainly in the Cape, following on the work of van Lier, he played an important role in stimulating a greater concern for the spiritual welfare of the unevangelized indigenous people and the slaves, thus preparing the way for the Moravian and LMS missionaries who arrived in the closing decade of the eighteenth century. Describing the work being done in Vos's parish of Roodezand, Jan van der Kemp wrote to Thomas Haweis, a founder of the LMS, "a thousand heathen were receiving instruction in the Christian religion, and among them there were many who appeared to have experienced in their lives the power of truth."[15]

The Re-establishment of the Moravian Mission

Despite the departure of George Schmidt from the Cape in 1744, the Moravians in Herrnhut never forgot about the Khoikhoi in the Cape. From time to time

---

15. Du Plessis, *History of Christian Missions*, 69.

they tried to revive the work there, but without any success until the time of van Lier and the change of attitude towards missions brought about by his ministry. When a Moravian bishop, Johann Reichel, called at the Cape in 1787 on his way back to Europe from Tranquebar, he was warmly received by van Lier and others of like spirit. Sensing the change of feeling in the Cape, Reichel counselled the Moravian Brethren to renew their application to re-establish their work in the Cape. This time they were successful, and in 1792 three Moravian missionaries – Marsveld, Schwinn and Kühnel – landed in the Cape.

The Moravian Brethren in Herrnhut were not the only ones who had not forgotten. Among the Khoikhoi converts of Schmidt, there were also those who remembered his promise to send other brethren. While waiting for them to arrive, they stayed in the vicinity, reading their New Testaments and teaching their children to read and pray.[16] The memory of George Schmidt and his teaching, however vaguely or imperfectly remembered, was still alive in a group of Khoikhoi, and these were the first to respond to the renewed labours of the Moravians in 1792.

On returning to the scenes of Schmidt's former labours, the missionaries were delighted to find a pear tree he had planted many years before. Even greater was their joy at finding an eighty-year-old woman, Lena, who turned out to be one of Schmidt's original converts, baptized nearly fifty years earlier.[17] Old Lena then produced a copy of the Dutch New Testament which Schmidt had given her. Her eyes were too weak to read it, and she gave it to a younger woman who read the story of the wise men from the East aloud with considerable fluency.[18]

News of the arrival of the Brethren spread quickly, attracting considerable numbers of Khoikhoi to Baviaanskloof. In 1793 one hundred adults attended the special Christmas meetings. Eight months later, two hundred were gathering for regular services of singing. Through the diligence and devotion of the three missionaries, Baviaanskloof was soon to develop into a Christian community that was widely admired and served as a model for many other missionary enterprises in southern Africa. In recognition of the evident blessing on the work of the Moravians, the name Baviaanskloof (Baboon

---

16. Krüger, *Pear Tree Blossoms*, 56.
17. Du Plessis, *History of Christian Missions*, 72.
18. Krüger, *Pear Tree Blossoms*, 52.

Ravine) was changed to Genadendal (Valley of Grace) by the governor of the Cape in 1806.

But it must not be imagined that everything was plain sailing. Accounts of the work at Baviaanskloof/Genadendal are replete with many instances of conflict, suspicions and accusations between the missionaries, the Khoikhoi converts, the local farmers, the governing authorities and the Reformed clergy. Many writers on the subject assume a strongly apologetic tone, defending or accusing this group, that church, or that community.

In retrospect, conflict and suspicions were inevitable. There were too many parties with deeply conflicting interests and with too little understanding of one another. In the eyes of the Khoikhoi, the farmers were often brutal oppressors, whose only interest in the Khoikhoi was as units of labour on their land, which had been stolen from their forefathers. In the eyes of the farmers, the Khoikhoi lacked initiative to develop or improve themselves by labour and industry and were only interested in stealing the hard-won fruits of the farmers' labour. As for the missionaries, the farmers viewed them as naive and prejudiced, ready to believe any false accusation against the farmers and providing havens of indolence for the idle, thieves and malcontents. In the clash between these conflicting communities, it was the Khoikhoi, powerless against the superior weapons of the farmers, who suffered the most.

Even between the Dutch Reformed clergy and the missionaries, little understanding and much prejudice existed. The Moravians were quick to judge the Dutch Reformed clergy as blind leaders without the Spirit. The Reformed clergy, for their part, often regarded the Moravians as an unhealthy sectarian movement, teaching false doctrine and given to emotional subjectivism.

The trouble with all the above perceptions and accusations is that there was just enough truth in them to sustain and justify the prejudices of the various parties. This has always been the tragedy of South Africa, a tragedy that has unfolded over the centuries as so many different tribes, races, religions and denominations with conflicting interests and perceptions have clashed with one another in a common arena. And yet this very same arena has witnessed wonderful triumphs of sacrificial love, faithful service, and costly reconciliation. Tragedy and triumph are interwoven in the story of South Africa's Zion and in the stories of the saints and sinners who laboured to build her.

Some Closing Reflections on the Dutch Period

We have already covered a century and a half of Christian presence in the Cape, nearly half the total period of South Africa's Christian history. In terms of church growth, it was a slow start. By 1800 there were only seven Dutch Reformed congregations, while the Lutherans and Moravians had one congregation each. Despite these small beginnings, however, deep roots were being put down. These few churches were to grow to thousands of congregations with millions of members by the end of the twentieth century.

Socially and culturally, profound changes had taken place. There is no knowing what the Khoikhoi population of the Cape was in the mid-seventeenth century, but their numbers had declined significantly by 1800, largely as a result of the ravages of smallpox among a people whose resistance to that disease was far lower than that of the European and slave immigrants. As was mentioned earlier, in 1806 the inhabitants of the Cape Colony numbered approximately 26,000 whites, 29,000 slaves, and 18,000 Khoikhoi.

Out of the social interaction between Dutch, Khoikhoi and slaves, two new entities emerged: a new language, Afrikaans, and a new people group, the coloureds. Afrikaans is a simplified form of Dutch, originally regarded somewhat disparagingly as "kitchen Dutch" – the language of communication between domestic servants, farm labourers or slaves and their employers or owners. The assimilation of the French-speaking Huguenots into the Dutch-speaking community also had an influence on the kind of Dutch spoken in the Cape. In time, this local dialect became the spoken language of virtually all "Dutch" speakers, white and coloured, although "high" Dutch remained the official language of the church, the law courts, government and learning.

One would have thought that this new language of Afrikaans would have bound its speakers together. But social pressures, cultural differences, and racial prejudices were to divide Afrikaans speakers into two main groups: the white Afrikaners and the brown coloureds. The division between these two groups was to be firmly maintained for another two centuries. Only after the collapse of apartheid, towards the end of the twentieth century, did the rigid barriers between white and brown Afrikaans speakers begin to crumble.

The roots of the coloured people are in all three communities of the early Cape Colony – the whites, the slaves, and the Khoikhoi. The slaves, in turn, came from widely diverse parts of the world, but chiefly from the East (Indonesia and Malaysia) and from Africa. This makes the so-called coloured people of the Cape a group with some of the most varied and divergent roots of any people in the world, drawn as they are from Europe, Asia and Africa. With the abolition of the slave trade in the early nineteenth century followed closely by emancipation, slaves, as a group, ceased to exist. And the demise of Khoikhoi as a spoken language led to the disappearance of the Khoikhoi as a distinct group. All of these were caught up in the umbrella term "coloured." It is the descendants of these peoples who now constitute the largest community in the Western Cape Province of South Africa.

3

The Start of the British Period

While life proceeded at a slow pace on the southern tip of Africa in the eighteenth century, storm clouds of unrest over Europe were unleashing violent and bloody conflicts that were to change the face of Europe and usher in a whole new era – the age of enlightenment and revolution.

The French Revolution, which began as a reasonably orderly reform movement in 1789, quickly degenerated into an orgy of violence in which extremist groups battled for power. In 1799 Napoleon took control in a military coup to save France from chaos, but his own ambition for military glory and conquest plunged virtually the whole of Europe into war. However, European wars had already begun before Napoleon came to power. In 1795 French troops invaded the Netherlands, forcing William V, Prince of Orange, to flee to Britain. To keep the Cape from falling into French hands, the British sent a fleet of warships to occupy the Cape, thus protecting the sea route to the East for the British navy. By the Treaty of Amiens, the Cape was returned to the Batavian Republic (as Holland had been renamed) in 1803. But with the renewal of hostilities between the French and the British in 1806, the British again took control of the Cape. In 1815, in return for a payment of two million pounds to the Netherlands, the colony was formally ceded to Britain, which became its controlling political power for the next century.

The change of authority from Dutch to British was to have profound implications for the Cape and the whole of southern Africa. While the Dutch were enterprising and commercially ingenious, their golden age had passed by the end of the eighteenth century and they did not have the resources or the will to expand their colony in the Cape. The British, on the other hand, had become the leading industrial nation in the world and were in the process of developing (whether by design or accident) the most extensive empire the world has ever seen. The nineteenth century was to witness the expansion of

British power and authority throughout southern Africa. The British Empire swallowed up the Xhosa territories in the east, the Zulu kingdom in the northeast, and the Boer republics in the north, and in the process created the borders of the modern South Africa. Indeed, British authority extended far beyond these borders, forming those countries now known as Zimbabwe, Zambia, Malawi, Tanzania, Uganda, and Kenya, not to mention the states in West Africa. But theirs is another story.

While earthly kingdoms and empires were rising and falling, the final decade of the eighteenth century saw another revolution taking place in the Protestant churches of Western Europe and North America. This was a quieter movement, but one with more lasting consequences.

From the time of the Reformation in the sixteenth century, Protestant churches had shown little interest in missions to non-Christian peoples. The fact that Roman Catholics were so active in promoting foreign missions around the world only increased Protestant hesitations. (If the Papists were for it, it must be suspect!) Theological reasons were advanced to show that such activities were presumptuous. It was argued that the Great Commission (Matt 28:19) was given to the apostles only and provided no mandate for the contemporary church to engage in foreign missions.

Despite the general apathy towards missions prevailing in Protestant circles, there were minority groups that believed the church had a responsibility to preach the gospel to all nations. As we have already seen, Pietists in Germany, Congregationalists in New England, and Moravians from Herrnhut were among those who laboured to spread the good news among non-Christian peoples. Towards the end of the eighteenth century their witness and labours began to bring about a change of heart in the Protestant world concerning missions. The catalyst of this change, it would seem, was an English Baptist minister named William Carey. A passionate believer in the "Obligations of Christians to use Means for the Conversion of the Heathens," Carey inspired the formation of the Baptist Missionary Society in 1792 and went to India as its first missionary the following year. His carefully written reports sent back to England were eagerly read and awakened a growing interest in his work and the cause of Christian missions in general. Within the space of a couple of decades, a host of missionary societies sprang into existence in Britain, France, Germany, Holland, Switzerland, Scandinavia and the USA, and the great Protestant missionary movement of the nineteenth century had been launched.

The London Missionary Society (LMS)

One of the earliest of the missionary organizations was the LMS, formed in 1795. Among the places it identified as a suitable field of labour was southern Africa, and so in 1799 four LMS missionaries arrived in the Cape. Kicherer, Edward, Edmonds,van and van der Kemp were the first of many missionaries who came to southern Africa under the auspices of the LMS, including some of the most illustrious names in mission history (Robert Moffat and David Livingstone).

The LMS began life as an interdenominational society, pledged "not to send Presbyterianism, Independency, Episcopacy, or any other form of Church Order and Government . . . but the Glorious Gospel of the blessed God to the Heathen." But as the Presbyterians and Anglicans soon set up their own missionary societies, the LMS became, to all extents and purposes, a Congregationalist society. The chief fruit of its work in southern Africa is the United Congregational Church of Southern Africa. The story of the LMS is perhaps best told through the lives of some of those associated with its work.

Dr Johannes Theodorus van der Kemp

A Dutchman who came to the Cape with this British missionary society, van der Kemp was a man of considerable intellectual abilities, undoubted devotion to Christ and unconventional views. Born in Rotterdam, Holland, in 1747, he was the son of a Lutheran minister but seems to have rejected orthodox Christian views in favour of Deism. Joining the army, he rose through the ranks to become a captain and was also a friend of the Prince of Orange. Yet all the time van der Kemp was, in his own words, "a slave to vice and ungodliness." Marriage brought a certain respectability into his life, and he proceeded to the University of Edinburgh to study medicine. After successfully completing his studies he returned to Holland to practise as a physician. A sudden tragedy in 1791 brought about a radical change in his life. His wife and only child were drowned in a boating accident, in which he also nearly died. Yielding himself to God, van der Kemp decided to devote the rest of his days to the cause of Christ. Hearing of the LMS, he offered his services to it, and was one of the first party of its missionaries sent to the Cape. Van der Kemp was to live a very different life from that to which he had previously been accustomed, enduring hardships, difficulties and heartbreaks for the sake of the gospel.

Michiel Vos was among those who warmly greeted the LMS missionaries on their arrival in Cape Town in March, 1799. Van der Kemp and his companion Edmond made note of the considerable goodwill and kindness they experienced from the Dutch colonists as they proceeded to the interior of the country. On 13 June 1799, for example, van der Kemp wrote:

> This morning we crossed the *Gamka* which though very broad, was quite dry. We arrived at the house of Samuel de Beer, who, when he heard what the object of our journey was, received us with uncommon joy. He summoned his family and slaves, communicated to them the news, and fell upon his knees, saying: "O Lord, Thou hast saddened me with inexpressible grief by taking from me my child, whom I buried today; but now Thou dost rejoice my soul with joy greater than my sadness, as Thou showest me that my prayers for the salvation of the Kaffirs[1] have been heard, and Thou grantest me at this time to see how Thy promises are beginning to be fulfilled."[2]

Unfortunately, in the years to come the goodwill between missionary and colonist was to be strained considerably and often replaced by hostility and bitterness.

Van der Kemp desired to bring the gospel to the Xhosa people dwelling on the eastern border of the Cape Colony, among whom no Christian missionary had yet laboured. He was advised against the attempt because of the highly unsettled condition of the border area, which was troubled by repeated hostilities between the Xhosa, the colonial authorities and the trekboers (Dutch/Afrikaans farmers). Edmond left van der Kemp and returned to the Cape, from where he proceeded to India. But van der Kemp was determined to pursue his goal of preaching to the Xhosa, and towards the end of 1799 he was able to make contact with the Xhosa chief Ngqika who gave him tentative permission to work among his people. For about a year van der Kemp lived among the Xhosa, but no real opportunity was afforded him to preach the gospel to them. He was only able to gather a few Khoikhoi women and children living in the area and instruct them. As a result of further outbreaks

---

1. Today the word "Kaffir" is pejorative and highly offensive. Then it was the normal word used for black people in Africa south of the Sahara. It was first used by the Arabs for black people, and learned from them by European traders and colonists. It means "unbeliever" in Arabic. It will be used in this book only when part of an original quotation.

2. Du Plessis, *History of Christian Missions,* 121.

of hostility and the failure to make meaningful contact with the Xhosa, van der Kemp withdrew to the town of Graaff-Reinet towards the end of 1800. This first attempt to evangelize the Xhosa had apparently ended in failure – but not quite. One of those who heard van der Kemp was a teenage herd boy, Ntsikana, who was deeply impressed by his message. Some fifteen years after van der Kemp left, Ntsikana was to have a profound spiritual experience that transformed him into a mystical, prophetic preacher of the Christian faith. He is justly celebrated as the morning star of the Xhosa church, and we will take up his story after we have finished that of van der Kemp.

At Graaff-Reinet van der Kemp was invited by the local Dutch Reformed Church to be their minister. He declined, however, convinced that his calling was to serve the indigenous people. Together with James Read, he began to labour among the Khoikhoi. But Graaff-Reinet was soon plunged into the same turmoil as the other eastern parts of the colony. The Xhosa, the farmers, the colonial authorities and the Khoikhoi were all drawn into the conflict. Van der Kemp and his congregation were obliged to move from place to place, and eventually settled in a place he named Bethelsdorp, close to the present-day Port Elizabeth. Many accusations were levelled against van der Kemp at this time, largely because of his close association with and sympathy for the Khoikhoi and Xhosa people.

Bethelsdorp was founded in the high hope that it would become another Genadendal, a haven of quiet and godly living, honest labour and Christian virtue in the midst of a wild and tumultuous country. In a letter to Governor Dundas dated 11 February 1801, van der Kemp enunciated thirteen principles upon which the new settlement was to be found. They included the following:

> 2. The chief object and aim of the missionaries under whose direction this settlement shall be established ought to be to promote the knowledge of Christ and the practice of real piety, both by instruction and example, among the Hottentots and other heathen, who shall be admitted and formed into a regular society; and, in the second place, the temporal happiness and usefulness of this society, with respect to the country at large.
>
> ...
>
> 3. Into this society only those ought to be admitted who will engage themselves to live according to the rules of the institution.
>
> ...

6. As we are of opinion that the rule laid down by Paul, "that if any would not work, neither should he eat," ought to be strictly observed in every Christian society, our intention is to discourage idleness and laziness; and to have the individuals of our institution, as much as circumstances shall admit, employed in different useful occupations, for the cultivation of their rational faculties, or exercise of the body, as means of subsistence, and of promoting the welfare of this society, and the colony at large.[3]

The high ideals envisaged in this letter were only very partially realized. One reason for this may be that the very poor quality of the land and the scarcity of water made proper agricultural development almost impossible. Indeed, several efforts were made to find a more suitable spot, though without any success. Others have seen in the character of van der Kemp himself a major reason for the shortcomings of Bethelsdorp. Even his warmest admirers admitted that he had eccentric views and lacked practical skills. It has been suggested that the doctrines of Rousseau to which van der Kemp had subscribed in his youth persisted in his mind even after he became a Christian. Rousseau maintained that "the life of the savage is the simplest and most perfect, whereas civilized communities are all degenerate, wealth a crime, government nought but tyranny, and social laws unjust."[4]

One thing is certain: Van der Kemp had the courage to put into practice the Pauline principle of being all things to all men. To the Khoikhoi he became a Khoikhoi, adopting their dress, food and mode of living. He also married the daughter of a slave from Madagascar. Thus van der Kemp lived in utter simplicity among the people he served. To his critics, instead of uplifting the Khoikhoi, he had simply "levelled himself with them, and adopted their habits of negligence and filth."[5] Bethelsdorp was described as a place where the small, low huts were "so wretchedly built, and kept with so little care and attention, that they have a perfectly ruinous appearance."[6] But an admirer describing a communion service at Bethelsdorp, says: "The hills outside are bare, the plain is bare, the houses of the folk are bare, the place of worship is bare but the Holy Catholic Church is here in all the opulence of

---

3. Hofmeyr, Millard and Froneman, *History of the Church*, 74–75.

4. As quoted in du Plessis, *History of Christian Missions*, 128.

5. Dr Henry Lichtenstein who visited Bethelsdorp six months after its establishment, quoted in Du Plessis, *History of Christian Missions*, 126.

6. Ibid.

the spirit, keeping the memory of her Lord and receiving from Him the grace that upbuilds men into eternal life."[7]

In his last years van der Kemp was assisted at Bethelsdorp by "Mother Smith," an extraordinary woman of abounding piety and good works, a veritable Dorcas of the early Cape church. Widowed at a comparatively early age, she was converted under the ministry of Helperus Ritzema van Lier and dedicated the rest of her life to promoting the interests of the kingdom of God. She laboured among the soldiers and the slaves in Cape Town and thereafter for a prolonged period among the slaves and the Khoikhoi at Roodezand (Tulbagh), the parish of Michiel Vos. Towards the end of 1805 she undertook the arduous journey to Bethelsdorp to assist in the work there, teaching the women and children the arts of sewing and knitting and other practical crafts. The sale of articles made at Bethelsdorp generated funds for the support of the institution. Mother Smith's spiritual input was also invaluable, as she taught the gospel to the children and women in particular. Unfortunately her stay at Bethelsdorp was cut short by a difference of opinion between her and the other missionaries over the issue of slavery. Like most other Dutch people at the Cape, she owned slaves, and to this her colleagues objected. Notwithstanding this difference, it was she who tended van der Kemp in his last days before he died in 1811.

The work at Bethelsdorp, continued by other LMS missionaries, was to weather many more fierce storms. Yet, in time, there was undoubted spiritual fruit, as reported by the Congregationalist historians Briggs and Wing:

> The most important signs of spiritual progress were that some of the Hottentot converts went out to evangelize their own people in the district, often preaching as acceptably to the white farmers as to their servants! We might fill several pages with the missionary activities of these men – Joachim Vogel and Cupido Kakkerlak and Kruisman, Boezak the buffalo hunter, Samson the converted agnostic, Jocham and Abraham the persecuted preachers whom not even flogging or imprisonment could deter. All were brave, devoted servants of their new master, but the achievements of brother Jacob eclipse the rest. He went to live in the *kraal* of David Stuurman, a notorious brigand much feared along the frontier, winning nearly the whole village to Christ.[8]

---

7. Martin, *Dr. Vanderkemp*, quoted in Davies and Shepherd, *South African Missions*, 141.
8. Briggs and Wing, *Harvest and the Hope*, 20.

The work done by van der Kemp, with all its imperfection, was not in vain.

Ntsikana – The Morning Star of the Xhosa Church

A man who had a mystical experience of Christ quite apart from any missionary, a man who emerged as a powerful prophet of the Christian message, an inspired writer of hymns, a leader of a Christian congregation, and one whose contact with missionaries was so minimal that he was never even baptized – such is the Melchizedek-like figure of this Xhosa prophet of Christ.

During van der Kemp's first abortive attempt to bring the gospel to the Xhosa in 1800, Ntsikana, then a teenage herd boy, heard him preach. What else he may have heard about the gospel is uncertain, but in about 1815 he had a dramatic experience that was to change the course of his life. In the words of an account reported by Crafford:

> One morning, at daybreak he was at the cattle kraal watching his favourite ox Hulushe when a strange light appeared above the horns of the ox. On the same day he and his people attended a dance at a certain homestead and, when he wanted to join in, a strong whirlwind suddenly blew up. Unexpectedly he ordered his wives to return home. On the way back he washed the red clay from his body in a stream. In this way he openly declared the fact that he had gone over to the Christian faith (even though he was never formally baptized).[9]

From the very next day, Ntsikana began to sing of his new-found faith, in keeping both with his status as a poet and praise singer and the African custom of celebrating special events in song and dance. Four of his hymns have survived. The so-called "Great Hymn" is truly remarkable and is still sung today.

> He is the Great God of the heaven.
> Thou art the only True shield.
> Thou art the only True fortress.
> Thou art the only True bush [hiding place].
> Thou art the only One who dwells in the highest.
> He is the Creator of life.

---

9. Crafford, *Trail-Blazers of the Gospel*, 20.

He is the Creator of the heaven.
He is the Creator of the stars.
A star fell from heaven and brought us the message.[10]
He is also the Creator of the blind.[11]
The trumpet was sounded to call us.
He is the great hunter of souls.
He gathers together the warring flocks.[12]
He is the great Leader who leads us.
He is the great Kaross that covers us.
Why art Thy hands covered in wounds?
Why art Thy feet covered in wounds?
Why dost thy blood flow so?
Thy blood was shed for us.
Is that what it cost thee to save us?
The people of Khanwana (Soga), did we call them?[13]

In 1816 another attempt was made to establish a mission among the Xhosa people, this time by an LMS missionary named Williams, a simple and devout man who succeeded in gaining the trust of Ngqika. Soon more than a hundred people, Xhosa and Khoikhoi, were residing on the mission Williams had established. Among those who received instruction from him was Ntsikana, although he never took up residence at the mission station. He would visit Williams for a few days at a time, and the influence of the missionary undoubtedly helped Ntsikana in his understanding of the gospel.

Williams was not to stay long among the Xhosa. In 1818 he died, leaving his wife and two children. His wife was willing to continue the work, but friends persuaded her to leave. It was two years before the LMS was able to send someone to replace Williams, and during this period Ntsikana became the leader of the group of Christians, none of whom had yet been baptized. He would hold services at his kraal mornings and evenings, as well as on Sundays, summoning his flock with his "bell" song. Sometimes large numbers would come to hear him, including Ngqika, who, according to some witnesses, was deeply impressed by the gospel of God's grace and

---

10. Was this star a reference to van der Kemp? Or perhaps Christ?

11. Implying that blindness is not necessarily the result of sorcery

12. Conflict had been stirred up between Ngqika and Ndlambe. Ntsikana urged Ngqika not to wage war on Ndlambe.

13. Crafford, *Trail-Blazers of the Gospel,* 26.

only prevented by his senior counsellors from becoming a convert. Another leading Xhosa official to be influenced by Ntsikana was Soga, whose son Tiyo Soga was later to become the first ordained black minister in southern Africa. His story will be told later.

The main theme of Ntsikana's message seems to have been the greatness of God and the coming of Jesus to bring forgiveness of sins through his blood. He also received visions and seemed to have had the gift of foresight. On one occasion he warned his chief, Ngqika, not to wage war on a neighbouring chief and told him that he had seen the fields strewn with the rotting corpses of Xhosa warriors. Ngqika did not heed his counsel and in the ensuing war suffered a crushing defeat in which there was a great loss of life on both sides.

In 1820 the LMS sent Brownlee to replace Williams. But before he had a chance to meet the new missionary, Ntsikana died at a comparatively early age. Brownlee describes his death as follows in a letter dated 3 August 1822:

> There is here a kraal of about a hundred inhabitants who, from the time of his [Williams'] death, until my arrival in Xhosaland (a period of nearly two years) were accustomed to assemble regularly for religious services, mornings and evenings, as well as to keep the day of the Lord. The head of the kraal, who led these services, died approximately two years ago. He composed a hymn in their own language which is still regularly sung at their services. On the day of his death (which he had apparently foreseen), although he was still able to lead the service, he spoke like somebody about to pass over into eternity. He intimated that he had contented himself with the will of the Lord (referring to his illness) and professed a humble faith in the grace and mercy of God. He was deeply concerned over the redemption of his compatriots and seriously admonished his followers to prefer the most horrible death above losing their faith.[14]

Ntsikana's remarkable achievement in indigenizing the gospel in the context of Xhosa culture and society was not sufficiently noted or appreciated in his time. It took a long time before the importance of the contextualization of the gospel for a given culture was fully appreciated in missionary circles. Ntsikana's ministry remains an early example of how the gospel can be

---

14. Ibid., 23.

efficiently communicated within the language, idioms, thought forms, cultural traditions and social practices of a particular people.

John Philip

In the closing days of van der Kemp's ministry, the LMS became aware that the various projects of its mission in southern Africa were in dire need of more efficient supervision. The man they eventually appointed to take charge of their work in southern Africa, John Philip, was to become one of the most controversial religious figures in South African history. In the words of the eminent church historian of South Africa, Peter Hinchliff, Philip has been

> reviled as a liar, a slanderer, a prejudiced and insidious politician. He has been lauded as the first and most vigorous champion of the underprivileged people of South Africa. Perhaps the fairest and least emotionally distorted judgement sees him as an honest, sensible man, too far ahead of his contemporaries, sometimes making mistakes, but genuinely concerned with finding the just and practical solution.[15]

Born in 1775 in Kirkcaldy, Scotland, Philip was the son of a weaver and passed his earlier years at the loom. While managing a mill at Dundee, Philip experienced a religious conversion and joined a Congregational church. Feeling a call to the ministry, he studied theology in London, later accepting a call to a Congregational church in Aberdeen, where he served as pastor for fifteen years. An incident that directed his thoughts to mission work was the challenge of a man who asked him if he believed Acts 4:12, "Salvation is found in no one else, for there is no other name under heaven given to mankind by which we must be saved." When Philip replied that he did, the man responded: "Whoever believes that, ought to go to the ends of the earth to preach the Gospel."[16]

As a result of Philip's ministry in Aberdeen, several members of his congregation volunteered for missionary work. Among them was Dr George Thom, who originally intended to go to India, but who, when stopping over in Cape Town, was persuaded to stay there to minister to soldiers and others. It was he who pointed out to the LMS some of the defects of its work there.

---

15. Hinchliff, *Church in South Africa*, 28.
16. Du Plessis, *History of Christian Missions*, 142.

Shortly after this, in 1820, the LMS appointed Philip as superintendent of its work in southern Africa. The same year he was called to be the pastor of an independent congregation in Cape Town. He accepted this position on the clear understanding that his missionary duties had the first call on his time.

For nearly thirty years Philip devoted his many gifts and great energy to the work of the LMS. It was a period crammed with some of the most dramatic and far-reaching events in South African history, including the following:

1. The massive social and demographic dislocation brought about by the rise of Shaka's Zulu kingdom.
2. The arrival in 1820 of 4,000 British colonists, most of whom were settled on the eastern frontier, the border area between the Cape Colony and the Xhosa chiefdoms.
3. The emancipation of slaves in 1834.
4. The Great Trek of dissatisfied Dutch farmers (Boers) into the interior, beyond the reach (they hoped) of British rule.
5. The British occupation of Natal and temporary annexation of the Orange River Sovereignty (1848–1854).
6. The outbreak of three wars on the eastern frontier.

In addition to these major events, there were continual disturbances within the Cape Colony as many conflicts and grievances arose between the British government in Cape Town, the Dutch farmers, the British settlers, the Xhosa people, the Khoikhoi, the slaves and other people of colour.

The plight of the Khoikhoi was particularly tragic. Deprived of virtually all their land and therefore also of their traditional way of life, all that was left to them was to become vagrants in their own country, to work as farm labourers, or find refuge on a mission station. It was for the rights of these "coloured" people in particular that Philip exerted himself, and in the process made himself deeply unpopular with colonists, farmers, governors and even many missionaries. He had considerable influence with the administrators in England responsible for the Cape Colony, and he used this effectively. Philip played a major role in the passing of Ordinance Fifty in 1828 which gave legal equality "to Hottentots and other free persons of colour,"[17] thereby greatly improving the status of the Khoikhoi and coloured peoples.

According to his critics, the many reports, representations and other publications produced by Philip tended to malign the colonists, painting a one-sided picture and laying the blame for the various wars and troubles

---

17. Hofmeyr and Pillay, *History of Christianity*, 55.

wholly at their feet. Indeed, at one stage a libel case was brought that resulted in a judgment against him and a considerable fine. In response to those who accused him of meddling in politics Philip replied,

> If a minister is guilty of dereliction of his duty in advocating the cause of the oppressed, or in relieving the necessities of the destitute, I plead guilty to the charge . . . I could not see the Mission destroyed, nor the aborigines trampled in the dust, nor the settlers left to perish, without attempting to relieve them by legal means.[18]

Philip was certainly not guilty of concerning himself exclusively with the spiritual welfare of converts while ignoring their social, economic and political condition. That charge is often brought against missionaries, yet often with very little justification. It is true that the missionaries did not always agree with one another as to the best methods of advancing the interests of the people they sought to help, but they were at one in desiring the greatest possible good, spiritually, physically and materially, for those to whom they preached the gospel. For Philip, a vigorous engagement in political activities on behalf of the coloured people was an intrinsic part of his calling to serve them. For others it was impossible to become so deeply involved in political matters without becoming influenced by the prejudices, deceits and corruption of political life. Furthermore, it was argued, the spiritual issues of salvation, forgiveness of sins, and reconciliation to God were far weightier than any temporal, social or political issues. Spiritual issues had eternal consequences, and therefore required the primary attention of those called to preach the gospel. In practice, however, most missionaries laboured for both the temporal and spiritual welfare of their converts, even while, in the frailty of limited understanding and imperfect motives, they often differed with one another concerning the best means of attaining such goals. In this, the nineteenth missionaries were no different from other Christian leaders before and after their time.

In 1833, Jean-Eugène Casalis, one of the pioneer French missionaries with the Paris Evangelical Missionary Society who first took the gospel to the Sotho people, met with Philip and has left us this interesting record of his impressions:

---

18. Briggs and Wing, *Harvest and the Hope*, 37.

He was then a little over fifty years of age. His height, his fine frame, sonority of voice, his high forehead wrinkled with the force of thought, his intelligent eyes shadowed by heavy eyebrows, created an overall impression that suited perfectly his titles of "doctor" and "superintendent." But an expression of unspeakable kindliness and Christian simplicity immediately gained confidence and affection for him. He belonged to this fine type of British piety, full of vigour and originality . . . He was a generous and liberal spirit, who grasped the main threads of complicated issues. He had become in South Africa the protector of all indigenous peoples, applying himself to obtain missionaries for them.[19]

The LMS sent many others to southern Africa who gave their lives for the cause of Christ and his kingdom, people such as Robert Moffat and David Livingstone. But before their stories can be told, we need to return to Cape Town and look at some of the new developments in the life of the church as a result of the British takeover of the Cape.

Churches of British Origin

Before the year 1800 English was a completely foreign language in southern Africa. The first English-speakers were the British governor and his administrators, together with the British soldiers and their officers. And with the English, Scottish and Irish soldiers came their churches: Anglican, Methodist, Presbyterian, Roman Catholic, Congregational and Baptist. All these were transplanted into South African soil and have been growing ever since, some more vigorously than others. We shall now trace the beginnings and development of these churches and tell the stories of some of those who built them.

Anglicans

The spiritual needs of Anglicans were first met through the ministry of the chaplains who accompanied the British troops. In Cape Town, the Dutch Reformed Church building was made available to the Anglicans for their

---

19. Quoted from Casalis, *Mes Souvenirs*, in Davies and Shepherd, *South African Missions*, 113.

services. This arrangement, which lasted until 1834 when the Anglicans acquired their own building, demonstrated the friendly relations at that stage between the two denominations.

Episcopal churches, such as the Anglicans, cannot function well without bishops, as only a bishop can confirm the young and ordain priests for the ministry. This meant that the Anglicans in the Cape depended on the occasional Anglican bishop stopping over at the Cape on his way to the East to carry out these important functions. The need for their own bishop was felt keenly by Anglicans in the Cape. From the eastern part of the colony there came a complaint in 1830: "Leave us to ourselves a little longer and we will all be Methodists – or what is worse – nothing!"[20] Fifteen years later the priest at George complained that the young people were asking to be admitted to the Dutch Reformed Church as there was no bishop to confirm them as Anglicans.[21] Finally, in 1848, the Cape Anglicans received Robert Gray as their first bishop, a man whose ministry profoundly influenced the course of Anglicanism in southern Africa.

Robert Gray

The seventh son of an Anglican priest who later became the bishop of Bristol, Gray was born in 1809 and educated at Eton. Going up to Oxford in 1828, he experienced the excitement of the early beginnings of the Oxford Movement. As Gray was clearly influenced by this movement, it is important for us to recall some of its principles and goals.

The leaders of the Oxford Movement believed the church to be a divinely instituted body, governed by bishops standing in true apostolic succession and administering sacraments that were effective means of grace instituted by Christ himself. These Tractarians or Anglo-Catholics, as they were also known, were opposed to state control of the church and were critical of the Protestant Reformation with what they saw as its anti-Catholic tendencies. They sought to revive the doctrines and practices of the early and undivided Catholic Church of the fourth century, before the corruptions of the medieval papacy and the divisions and heresies of Protestantism.

To what degree Gray embraced the ideals of the Oxford Movement is debatable, but it cannot be doubted that they influenced him. After his ordination in 1834, he served two parishes in England for about thirteen

---

20. Hofmeyr and Pillay, *History of Christianity*, 82.
21. Ibid.

years, during which time he also became secretary of the Society for the Propagation of the Gospel, an Anglican missionary society founded in 1701 with a special responsibility for congregations in British dependencies. Gray's interest in missions was surely a factor that led to his appointment as the first bishop of Cape Town. Some of his observations on his arrival in 1848 illustrate his thinking and contain portents of future struggles and conflicts awaiting him.

> I landed in the afternoon with Sophy [his wife] and Douglas [the ordained son of an Earl], and Douglas read prayers in the Cathedral in the evening, where there was a tolerable congregation. St. George's is decidedly the best ecclesiastical building in the town. Church matters are in a bad state. I am told there is a party ripe for anything, and full of suspicions and jealousies.
>
> The Baptismal Regeneration controversy is raging, and the pulpit of the Cathedral has been used for proclaiming pamphlets against that doctrine of the Church. I feel the great need there is of judgement, prudence, and forbearance, and how much I shall need all your prayers in a very trying and delicate position…
>
> As to our Church here, the only two clergy belong to a little evangelical alliance, one holds prayer meetings in a school, the other officiates in a school at Green Point, turn about with dissenters. In the Cathedral last Sunday a school was taught with an American catechism… I have declined to interfere, choosing to take time for everything.[22]

Gray's somewhat critical references to his clergy and their evangelical tendencies (fraternizing with dissenters – presumably Methodists, Congregationalists, or Presbyterians – and opposing the doctrine of baptismal regeneration) reflects the war of words that was being waged within the Church of England at that time between Anglo-Catholic Tractarians and Protestant Evangelicals. The latter saw in the Oxford Movement a Romanizing tendency which they feared would ultimately undermine the Protestant character of the English people and their national church. This conflict was to produce a division among South African Anglicans that has persisted to the present time.

---

22. Hofmeyr, Millard and Froneman, *History of the Church*, 91.

Gray was indefatigable in his efforts to consolidate and develop the Anglican Church in southern Africa. His vast diocese included the Cape Colony, British Kaffraria, Natal, the Orange River Sovereignty, and St Helena – and he was determined to visit all of it. His third visitation took him on a journey of 6,400 kilometres (4,000 miles) on horseback, which he completed in nine months. Convinced of the need to subdivide such a vast diocese into smaller, more manageable units, Gray returned to England in 1852 in order to arrange for such a division. When this had been done, Bishop Armstrong was appointed to the Eastern Province and Bishop Colenso to Natal. Both bishops were also to develop missions to the indigenous people in their dioceses.

Returning to Africa, Gray devoted himself to the organization of the church as an autonomous, self-governing church within the Anglican Communion, recognizing the Archbishop of Canterbury as "first among equals" but firmly rejecting any judicial authority of the British state over the church in South Africa. These moves were entirely in keeping with the ideals of the Oxford Movement, and for that reason they were staunchly resisted by some of Gray's clergy. They feared that he would steer an autonomous church in a Rome-wards direction unacceptable to Anglicans of Low Church and evangelical sympathies. For this reason they fought to keep the ties with the home country that they believed would safeguard the rights of Protestant and Reformed views within the Church of England. This fundamental conflict between Gray and some of his clergy was to lead to many unedifying court cases in which the various parties struggled over property rights, rights of appointment and such like. It also contributed to the tremendous struggle between Gray and Colenso over matters of doctrine and polity, a conflict that reverberated around the Anglican Communion throughout the world. That is such an interesting story in itself that we will take it up later in more detail.

Notwithstanding all these difficulties, Gray was able to achieve his goal when in 1870 the first provincial synod was held and a constitution for the Church of the Province of South Africa (CPSA) approved. By the famous "Third Proviso" in the canons of this constitution, the privy council of Britain was excluded as a court of appeal for the South African church. Gray was confirmed as the metropolitan of the Church of the Province. The title "metropolitan," common in the church of the fourth century, was later dropped in favour of the more familiar "archbishop."

Those clergy and congregations who refused to recognize the 1870 synod, or the Church of the Province born out of it, eventually formed the Church of England in South Africa (CESA) and claimed to be the continuation of authentic Anglicanism in South Africa. Despite many attempts to unite these two bodies, they still remain apart. The CESA is much smaller than the CPSA and is not recognized by the Archbishop of Canterbury and the Anglican Communion. It nevertheless maintains links with like-minded Anglicans worldwide and has produced many worthy labourers who have made an honourable contribution to building the walls of Zion in South Africa.

By the time Gray died in 1872, Anglicanism in South Africa had been transformed from a weak and disorganized body into an independent, disestablished province of the Anglican Communion with five synodically governed dioceses, all vigorously engaged in promoting missions, education and many other good works.

Methodists

Methodism was still enjoying its springtime of youthful enthusiasm when the first Methodists arrived in the Cape. And the zeal which characterized that movement in Britain and the USA was fully manifested here as well.

While Methodism, as a movement, was bigger than any one man, to a large extent it was the fruit of the life and work of one Church of England clergyman – John Wesley. As an earnest but disappointed young priest, Wesley was challenged by his contact with certain Moravians to find full assurance of salvation through faith. This he found in a meeting in Aldersgate in 1738 when his heart was "strangely warmed" while listening to a reading from Luther's preface to the book of Romans. Thereafter he dedicated the rest of his life to preaching the gospel up and down the British Isles, labouring "to spread Scriptural holiness over the land."[23] Having no desire to start a new sect, he remained loyal to the Church of England until his death, striving only "to promote so far as I am able, vital, practical religion; and by the grace of God to beget, preserve, and increase the life of God in the souls of men."[24]

To conserve the gains of his evangelistic efforts, Wesley gathered his converts into societies in which they might encourage one another to faith and good works. Although these societies had become, de facto, a separate church even during Wesley's lifetime, it was only after his death that the societies formally separated from the Church of England in 1795.

---

23. Skevington-Wood, "John Wesley," 1034.
24. Ibid.

The first Methodist meetings in the Cape were held by some of the British soldiers stationed there. One of these, a Sergeant Kendrick, became known for his spiritual zeal and efforts to promote the gospel among his fellow soldiers. An earthquake in 1809 provoked seriousness about religious matters, and Kendrick noted in his journal concerning the 83rd Regiment at Saldanha Bay:

> The spark of grace soon began to catch from soul to soul. Prayer meetings now commenced among them and such a cry for mercy followed as is most wonderful. The room frequently has been so crowded that many have been unable to reach the door.[25]

The group of Methodists soon grew until they numbered 120, but not without encountering considerable opposition. A small church the soldiers built for themselves in Wynberg was burned down by order of the colonel of the regiment. The first Methodist minister sent to assist the work in 1814 was refused permission to preach by the governor, Lord Charles Somerset, and had to leave the Cape. The Methodists repeated their request for a minister, but the second one sent out in 1816, Barnabas Shaw, was also refused permission to preach. Ignoring this, he did so anyway. It would seem that the attitude of the British authorities to the Methodists at this stage was not much different from that of the Dutch authorities to the Moravians nearly a century earlier. Shaw's intention, however, was not just to labour in Cape Town; his heart was set upon regions beyond, to take the gospel to those who had not yet heard it. An opportunity arose to join an LMS missionary named Schmelen, who intended to find a place to work among the Namaquas, northwest of Cape Town. On their way, after a journey with many difficulties including intense, scorching heat, a remarkable incident occurred, which is best told in Shaw's own words:

> On leaving the banks of the Elephant River, we commenced our journey in the Karree or arid desert. When we had travelled for a short time, it was announced that the chief of the Little Namacquas and four of his people were approaching. We immediately halted and entered into conversation with them, when they proposed that we should remain together for the night. This request was complied with, and the chief stated, that having heard of the Great Word, and other tribes having received it, he was also anxious to have it, and had commenced this journey in search

---

25. Orr, *Evangelical Awakenings*, 8.

of a teacher. They had already travelled two hundred miles [320 km], and had designed proceeding to Cape Town, which would have been between two and three hundred more. It was certain that they could have obtained no missionary at Cape Town, and it appeared a peculiar Providence that we should thus meet with them in the wilderness; for had we commenced our day's journey half an hour sooner or they theirs half an hour later, we should have continued our route towards Great Namacqualand, and should consequently have missed them coming from Little Namacqualand. As the finger of God was evidently perceptible throughout the whole of this event, it was proposed that I should accompany the chief to his kraal; at this he was highly delighted, and willingly accepted the offer. At our evening's service he with his people bowed their faces to the ground, and when Jesus was set forth as the Great Shepherd, who had black sheep as well as white . . . the chief wept aloud and appeared to rejoice as one who had found great spoil.[26]

The Namaqua were a Khoikhoi tribe, most of whom had learned some Dutch through employment by Dutch farmers. Shaw therefore taught the Namaqua in this language, having learned it before coming to the Cape. Ten fruitful years were spent among them during which time he not only taught them the Word of God but also introduced to them agricultural methods which greatly enhanced their output. Leliefontein, as Shaw's mission station was called, not only became a flourishing centre of Christianity but also the springboard for further missionary advances among the Great Namaqua tribes and even further north among the Tswana-speaking people.

After returning to Cape Town, Barnabas Shaw continued to minister to the slaves. From 1826 until 1837 he was in charge of Wesleyan ministries in the area from Simonstown to Cape Town. Work was also extended to Stellenbosch and Caledon. Then, after spending six years in England, in 1843 Shaw sailed back to the Cape, still active in Christian ministry. He died in the Cape in 1854. He must be reckoned as one of the great pioneers and founders of Methodism in South Africa. The other, even greater, founding figure of South African Methodism was also a Shaw, but no relative of Barnabas.

---

26. Shaw, "Memorials," in Davies and Shepherd, *South African Missions*, 107–108.

William Shaw

With rising unemployment in Britain after the Napoleonic wars and continual conflict with the Xhosa tribes on the eastern border of the Cape Colony, the British government devised a plan which, it believed, would kill two birds with one stone. Fifty thousand pounds was voted by parliament to finance a scheme whereby British people would be settled in the eastern border area of the Cape Colony, providing a buffer against the Xhosa while at the same time strengthening the English element in the colony. There were 90,000 applicants and 4,000 were selected. Thus the 1820 Settlers came to South Africa, introducing yet another major component to the increasingly complex mosaic of peoples inhabiting the region. Among them was a young Methodist minister whose spiritual impact on the area was to be one of the most important in its history.

Born in Glasgow in 1795, William Shaw was the eleventh child of devout Anglican parents and initially intended to follow his father's career as a soldier in the British army. A conversion experience in 1812 led him into a Methodist society, and he later became a teacher and a lay preacher. Hearing that one of the parties emigrating to South Africa wanted a chaplain, Shaw successfully applied for the post, being ordained by the Methodist Conference for the purpose of ministering to the needs of the settlers as well as initiating missionary work when the opportunity arose.

The experience of the settlers was one of bitter disillusionment after the high hopes that had brought them to Africa. The land was unsuitable for agriculture and their living conditions were wretched. A man who escorted them to their land gave them the following parting advice: "Gentlemen, when you go out to plough, never leave your guns behind." They had not been aware of the dangers of the territory or that they were expected to serve as a buffer between the colony and aggrieved and hostile Xhosa tribes. Many left the area, and for those who stayed, the first few years were hard and difficult. The twenty-two-year-old Shaw gave the following description of their living conditions:

> After a while a great variety of fragile and grotesque-looking huts or cottages began to arise. These were generally built in the style called by the settlers "wattle and daub.". . . At first there was no plank for doors, or glass for windows hence a mat or rug was usually hung up in the void doorway . . . and a piece of white calico, nailed to a small frame of wood and fastened into two or three holes left in the walls for the purpose, admitted light

> into the dwelling during the day . . . I have described the better class of structure erected by the settlers at the beginning; but there were many whose first attempts were miserable failures, and hardly served to protect them from the weather. Some, taking advantage of particular spots favourable to their purpose, thought they saved themselves labour by digging out holes, and burrowing in the ground, placing a slight covering over their excavations . . .[27]

Shaw was the only chaplain who had accompanied the settlers, and his first three years were devoted to ministering to their needs and establishing the church among them. Chapels were built and local preachers and class leaders appointed. Shaw was a man of a generous, catholic spirit and gladly assisted those of other denominations. The Anglicans held services in the chapels built by the Methodists, and the Dutch Reformed people brought their children to be baptized by him. Of the first fifty-seven baptisms recorded in the Grahamstown chapel, fifty-three were those of children of Dutch parents.[28]

But Shaw could not limit his ministry to the Europeans. His vision was filled with the regions beyond and the tribes that knew not Jesus, and his firm purpose was to reach out to them. As he wrote in his autobiography, *The Story of My Mission among the Native Tribes of South-Eastern Africa*:

> From the time when I received my appointment to Southern Africa, as Chaplain or Minister to a party of British settlers, my mind was filled with the idea that Divine Providence designed, after I had accomplished some preparatory work among the settlers who were located on the borders of Kaffraria, that I should proceed beyond the colonial boundaries, and establish a Wesleyan Mission among the Kaffirs. Hence I resolved not to be disobedient to the heavenly call; but while steadily pursuing the work of the day, my eye was constantly fixed on Kaffraria, as a great field for future Missions.[29]

Shaw then quoted from a letter which he had written to the Wesleyan Missionary Committee in 1820, only a few months after his arrival:

---

27. Hinchliff, *Church in South Africa*, 31.
28. Hofmeyr and Pillay, *History of Christianity*, 64.
29. W. Shaw, *Story of My Mission*, 59.

I hope the Committee will never forget that, with the exception of Latakoo, which is far in the interior, *there is not a single Missionary Station* between the place *of my residence* and the *northern extremity* of the *Red Sea*; nor any people professedly Christian, with the exception of those of Abyssinia. Here, then is a wide field – *the whole eastern coast of the continent of Africa!* If ever the words of the Saviour were applicable to any part of the world at any time, surely they apply to Eastern Africa at the present time: *The harvest is great, but the labourers are few.*[30]

The "Latakoo" mentioned by Shaw was Robert Moffat's mission station. Furthermore, his claim of "not a single Missionary Station" between himself and the Red Sea was obviously a reference only to Protestant establishments, for there were many Roman Catholic missionaries labouring in Africa.

Shaw dreamt of establishing a chain of mission stations along the coast from the Eastern Province to Natal, and the following list of stations with the dates they were founded shows how far his dream was realized:

Wesleyville (1823)
Mount Coke (1825)
Butterworth (1827)
Morley (1829)
Clarkebury (1830)
Buntingville (1830)

Other stations were also established but, as could be expected in the troubled circumstances of the Eastern Cape, the work did not always progress smoothly. When one of the border wars broke out in 1834, many of the stations were burned down and the missionaries dispersed. But destruction was followed by patient rebuilding, and the gospel became increasingly rooted in the hearts of a growing number of Xhosa people. The achievement of William Shaw and the Methodist missions can be seen in the following statistics. By 1860 after forty years' labour, starting from scratch, there were thirty-six Methodist missionaries, ninety-six school teachers and catechists, about five thousand church members, eighty Sunday schools and forty-eight day schools, seventy-four chapels and 183 preaching stations.

One last incident in this remarkable man's life must also be told. During a severe drought, a debate took place between Shaw and Gqindiva, the official

---

30. Quoted in Davies and Shepherd, *South African Missions*, 109.

rain-maker, in the presence of the Chief Pato, his counsellors and many of his subjects. In the course of their discussion, Gqindiva accused Shaw of hindering the rain, stating

> I have slaughtered cattle, and offered to the spirits; I have often burned herbs. When the clouds come up from the sea, and spread all over the land, and the rain is ready to fall, *that thing* which you have brought into the country and set up on a pole on the hill at Etweca [Wesleyville] goes *tinkle-tinkle-tinkle;* and immediately the clouds begin to scatter, they disappear, and no rain can fall.

This accusation generated considerable discussion in the community, with opinions being divided. When some of the Xhosa residents of the Mission village suggested that the church bell should not again be used until after rain had fallen, Shaw felt led to call for a day of prayer and fasting for rain. The fast was vigorously observed and the several services were attended by a large number of people, including the principal chiefs, with many fervent prayers being offered. Then

> ... just as the people were beginning to assemble for the evening service (the last for the day) drops of rain began to fall slowly, and without any great promise of a copious flood. But, while the service was proceeding, the clouds were rolling up from the direction of the great Southern Ocean; and, at the time of its close, the rain was falling in heavy showers. It increased during the night, and became continuous, coming down heavily hour after hour. All the smaller streams were speedily overflowing; and on the third day some of the people came to the Missionary and said, "The rivers are overflowing their banks, and washing away some of the gardens: would it not now be well to thank God, and tell Him that it is enough, and pray that He may now withhold His hand?" Truly all acknowledged that this was "God's Rain." Gqindiva and his profession fell into disrepute in all that neighbourhood; and, for many years after, the Chiefs and counsellors or the Amagonakwaybie never made another application to a rain-maker.[31]

Criticism was sometimes levelled at the rapidity with which Shaw's chain of missions expanded. Thoroughness, it was felt, was sacrificed to speed. But

---

31. Shaw, *Story of My Mission*, quoted in Davies and Shepherd, *South African Missions*, 168.

there is no evidence that depth was sacrificed to breadth in the work of the Methodist missions.

The story will be told later of an African boy, Charles Pamla, born in Butterworth in 1834, who was destined to become a powerful instrument for the reviving and expansion of the church in the 1860s.

Presbyterians

Like the Dutch Reformed, the Presbyterians are children of the sixteenth-century Protestant Reformation, and particularly of the Calvinist or Reformed branch of that movement. On the continent of Europe, churches following the form of church government advocated by Calvin became known as "Reformed," whereas in the British Isles churches of the same polity became known as Presbyterian (from the Greek word for elders, *presbyteroi*). Most Presbyterians in Britain are of Scottish descent, as the National Church of Scotland adopted a Presbyterian (or Reformed) form of church government.

A group of Scottish soldiers stationed in the Cape formed a Calvinist Society in 1806, in which they met for Bible study and prayer. In 1812 they persuaded George Thom, an LMS missionary, to stay in the Cape and minister to them. It was he who formed the first Presbyterian church in southern Africa. When the Scottish regiment was recalled to Britain in 1814, Thom accepted a call to the Dutch Reformed Church in Caledon. Quite a number of Scottish Presbyterian ministers served in Dutch Reformed churches in the early nineteenth century. Indeed, when the shortage of ministers in the Dutch Reformed churches became acute in 1820, Thom was requested to inquire about suitable candidates from Scotland as the evangelical piety of the Scottish Presbyterian ministers was more acceptable in the Cape than the more rationalist theology prevalent in Holland.

But the few remaining English-speaking Presbyterians in the Cape still hankered after a church and a minister of their own. Finally in 1829 St Andrew's Presbyterian Church was opened with John Adamson as its first minister. At about the same time a church was built in the Eastern Cape by a group of Scottish Presbyterians who had come with the 1820 Settlers. From these beginnings, further Presbyterian churches were established in various parts of the colony leading to the formation in 1897 of the Presbyterian Church of Southern Africa.

Presbyterians participated fully in the great Protestant missionary movement of the nineteenth century and were to make a noble contribution to the extension of the gospel in southern Africa, and elsewhere. They were the first to ordain a black man, Tiyo Soga, to the Christian ministry, and they established at Lovedale the most important educational institute in the Eastern Cape.

Lovedale

Founded as a mission of the Glasgow Missionary Society in 1824, the first decade of Lovedale's existence was stormy and precarious. Destroyed during the frontier war of 1834–35, it was later rebuilt. In 1841 a theological seminary was established at Lovedale with Dr William Govan as its first principal. He continued to serve in that capacity for twenty-nine years. Two important decisions that he made were that Lovedale should be interdenominational, accepting students from other missions, and second, that it should be multiracial.[32] The first class consisted of eleven black and nine white students. Despite the disruption caused by the War of the Axe in 1846 and Umlanjeni's War in 1850, the work continued. In 1870 Govan was replaced as principal by James Stewart, under whose capable leadership Lovedale continued to develop, becoming the most important educational institution for Africans in South Africa. Many future leaders of the ANC received their training and education there.

Something of Stewart's intellectual ability can be seen in the fact that, while studying theology at the University of Edinburgh, he published two books on botany which were widely used as textbooks for many years. Stewart's zeal for missions was fired by Livingstone's *Travels and Researches in South Africa*. He later met that famous missionary in 1862 and wrote of the encounter: "It seemed to me the realizing of some strange dream to be rambling through the grassy delta and mangrove forests of the Zambesi on this African summer evening with Livingstone."[33]

For thirty-five years Stewart was at the head of Lovedale. In addition to his labours there, he was actively involved in establishing a new missionary institution at Blythswood in the 1870s. During the following decade Stewart pioneered the Church of Scotland mission in Malawi, and in the 1890s he led a mission to East Africa.

---

32. Hofmeyr and Pillay, *History of Christianity*, 75.
33. Davies, *Great South African Christians*, 115.

Tiyo Soga

In the days when Ntsikana (about whom we heard earlier) was preaching, Ngqika, the Xhosa chief, sent one of his foremost counsellors and warriors, Soga, to listen to him. Soga was impressed and, though never baptized, he became deeply sympathetic to the gospel, and most of his children were converted to Christianity. Tiyo was the seventh child of Soga's chief wife, Nosuthu, a devout believer who encouraged her children to study.

Tiyo attended the school run by William Chalmers, a United Presbyterian Church missionary. From there he went on to study at Lovedale, where he excelled. Religious instruction was by means of the Westminster Catechism, which Tiyo learned by heart to the delight of his Scottish teachers. Lovedale was closed down during the War of the Axe in 1846. Govan, the principal, returned to Scotland for a while and offered to take Tiyo with him to further his education. Permission was granted, and Tiyo went to Scotland, where he was baptized in 1848. Returning to South Africa towards the end of the same year, he worked for a while as an interpreter and an evangelist teacher. But the outbreak of the 1850 border war again disrupted the work of the mission. In Port Elizabeth Tiyo was offered a job as a court interpreter with a good salary. An opportunity also arose for him to return to Scotland to study theology in preparation for the ministry. Choosing the latter, he found himself immersed in the study of Greek, Latin, Hebrew, philosophy, history, and theology. These he successfully mastered, and was ordained into the ministry of the United Presbyterian Church in 1856, the first black man from southern Africa to receive formal training before ordination into the Christian ministry.[34]

In 1857 Tiyo married a Scottish girl, Janet Burnside, and returned to South Africa. The Eastern Province he returned to was suffering the consequences of the tragic cattle killing episode (see next section), and in these sad circumstances he began work as a missionary to his own people at Mgwali. He had hoped to witness a widespread turning to Christ among the Xhosa people, but in this he was disappointed. It is possible that his Scottish wife and the years he had spent in Scotland had alienated him to some extent from his own people. He also struggled with poor health, which eventually led to his death at the age of forty-seven.

Notwithstanding these and other difficulties, his ministry was certainly not without fruit. Alexander Duff, the famous Scottish missionary to India,

---

34. It has been claimed that Arie van Rooyen was ordained to co-minister with James Read in 1849, and that Jacob Links and Johannes Jager of Leliefontein mission were also ordained. But Tiyo Soga remains the first to be ordained after formal theological training.

commented after visiting Soga's work at Mgwali that the standard of the spiritual work there was of the highest he had witnessed in South Africa. Soga's literary output was prodigious. He was a prolific hymn writer, and about thirty of his hymns found their way into hymnbooks. He also assisted in the revision of the Xhosa Bible. His isiXhosa translation of Bunyan's *The Pilgrim's Progress*, *uHambo lomhambi*, became the most widely read religious book in that language after the Bible, and it is often reprinted to this day.

Was Tiyo Soga a "black Scotsman" as some allege, or the father of black nationalism, as others have claimed? On the one hand, he was certainly deeply committed to the Reformed faith of his Presbyterian church and critical of many tribal customs. His marriage to a Scot and consequent adoption of many European cultural forms distanced him to some extent from the Xhosa culture of his birth. On the other hand, he was proud of being a Xhosa and rejected feelings of racial superiority or inferiority in any form. His advice to his children was:

> You will ever cherish the memory of your mother as that of an upright, conscientious, thrifty, Christian Scotch woman. You will ever be thankful for your connection by this tie to the white race. But if you wish to gain credit for yourselves – if you do not wish to feel the taunt of men, which you sometimes may well feel – take your place in the world as coloured, not as white men; as Kafirs, not as Englishmen. . . . For your own sakes never appear ashamed that your father was a Kafir, and that you inherited some African blood. It is every whit as good and as pure as that which flows in the veins of my fairer brethren.[35]

Many years after the death of Tiyo Soga, at the historic founding of the South African Native National Congress – the forerunner of the African National Congress (ANC) – in Bloemfontein in 1912, the conference opened with the delegates and observers singing together a moving rendition of Tiyo Soga's hymn *Lizalis'idinga lakho* (*Fulfil Thy Promise*). Thus it was that the life and work of this pioneer African missionary and minister was seen as a symbol of hope for all African people longing for justice and freedom in the land of their birth.

---

35. Saunders, *Illustrated History*, 151.

The Cattle Killing Tragedy

Shortly after the middle of the nineteenth century a tragedy befell the Xhosa people more terrible, perhaps, than any other event in the history of that troubled nation. Eight frontier wars between the colonists and the Xhosa tribes had resulted in the humiliating defeat of the latter and the loss of much of their former territory. Expanding Zulu power in the north caught the Xhosas between the pincers of two military powers. Seeing that no natural means of defeating their enemies seemed effective, a longing arose in the hearts of the people for a supernatural intervention that would drive the foreign invaders back into the sea from whence they had come. This longing rendered the Xhosas vulnerable to a delusion that was to have more devastating consequences than all the guns of their enemies.

In 1856 a young girl, Nongquase, claimed to hear voices declaring apocalyptic events that would bring about the utter defeat of the whites and the restoration of the Xhosa people. Her uncle, Mhlakaza, a renowned seer, supported and promoted her prophecies. Such claims were not entirely new. During the time of Ntsikana a certain Makanna (also known as Nxele) had also listened to van der Kemp but had developed a theology very different from that of Ntsikana. Makanna became an uncompromising war doctor who also proclaimed that the ancestors would rise from the dead to help the Xhosa drive the whites into the sea.

Nongquase and her uncle Mhlakaza designated 18 February 1857 as the day of deliverance and restoration. But let us hear the story in the words of Brownlee, Chalmers and Govan, contemporary witnesses of the events:

> [Nongquase] professed to have held converse with the spirits of the old heroes of the tribe, who intimated that they had witnessed with sorrow the ruin of their race through the oppression of the conquerors from overseas; and as they would no longer be silent spectators of the wrongs and insults, it was their intention to come to the rescue and save their progeny from destruction.

They would appear once more in the flesh among their people, but they would not do so unless and until the nation would exterminate all animals both great and small with the exception of horses and dogs. The corn pits in the cattle-folds were to be emptied of grain, which must be cast away, and the fields were to be left untilled. As soon as these commands were obeyed, vast herds would emerge from the ground, the country would smile again with corn, and there would be plenty for everyone. There was, in short, to be a resurrection of men and of cattle for their subsistence. The advent of the resurrection would be preceded by a frightful whirlwind, which would sweep all unbelievers who had refused to obey the orders of the spirits, and along with them all White men, into the sea.

Soon the country was resounding with stories of the wonders witnessed at the prophet's village. The horns of oxen were said to be seen peeping from beneath the rushes which grew round a swampy pool near the village of the seer. . . . Additional reports were that thousands of cattle were heard knocking their horns together and bellowing in caverns, impatient to rise, waiting only until all their fellows who still walked the earth were slain; dead men, years in the grave, had been met, who sent pathetic appeals to their kindred not to delay their coming back to life by refusing to obey the prophet. . . . Soon indeed all over the country, and particularly among the Gcaleka tribe, cattle began to be slaughtered. Traders bought hundreds of hides in a day. Feasts were everywhere, but it was impossible to consume all. Dogs were gorged on fat beef, vultures were surfeited, whole carcasses were left to putrefy, and the air became tainted with corruption.

After the delusion had been at work for ten months, an order came from the prophetess that within eight days all cattle must be killed. The preparations made during these days kept everyone busy. Cattle kraals were immensely enlarged so as to receive the huge herds that were to arise out of the ground. Corn pits were cleaned in readiness for the abundant corn that would pour in. Huts were rethatched so as to resist the coming storm. Not even a fowl was left alive to disturb the awaited, awesome morn. On the eighth day – 16 February 1857 – heaven and earth, it was said, would come together amid darkness, thunder, lightning, rain and a mighty wind, by which the unbelievers would perish. The sun would rise blood-red and double, and at noon would suddenly descend not to the west but to the east.[36]

The great day came and went, and the joyful hope and expectation of thousands was turned into the darkness of despair and starvation. It is estimated that some 40,000 people died of starvation, with about another 40,000 being forced to enter the colony as labourers. The population of the frontier areas was reduced to nearly a third of its former number. It was indeed a dark hour for the Xhosa people, but a brighter day was coming. In the years following the disaster of the cattle killing, remarkable spiritual movements were to advance the cause of Christ among the Xhosa. That story will be told later. And looking even further ahead, who would have guessed in the dark days of 1857 that in 1994 the first black African president of a united, liberated and democratic South Africa, Nelson Mandela, would be a son of the very Xhosa people so tragically decimated some hundred and thirty years before?

---

36. Davies and Shepherd, *South African Missions*, 38–41. Abbreviated from Brownlee, Chalmers and Govan.

Baptists

The first Baptists to reach southern Africa arrived among the 1820 Settlers. They were few in number and without a minister. William Miller took the lead in holding the first Baptist services on South African soil under a tree in the Albany district. Once planted, the Baptist faith continued to grow and spread throughout South Africa. In numbers, though, Baptists lagged behind the Methodists and Anglicans and remained one of the smaller Protestant denominations in southern Africa. Ecclesiastically, Baptists are close cousins of the Congregationalists. The first English-speaking Baptist church was formed in Holland in the early seventeenth century after an English Independent minister, John Smyth, began to doubt the validity of infant baptism. As a Congregationalist, he was already convinced that the local church consisted of believers in Christ freely gathered and covenanted together to serve the Lord, and that such a church was autonomous, subject only to Christ and not to any other external authority, whether civil or ecclesiastical. To these Congregationalist (or Independent) principles, Smyth joined the conviction that only those who freely and consciously believed in Christ were eligible for baptism, which he understood to be a personal pledge of commitment to Christ. By these principles, baptism could not be given to infants who were incapable of asking for it or understanding its meaning.

Smyth's convictions were almost certainly influenced by his contact with Dutch Anabaptists, a small group of whom had managed to survive in the somewhat more tolerant environment of the Netherlands. From their earliest beginnings, English-speaking Baptists were divided into two groups, the Particulars, adhering to the more Calvinistic theology of English Puritanism, and the Generals, who were more Arminian in their theology. It was precisely these tensions that brought about a schism in the very first Baptist church in Grahamstown, a division that took many years to reconcile and which doubtless hampered the early growth of the Baptists in South Africa.

In 1857 about 2,400 German soldiers who had fought for the British in the Crimean War were permitted to settle in the Eastern Cape. These were followed shortly afterwards by a larger group of north German immigrants. Among these German settlers were some Baptists who made application to Johan Oncken in Germany for a minister. In 1867 Oncken, who can be considered the founder and apostle of Baptist work in Germany and eastern Europe, sent out Hugo Gutsche, who became one of the most significant pioneers of Baptist work in South Africa.

Hugo Gutsche

Born in Saxony, Gutsche received a sound education and qualified as a pharmacist. Though brought up in the state Lutheran church, his own spiritual search and pilgrimage led him to Baptist convictions and so he was baptized in 1864. In the following year he met Oncken who recognized Gutsche's qualities and encouraged him to preach. In 1866 he became Oncken's assistant.

When the request from the German Baptist settlers for a minister reached Oncken, their requirements were so demanding that he protested: "Such men do not grow on apple trees, nor are they produced as a baker produces loaves of bread." Nonetheless, Gutsche was selected, and in 1867 he arrived in King William's Town to begin his ministry.

Under his leadership the German Baptists experienced considerable growth and their organization consolidated. At the time of his arrival there were no Baptist church buildings in British Kaffraria. Within twenty-five years he had built twenty-five churches, every one free of debt when opened. But Gutsche was more than a builder in brick and stone. Something of the spirit of the man is seen in this entry in his journal, written in February 1868:

> The cure of souls is the gravest task of the minister. May God have mercy on me should I take this lightly! How heavy this burden rests on me, and how much pain and fear I suffer, God alone knows. So many people are my responsibility. Oh that some would help and understand. I have to give an account of my work before God, my own salvation is involved, if I do not faithfully preach the truth. If some think other preachers would make it easier to follow Christ then let them go. I am bound to proclaim the Gospel not counting the cost.[37]

So effective was the work of Gutsche that at the time of the formation of the Baptist Union of South Africa in 1877 there were more German-speaking than English-speaking members.

Indeed, the fact that German and English Baptists were able to come together in the Baptist Union is a testimony to the patience, sacrifice and vision of Hugo Gutsche. There were several issues on which German and English Baptists did not see eye to eye, resulting in not a little suspicion and tension between them. English Baptist congregations were more independent

---

37. Hudson-Reed, *Together for a Century,* 23.

in character, while the German Baptist churches were bound together in closer unity. The German churches practised "closed membership" and a "closed table" (allowing only baptized believers into church membership and to share in Holy Communion). The English churches, on the other hand, generally favoured an "open table," welcoming all believers to Holy Communion, and some of them even an "open membership," taking into membership believers who had not received believers' baptism. For these reasons the Germans were hesitant to unite with the English churches. Gutsche, who was a champion of unity, received much criticism and at one stage was refused communion in one of the German churches. Such things pained him very deeply, but he persevered in promoting the welfare of both his fellow German Baptists and the wider family represented by the Baptist Union.

It is interesting to note that in 1880, when a proposal was made to merge the Baptist Union with the Congregational Union, Hugo Gutsche spoke strongly against the idea. Doubtless he had a shrewd idea as to the limits of what his fellow German Baptists could be expected to accept.

Further Baptist Developments

From their early beginnings in the Eastern Cape, the Baptists gradually spread to other parts of South Africa, especially where English-speaking people were to be found.

The first Afrikaans Baptist church was established in 1886 by J. D. Odendaal. In his youth he had studied at Stellenbosch to prepare for the Dutch Reformed ministry. Doubts about the validity of infant baptism led him to discontinue his studies. Some years later, while farming at Burgersdorp in the Orange Free State, he heard about the Baptists in the Eastern Cape and undertook the 300 kilometre journey to visit them. At Frankfort he met Hugo Gutsche, who had arrived in the country only fourteen days previously, and was baptized by him. About ten years later Odendaal was ordained by the German Baptists, and became the leader of the first Afrikaans Baptist church in South Africa. Although never large, the Baptist work grew slowly among Afrikaans-speaking people.

Inspired by the example of William Carey, Baptists in southern Africa were eager to impart the gospel to the indigenous people of the land. The first to do so was a German farmer, Carl Pape, who had learned to speak Xhosa fluently. After having a dream in which he watched a native hut sinking in the waves while hands stretched out appealing for help, he felt called to preach the gospel to the Xhosa people.[38] In this work he was greatly encouraged by Hugo Gutsche who persuaded the German churches to recognize his ministry officially in 1868. The work of Pape and Gutsche played an important role in the formation of the South African Baptist Missionary Society in 1892.

An acute labour shortage in Natal led to about 150,000 Indians being brought to Natal as indentured labourers between 1860 and 1911. Less than 2 percent of these were Christians and very few were Baptists. They kept their faith, however, and in 1903 wrote to India requesting the services of a Baptist minister. In response, the Telegu Baptist Home Missionary Society sent John Rangiah who laboured faithfully until his death in 1912. His first convert in Natal was a Telegu-speaking man named Subbadoo, who was awaiting execution for murder. With characteristic patience and persuasion, Rangiah won the heart of the condemned man, and Subbadoo was baptized in the prison bath. With Rangiah standing beside him on the gallows, Subbadoo cried, "I am going to the Lord Jesus Christ."[39]

The work of the Indian Baptists was troubled by a number of divisions – a weakness often observed among Baptist people, perhaps accentuated by their strongly independent outlook and the emphasis placed on the autonomy of the local church. Nevertheless, Indian Baptist churches were able to maintain themselves and achieve modest growth.

Roman Catholics

Roman Catholics were the first Christians to make contact with southern Africa, as witnessed by the three large stone crosses planted by Bartholomew Diaz on South African soil in 1488. But the fact that Dutch Protestants were the first to establish themselves in the Cape meant that Roman Catholicism was virtually excluded from the area for a century and a half. This ought not to surprise us, given the deep-seated animosity between Catholics and Protestants in the centuries following the sixteenth-century Reformation. For Protestants, Catholicism was an idolatrous corruption of the true Christian faith in which the good news of salvation by faith in Christ had been obscured, or even eclipsed, by a host of superstitious and extra-biblical doctrines and practices, such as the primacy of the pope, the cult of Mary and other saints, the sacrifice of the Mass, and the doctrine of transubstantiation. Protestants

---

38. Ibid., 22.
39. Hudson-Reed, *By Taking Heed*, 273.

believed it was their duty to hold fast to the true and saving gospel of Christ in all its purity according to the Scriptures. Catholics, for their part, regarded Protestants as heretics and schismatics who had rebelled against the church and its lawful pastors, shattering the unity of the church in the process and giving birth to dozens of competing sects that differed among themselves. The very diversity of Protestant churches and their conflict with one another was proof to Catholics that such churches were in error, for they held that truth could only be one, while error was always multiform. Catholics saw it as their duty to remain loyal to the one true church established by Christ himself and to uphold the traditions and teachings held by all the faithful down the ages and preserved in their fullness in the one holy catholic and apostolic church spoken of in the Nicene Creed.

The deep-seated antagonism between these two competing versions of Christianity meant mutual exclusion from each other's territory during the sixteenth, seventeenth and eighteenth centuries. Only in the nineteenth century did a thaw in relations begin, developing in the latter half of the twentieth century to a degree of mutual cooperation and respect unprecedented in more than four hundred years.

While there were a few Roman Catholics in the Cape before 1800, they were not permitted by the Dutch authorities to practise their faith openly but were allowed to have their children baptized in the Reformed church. Then, during the brief time of the Dutch Batavian Republic (1803–1806) religious toleration was extended to all denominations, and three Catholic priests arrived from Holland. A room in the castle was put at their disposal to serve as a chapel for the celebration of Mass. But when the Cape was recaptured in 1806, the priests were expelled by the British commander, David Baird, a staunch Scottish Presbyterian. Not long after that, however, there were again Catholic priests serving in the Cape.

As we previously observed with the Anglicans, episcopal churches do not function well without bishops. Only with the arrival in 1838 of the first resident bishop, the Irish Dominican Raymond Griffith, did the Roman Catholic Church begin to make significant progress in southern Africa. Griffith worked tirelessly, travelling around the colony, seeking out Roman Catholics who had lapsed in the practice of their faith, appointing clergy to various parts and establishing churches and schools for the spiritual care of the faithful. There were an estimated 700 Catholics in the Cape Colony when Griffith arrived, and by 1841 their number had grown to 2,500. Soon further bishops were appointed to share in the spiritual oversight of the growing church. Aidan Devereux was consecrated bishop of the Eastern Province. He had been a professor of Latin at St Peter's College, Wexford, and after coming to South Africa he became the principal of the Mercantile and Classical Academy, a school in Cape Town.

Roman Catholics enjoyed the advantage of being able to draw upon the various religious orders within the Catholic Church to staff their schools, hospitals, mission stations and parishes. These communities consisted of dedicated men and women gathered into societies that had often been founded by outstanding spiritual leaders. While organized as special bodies with their own constitutions, elected leaders and special institutions, they were all subject to the hierarchical leadership of the church, that is, to the bishops and the pope. The best known among these religious orders are the Franciscans (founded by St Francis), the Dominicans (founded by St Dominic), and the Jesuits (founded by St Ignatius of Loyola). But there are hundreds more. The religious orders that came to work in South Africa included the Dominicans, the Holy Family Sisters, the Augustinian Sisters, the Filles de Jésus de Kermaria, the Sisters of Hope, the Sisters of Nazareth, the Marist Brothers, the Christian Brothers, the Jesuits, the Precious Blood Sisters, the Pallotine Fathers, the Sacred Heart Fathers, and the Trappists.[40]

The first convent school in South Africa was established by an exceptionally capable nun, Marie-Gertrude, a member of a newly founded religious order, the Assumption Sisters. Born into a French aristocratic family that survived the Revolution, she received an excellent education in Brussels and London. In England she met Coleridge and Byron. The school she established in Grahamstown was so popular that many Protestants sent their children to it, resulting in the Anglican Bishop Gray warning his members against its influence. Marie-Gertrude was not at first willing to come to South Africa but, as a nun under vows of obedience to her superior, she felt obliged to obey the call. She afterwards commented,

> An English colony was distasteful to me, the next thing to the Chinese missions. Since it was God's will I must accept. I have lived to see no country offer so much personal religious and political liberty as those under English rule.[41]

---

40. Brain, "Moving from the Margins," 196.
41. Brown, *Catholic Church*, 46.

The first Catholic bishop in Natal was François Allard, who arrived there with a company of French-speaking Missionary Oblates of Mary Immaculate. As he was reminded a few years later, he had been sent to Natal "not to a few heretics who inhabit your towns but to convert the Zulus." His efforts to evangelize the Zulus, however, were not successful, but when he turned his attention to the Sotho people, greater success was achieved. Indeed, the Roman Catholic Church made greater progress in Lesotho than in any other area of southern Africa. To a large extent this was due to the selfless and dedicated labours of Father Gerard, the pioneer Catholic missionary to the Sotho people.

The Christian witness to the Sothos was, however, marred by animosity between the Catholic and Protestant missionaries. The Paris Evangelical Missionary Society had been active in Lesotho since 1835 and resented the intrusion of the Catholics into what they regarded as their territory. Father Gerard, on the other hand, felt no obligation to respect the prior claims of the Protestants as they were, in his view, not part of the true church. The wise Sotho king, Moshoeshoe, seemed to be torn between the competing Christian bodies – although perhaps, as some have suggested, he shrewdly played them off against each other in his own interests. Whatever the case, neither of them could claim him as a convert in the end; he died unbaptized.

In 1875 Allard was succeeded as bishop of Natal by Charles Jolivet, whose constant labours and many travels in the twenty-five years that followed resulted in considerable progress for the church. A newspaper report in 1899 stated that he had built ninety churches and chapels, eighty-two schools, and fourteen convents, orphanages and hospitals. The number of Roman Catholic clergymen increased from six to 114, and 284 lay brothers and 900 nuns were brought to South Africa as a result of his endeavours. One of those whom Jolivet brought to Natal was a Trappist monk, Franz Pfanner, who built up an institution that became the most famous Catholic mission station in southern Africa and the largest Catholic abbey in the world – Mariannhill.

Franz Pfanner and Mariannhill

Born in the scenic Austrian Tyrol, Wendolin Pfanner studied philosophy at the Universities of Innsbruck and Padua. Becoming convinced of a vocation to the priesthood, he began theological studies in the seminary of Brixen in Austria. From the beginning, his heart was inclined to missionary work. In his memoirs he wrote:

> As often as I recited the verse in the Miserere (prescribed in our rule for daily recitation), "I will teach the unjust Thy ways, and the wicked shall be converted to Thee," the yearning and desire to work in the badly neglected missions tormented me and gave me no rest.[42]

But Pfanner was dissuaded from missionary work on account of his physical weakness. After ordination to the priesthood, he served as parish priest of the village of Haselstauden for nine years before moving to the Balkans to take a post as chaplain to the Sisters of Charity. Meeting two Belgian Trappist monks in 1862, he found himself deeply attracted to the austere and strict discipline they followed.

The Trappists had their origin in a reform movement in the seventeenth century in the Cistercian abbey of La Trappe in Normandy, France. In reaction to lax practices, they emphasized liturgical worship and demanded absolute silence, with no allowance for recreation. The monks devoted themselves to liturgical prayer and contemplation, theological study, and manual labour. The ate no meat, fish or eggs.

On joining the Trappists, Pfanner received the religious name of Franz. Three years later he was commissioned to found a new monastery of the order on a site near the predominantly Muslim city of Banjaluka in Bosnia. When this was finally accomplished after much toil and many difficulties, the monastery was raised to the status of an abbey, and Pfanner was appointed its first abbot. The next day, at a general meeting of the Chapter of the Abbots and Priors of the Trappist order in France, Bishop Ricards of Grahamstown made an appeal for volunteers for missionary work in South Africa. When no one responded, Franz Pfanner finally spoke "If no one will go, I will."[43] And so it was that at the age of fifty-four, Pfanner embarked on yet another stage of his remarkable life, arriving in 1880 at Port Elizabeth.

The site the Trappists were allotted was so barren that it proved impossible to cultivate. It was then that Pfanner heard of Bishop Jolivet's desire for Trappists to settle in Natal, and so in 1882 they settled on a site close to Pinetown in Natal. At the end of the first year, Mariannhill, as their mission had been named, could boast a chapel, a chapter-room, a refectory, dormitory, bakery, a photographic studio, and a school for Africans, as well as workshops for tinsmiths, blacksmiths, wagon-makers and printers.

---

42. Davies, *Great South African Christians*, 86.
43. Ibid., 88.

In addition it had a guest-house, stables, and a small farm. By 1898, with a community of 285 monks, Mariannhill had become the largest abbey in the world and the centre of a number of other branches in other areas. Pfanner established a series of stations throughout southern Natal. Later on further stations were established in the Transkei, northern Natal and Rhodesia (now Zimbabwe).

But the very success of Mariannhill led to increasing tensions with the superiors of the Trappist order, which is contemplative rather than missionary. In 1892 Pfanner was suspended from office. Humbly he accepted this ruling and resigned his position, moving in 1894 to a remote place where he lived in great simplicity, rising at three in the morning for devotions and preparation for Mass, breakfasting at eight, spending most of the morning in manual labour, and the rest of the day in prayer, meditation and reading. After an hour's walk and final recitation of the Office, he would retire at eight in the evening.

After his death in 1909 the tensions between the Trappists and Mariannhill were finally resolved when the fathers and brothers of Mariannhill formed a new, separate order, the Congregation of Missionaries of Mariannhill. Pfanner was an outstanding example of the spirit of devotion, self-denial and obedience which characterized many of the nuns, lay brothers and priests who dedicated their lives to building the walls of Zion in South Africa – Catholic style.

The Journey So Far

We have traced now the planting and initial growth of the main English-speaking churches that arrived in the early decades of the nineteenth century – Congregationalists, Presbyterians, Anglicans, Methodists, Baptists and Roman Catholics. There were smaller groups too, such as the Quakers and the Salvation Army, with as much zeal, faith and commitment as any other Christian body. Limitations of space, however, preclude the telling of all their stories. But before we leave the nineteenth century and the British period, there are some important and interesting stories still to relate: the work of Moffat and Livingstone, the Great Trek of Dutch farmers up north, the formation of two new Afrikaans churches, the life of Andrew Murray, the remarkable mid-century revivals, the life of Charles Pamla, the Colenso controversy, the origin of the Ethiopian churches, and the work of the Lutheran missionaries.

4

"Ethiopia Shall Stretch Out Her Hands"[1]

At the beginning of the last chapter, we considered the life and work of two outstanding missionaries associated with the LMS – van der Kemp and Philip. No account of the church in South Africa would be complete without mention of two of their colleagues, Robert Moffat and David Livingstone.

Robert Moffat

Like so many other missionaries in South Africa, Moffat was a Scotsman. He was raised in a devout Christian home where his mother read him and his six brothers and sisters exciting episodes from the narratives of the Moravian missionaries in Greenland and the East Indies. His education was scant, interrupted when he ran away to sea at the age of eleven, and concluded when he was apprenticed to a gardener at fourteen. But Moffat continued to pursue his studies at evening school. Contact with a Wesleyan Methodist society led to a conversion experience in 1815, when he was twenty years old. Shortly thereafter he made acquaintance with an LMS missionary and offered himself to the directors of the Society as a candidate. After brief theological instruction, he set sail for Cape Town, bidding farewell to his family who were not to see him again for twenty-three years.

The LMS intended to send Moffat to a position beyond the frontiers of the Cape Colony, but permission for this was refused by the governor, Lord Charles Somerset, who had prohibited the colonists from proceeding beyond

---

1. Psalm 68:31

the border and did not want to make an exception for missionaries. Moffat then spent some months in Stellenbosch with a farmer, during which time he acquired a working knowledge of Dutch. Permission finally being granted for him to leave the colony, Moffat set off with a companion for Afrikaner's Kraal in Namaqualand, an area ruled by a former brigand, Jager Afrikaner, who had recently come under the influence of the gospel. During this journey an incident occurred that well illustrates something of the social and religious situation of the time. The following account was written by his son, John Moffat:

> He had stopped for the night at the farm of a wealthy Dutch patriarch. When supper was over, the host convened the family prayers and invited the missionary to conduct them. "But where are the servants?" asked Moffat. "Servants! What do you mean?" countered the patriarch. "I mean the Hottentots," said Moffat, "of whom I see so many on your farm." Anger mounting, his host retorted, "Hottentots! Do you mean that then? Let me go to the mountains and call the baboons, if you want a congregation of that sort. Or stop, I have it: my sons, call the dogs that lie in front of the door. They will do." The missionary dropped an attempt that would then have led to a violent ending. The psalm sung and the prayer offered. Moffat read the lesson of the Syrophoenician women who asked Jesus to cure her daughter and chose as his text the words, "Yes, Lord, but even the dogs eat of the crumbs that fall from the master's table." His host interrupted quietly this time: "Will *Mynheer* sit down and wait a little? He shall have the Hottentots." The motley throng trooped in, many of whom had never heard a preacher before nor seen the inside of their master's house. When the service was over, the farmer turned to his guest and said, "My friend, you took a hard hammer and you have broken a hard head."[2]

After spending about a year at Afrikaner's Kraal, Moffat was asked by the LMS to assume control of its work among the Tswana people, and so he came to establish the mission station at Kuruman, which became the headquarters of all his activities for the next forty-five years. Putting his gardening experience to good account, Moffat built a five kilometre (three

---

2. Davies, *Great South African Christians*, 23.

mile) conduit to bring water to the mission station. Kuruman became famous for its beautiful and fruitful gardens. Concerning the use of cattle manure, Moffat wrote:

> When they first saw us employing people to convey the contents of cattle-folds to our gardens, the act being in their judgment too ludicrous to admit reflection, they laughed boisterously, supposing it to be one of our foolish customs, to charm the ground, as they were wont to do to their own gardens, by chewing a certain root, and spitting on the leaves to make the whole more fruitful. Thus from time immemorial millions of heaps of manure were turned to no useful account. It was very long before they were convinced, but at last they discovered that manured gardens did not "get old," but could be made "very young again," and, therefore, the veriest heathen may now be seen carrying manure on their backs and on the backs of oxen, to garden grounds. Lately, an individual remarked to me on this subject, "I cannot persuade myself that we were once so stupid as not to believe what we saw with our eyes."[3]

Before leaving England, Moffat had fallen in love with a certain Mary Smith, whose father had employed Moffat as a gardener. Her parents were at first unwilling to permit her to travel to Africa to marry Moffat, but at last they yielded and in 1819 the couple were married in Cape Town. In addition to their own children, they also adopted two San (Bushman) orphans in 1822. Moffat had come across a party of San digging a grave for a woman. They were proposing to bury the orphans with her, that they might be cared for by their mother in the shades of the other world, but Moffat begged to adopt them. Rejoicing in the names Dicky and Ann, they became an integral part of his own family.[4]

Despite some progress on various fronts, spiritually the work at Kuruman was disappointing. There was no perceptible response to the message preached by Moffat. He persevered in learning the Tswana language and by 1825 was able to send the manuscript of a Tswana spelling book to Cape Town to be printed.

---

3. Hofmeyr, Millard and Froneman, *History of the Church*, 135.
4. Davies, *Great South African Christians*, 25.

A couple of years before that, however, an incident occurred which greatly enhanced the status of Moffat in the eyes of the Tlhaping people among whom he lived.

The rise of the Zulu kingdom of Shaka led to massive disruption of societies in a large part of southern, central and eastern Africa. One of Shaka's generals, Mzilikazi, clashed with him and then fled with a large following, cutting a swath of destruction from present-day KwaZulu-Natal into the interior and up to present-day Zimbabwe, where he finally settled. As one tribe was dislodged from its territories by invading impis (warriors), it would in turn invade the territory of neighbouring tribes. One such tribe was the Tlokwa, ruled by a woman called MaNthatisi. When Moffat heard that the Tlokwa warriors were planning to attack the Tlhaping, whom he judged would be no match for the invading army, he hastened to Griquatown and persuaded the Griqua chief, Waterboer, to come to their assistance. With a hundred mounted men armed with rifles, Waterboer was able to repel the much larger Tlokwa force and thus save the Tlhaping from possible extinction. The missionaries were now held in much greater respect among the people. Nevertheless, it took another six years before the hoped-for spiritual breakthrough finally took place in 1829, shortly after the people began to give greater attention to the preaching of the gospel. Johannes du Plessis describes the events as follows:

> Without any apparent antecedent agency a wave of strong emotion broke over the inhabitants. They crowded the place of worship long before the service was timed to begin. Men, women and children were bathed in tears. Some would listen with intense earnestness to the tones of the preacher's voice, and then suddenly fall down in hysterics, or suffer themselves to be borne away in a state of extreme prostration. At all hours of the day the missionaries would be beset in their homes by numbers of anxious seekers after salvation. Those who had found peace would gather for prayer and praise, and at early morn and late even the voice of rejoicing and salvation was heard in the tabernacles of the righteous.[5]

From this time on, the work progressed steadily. A large church building was erected which could seat 500. There, the baptism of the first six converts took place, followed by the first celebration of Holy Communion at Kuruman.

---

5. Du Plessis, *History of Christian Missions*, 161.

After thirteen years a church in which the sacraments could be observed had been established among the Tswana people.

Towards the end of 1829 Moffat made the first of his visits to Mzilikazi who, after his flight from Shaka in Natal, had established his Ndebele people as the dominant power in the highveld of the northern Drakensberg. From his base in the Magaliesberg, Mzilikazi sent two of his indunas (counsellors) to visit Moffat. He returned with them to meet the great king whose very name struck feelings of awe or terror in the hearts of thousands. On his way to Mzilikazi, Moffat could not help but note the many evidences of warfare that had ravaged the entire region in recent years – the ruins of many villages and piles of bleaching bones.

Moffatt was well received by Mzilikazi who, laying his hand on his shoulder, said, "My heart is all white as milk: I am still wondering at the love of a stranger who never saw me. You have fed me, you have protected me, you have carried me in your arms. I live today by you, a stranger." Moffat replied, "But when did I do all that for you?" Pointing to the indunas who had visited Kuruman, the chief answered, "These are great men. Umbate is my right hand. You fed them and clothed them, and when they were to be slain, you were their shield. You did it unto Mzilikazi, the son of Machobane."[6] One cannot but be reminded of the words of a greater king recorded in Matthew 25: "Whatever you did for these . . . you did for me."

Moffat developed a friendship with Mzilikazi that was to last over thirty years. Four times the missionary visited the chief. On the last occasion the Ndebele king was residing in Bulawayo (in present-day Zimbabwe), his headquarters north of the Limpopo which he had withdrawn after being defeated by the Voortrekkers in 1837. Moffat was not, however, to have the satisfaction of seeing his friend accept the Christian faith.

By the 1850s Moffat had translated the entire Bible into Tswana and spent some time in England to see it through the printing press. It was during this time that David Livingstone heard him speak and felt inspired to come to Africa.

In the 1860s Moffat and his wife suffered a series of blows: the deaths of their son, their daughter and a son-in-law, and a personal attack on Moffat that nearly killed him. In 1870 he and his wife finally left Kuruman to spend their remaining years in England. He was greatly honoured in the land of his birth. Twice he was summoned to meet Queen Victoria; twice he breakfasted

---

6. Ibid., 162.

with William Gladstone, renowned statesman and several times Prime Minister of the United Kingdom. Moffat died in Kent in 1883.

David Livingstone

It is a phenomenon of human history that the public gaze is sometimes focused on certain persons who are accorded a disproportionate measure of praise and honour, while worthy contemporaries are often passed by in silence. Such is possibly the case of Livingstone. Davies' statement that "he was probably the most distinguished missionary in history with the single exception of Saint Paul" is surely an exaggeration. However, even a more sober estimate of the man, must recognize his greatness of spirit and the impact he made on his generation.

Born in Blantyre in 1813 of humble Scots stock, Livingstone left school at the age of ten to toil long hours in a spinning mill but continued his studies at night after work. His shortcomings in formal education doubtless account for the atrocious spelling in his later writings. A conversion experience at seventeen led him to dedicate his life to spreading the gospel in other lands. When Livingstone offered himself to the LMS he had China in mind, but after listening to Moffat he decided to go to Africa. He studied medicine and theology at Glasgow and then proceeded to the Cape, arriving at Kuruman in 1841.

Livingstone married Moffat's daughter, Mary, and for the first few years worked at Mobatsa with Moffat. But there was a restlessness about Livingstone that made it difficult for him to remain in one area for long. He also did not find it easy to work under the older Moffat. In 1843 Livingstone moved north to work with the Kwena people. His first convert was the Kwena chief, Sechele, whose only son had been cured of a serious illness. Sechele initially made encouraging progress in the Christian faith, gaining considerable knowledge of the Scriptures. But few of the Kwena followed him in his faith, and this caused unbearable tensions between his desire to follow Christ and the expectations of his role as a traditional African chief, who was expected to be a rain-maker.

A missionary contemporary of Sechele, John Mackenzie, has left us a report which casts light on the question of contextualization that continues to provoke much debate in African Christian circles to the present day: To what extent must the Christian message be adapted to local culture and customs?

His position seemed to be one which he has not been by any means the first to occupy – that Christianity might be engrafted upon heathen customs, and that the two could go together. For instance, he himself would go with the people in their rain-making ceremonies, but he would not neglect at the same time to pray to God. He would use charms and incantations, washings and purifyings, according to the old rule, and yet profess faith in Him whose blood cleanseth from all sin. The Bible, in short, did not require him to give up the customs of his ancestors, although it required him to believe in the Lord Jesus Christ. He could be an orthodox Mochuana and a good Christian at the same time. This was the position which he took up, and the tenor of many of his discourses. I have spent many hours of the night with this clever chief in the earnest discussion of these points. When one after another his arguments failed him, he has said to me: "You have conquered, your idea of the Christian life is the right one, but was I not alone? What is one man against all the Bakwena?"

"How hard it is for us all, Sechele, for me as well as for you, to believe that God with us is greater than all who can be against us!"

"Monare" (Sir), he replied with feeling, "not hard for you: you are a missionary; your faith is great; but hard for me, who am chief of a heathen town."[7]

Mackenzie's report finds fault with Sechele, but most modern missiologists would find equal (if not more) fault with the rigidity of the missionaries. As a chief, Sechele naturally had several wives, according to African law and custom. Although he was fully convinced of the truth of Christianity, desirous of baptism and enthusiastic to serve the Lord, he was refused baptism for five years by Livingstone until he had put away his "superfluous wives." When one of Sechele's "ex-wives" became pregnant by him, he was "cut off for a season" by the missionary. Soon after, Livingstone left Sechele and the Kwena for further explorations into Africa. His affection and compassion for his African friends was sincere, but if he had only settled down for a longer period with the Kwena and showed greater sensitivity to the need of grafting the gospel onto African culture, what good fruits for the Kwena people might not have resulted?

---

7. Davies and Shepherd, *South African Missions*, 85–86.

In 1849 Livingstone set off on a journey to discover Lake Nagami. This exploit earned him a gold medal from the Royal Geographical Society and was the beginning of his public fame, but the toll on his family was high. His wife's newborn baby died in the Kalahari Desert. So that he might be free to continue his expeditions, Livingstone sent his wife and children to Britain in 1852. It was to be four years before he saw them again. In the stress and hardships of managing her family alone, Mary developed a drinking problem and her religious faith was undermined.

Livingstone's next accomplishment was an epic three-year trip from coast to coast, during which he "discovered" the Victoria Falls, shown to him by his African companions. "The scene was so lovely," he later wrote, "that it must have been gazed upon by angels in their flight." Just as he was entranced by scenes of natural beauty, so Livingstone was appalled by the cruelty of the slave trade, for he frequently encountered chained and shackled parties of slaves. By this time almost all the major seafaring nations had outlawed the trade, but Arabs merchants on the east coast of Africa still plied a lucrative trade in slaves from countries like Zanzibar. Slaves could be sold for at least ten times their purchase price in the slave trading ports of East Africa. For African chiefs, the taking and selling of slaves was the easiest and quickest way of earning the hard cash necessary for the purchase of the firearms so much desired for military purposes.

Livingstone realized that acts of parliament alone could not halt this trade. Africans needed alternative and more legitimate means of commerce. Furthermore, he believed, the establishment of a chain of British colonies up the spine of Africa, from South Africa through Uganda and the Anglo-Egyptian Sudan to Egypt, would provide the necessary muscle and infrastructure for the suppression of slavery and the economic development of the region. Hence his famous call for "Commerce and Christianity." Livingstone was certainly naive in his expectations of the benefits of colonization, and he clearly had no idea how much colonial rule would be resented by the Africans. Still, his personal motives were sincere; he desired the liberation, development and blessing of the African peoples.

Returning to England in 1856, Livingstone found himself a hero and was showered with honours and awards. In a private audience, Queen Victoria was delighted to hear that Africans wanting to know about the white Queen's wealth always inquired how many cows she possessed. Livingstone's fame increased even more with the publication of his *Missionary Travels and*

Research in South Africa. It became a bestseller and brought welcome financial relief to his family.

The LMS, however, was not happy with the direction Livingstone's career was taking and wanted him to return to more regular missionary work. To enable him to pursue his heart's desires, Livingstone severed his relationship with the LMS and in 1858 set off on a voyage of discovery on the Zambezi. This expedition with its tons of supplies and equipment was funded at enormous cost by the British government. Yet it was to prove a colossal failure. The steamship provided for them could not navigate the Zambezi. Livingstone fell out with most of his fellow explorers, and his wife Mary died five months after joining him. One disaster followed another until the expedition was recalled in 1864.

Undaunted by all these setbacks, Livingstone scorned advice to settle down in England and in 1866 set off on his last journey, an expedition sponsored by the Royal Geographical Society to discover the source of the Nile. He never found the source and in 1873, at the age of sixty, died at Chitambo's village in the Ilala district of present-day Zambia. His faithful companions Chuma and Susi, who had been freed from slavery by Livingstone, prepared his body for the long trip back "home" and he was finally buried in London's Westminster Abbey.

In many ways Livingstone was a failure. His preaching produced few converts. He lamented his neglect of his family and clashed with fellow missionaries. The Zambezi expedition he led and the Universities Mission he inspired were failures. Yet his indomitable spirit and his vision for an Africa truly liberated by the gospel inspired thousands. He also influenced the British government to take stronger measures to suppress the slave trade. Thus the Sultan of Zanzibar was threatened with a naval blockade if he did not close his slave market forever. He complied, thirty-five days after Livingstone breathed his last while on his knees beside his bed in the heart of Africa.

The Great Trek

Between 1835 and 1840 approximately 15,000 people left the eastern frontier area of the Cape Colony and established their own states in the interior. Known to the English as the Dutch, they called themselves Afrikaners (they spoke Afrikaans, a dialect that had already diverged significantly from its Dutch origins) or Boers (farmers). Later they were to be referred to as the

Voortrekkers ("those who go on ahead"), and their epic emigration was to be known as the *Great Trek*.

The reason for their leaving was their dissatisfaction with British rule and the conditions in the Eastern Cape. A number of factors contributed to this dissatisfaction. The Boers felt that the newly established British government in the Cape could not adequately protect them from Xhosa raids, yet at the same time it forbade them to take military action of their own. Furthermore, laws recently passed tended to treat the white and coloured communities as equal. This was resented by the Boers as it disturbed the long-established pattern of relationship between master and servant so essential, in their view, for the peaceful ordering of society. Yet another aggravation was the emancipation of slaves in 1834. The Boers were not merely opposed to the emancipation as such but also complained that they had not received adequate financial compensation for their freed slaves and had therefore suffered considerable economic loss. These were some of the principle reasons for their exodus from the Cape Colony. On 2 February 1837 the following manifesto, in which the Boers gave their reasons for quitting the colony, was published in *The Grahamstown Journal*:

> 1. We despair of saving the colony from those evils which threaten it by the turbulent and dishonest conduct of vagrants, who are allowed to infest the country in every part; nor do we see any prospect of peace or happiness for our children in a country thus distracted by internal commotions.
>
> 2. We complain of the severe losses which we have been forced to sustain by the emancipation of our slaves, and the vexatious laws which have been enacted respecting them.
>
> 3. We complain of the continual system of plunder which we have ever endured from the Kafirs and other coloured classes, and particularly by the last invasion of the colony, which has desolated the frontier districts, and ruined most of the inhabitants.
>
> 4. We complain of the unjustifiable odium which has been cast upon us by interested and dishonest persons, under the cloak of religion, whose testimony is believed in England to the exclusion of all evidence in our favour; and we can foresee as the result of this prejudice, nothing but the total ruin of the country.

5. We are resolved, wherever we go, that we will uphold the just principles of liberty, but whilst we will take care that no one shall be held in a state of slavery, it is our determination to maintain such regulations as may suppress crime and preserve proper relations between master and servant.

6. We solemnly declare that we quit this colony with a desire to lead a more quiet life than we have heretofore done. We will not molest any people, nor deprive them of the smallest property; but, if attacked, we shall consider ourselves fully justified in defending our persons and effects, to the utmost of our ability, against every enemy.

7. We make known, that when we shall have framed a code of laws for our future guidance, copies shall be forwarded to the colony for general information; but we take this opportunity of stating, that it is our firm resolve to make provision for the summary punishment of any traitors who may be found among us.

8. We purpose, in the course of our journey, and arriving at the country in which we shall permanently reside, to make known to the native tribes our intentions, and our desire to live in peace and friendly intercourse with them.

9. We quit this colony under the full assurance that the English government has nothing more to require of us, and will allow us to govern ourselves without its interference in future.

10. We are now quitting this fruitful land of our birth, in which we have suffered enormous losses and continual vexation, and are entering a wild and dangerous territory; but we go with a firm reliance on an all-seeing, just, and merciful Being, whom it will be our endeavour to fear and humbly obey.

By authority of the farmers who have quitted the Colony,

(Signed) P. Retief[8]

The "more quiet life" which the Voortrekkers hoped for was not destined to be. They were under the impression that there were large tracts of uninhabited land that could be peacefully occupied. Such impressions were

---

8. Hofmeyr, Millard and Froneman, *History of the Church,* 115.

created, in part, by the widespread devastation and depopulation resulting from the wars and troubles accompanying the rise of Shaka's Zulu kingdom in the early decades of the nineteenth century. When setting off for the interior the Boers little anticipated the hardships, conflicts and losses they would endure. The story of the Voortrekkers, the various routes taken by different leaders, the bloody clashes with Dingaan and Mzilikazi as well as their internal quarrels, is one full of high drama and fascination. But our concern is primarily with the story of the church, and so we shall focus only on the religious developments associated with the Great Trek and its aftermath.

The Dutch Reformed Church was not initially sympathetic to the emigration. In a meeting of a synod in October 1837, a pastoral letter in which the Trek was sharply criticized as an unlawful act of resistance against the British authorities was approved by the great majority of the delegates. The synod also expressed its concern that the Trekker's religious faith would suffer in the wild interior of the country.

To the disappointment of the Trekkers, no ordained minister from the church accompanied them. But they were able to procure the services of a former LMS missionary, Erasmus Smit, who had married a sister of one of the Trek leaders, Gert Maritz. Smit's origins with the LMS did not endear him to many of the Trekkers who regarded the "meddling and interfering missionaries" as one of the principle causes of their departure from the Cape Colony. Moreover, many of the Trekkers felt that Smit had never been properly ordained. It was alleged that Smit did not enjoy good health and was addicted to liquor. For these reasons he was never a popular minister and was eventually retired in 1840. Ironically the man who replaced him was another missionary, the American Daniel Lindley. Unlike Smit, Lindley was loved by the Voortrekkers and had a deep impact on the development of Christianity among the Afrikaners and the Zulus.

Daniel Lindley

The son of a Presbyterian minister, Daniel Lindley was born in 1801 in Pennsylvania. His ordination at the age of thirty was followed by two fruitful years of ministry in a Presbyterian church in North Carolina. Feeling a call to missionary service, Lindley and his wife were sent out to South Africa by the American Board of Commissioners for Foreign Missions (often referred to as the American Board, or ABM) and arrived at Cape Town in 1835.

Not long after their arrival the Lindleys again embarked on a long journey of 3,220 kilometres (2,000 miles) into the interior of the country to reach the Ndebele people of Mzilikazi, who at that time had his headquarters at Mosega in what is today the North West Province, about fifteen kilometres (nine miles) south-west of present-day Zeerust.

Despite a promising beginning, the mission to the Ndebele was soon disrupted by violent conflict between Mzilikazi and the Boers. Mzilikazi was suspicious of the arrival of so many whites (the Voortrekkers coming from the south). In October 1836 he launched an attack on them at Vegkop. The following January the Voortrekkers attacked Mzilikazi at Mosega. Lindley was awakened before dawn by the sound of gunfire and the shouts and screams of fleeing men and women. Mzilikazi and his Ndebele warriors were routed and soon afterwards withdrew across the Limpopo River to set up a new capital at Bulawayo, in the eastern part of what is today called Zimbabwe, where the Ndebele have lived to the present time.

His hopes of reaching the Ndebele having been dashed, Lindley decided to throw in his lot with the Voortrekkers in the hope of accompanying them to the Natal coast where fellow missionaries from the American Board were seeking to start a work among the Zulus. He came to be admired by the Boers, both as a man of God and as a crack shot with a rifle, a skill he had perfected in his youth in the woods of Ohio.

Hardly had Lindley arrived in Natal when his prospects for a settled ministry were again disrupted by conflict. A group of Boers had negotiated an agreement with the Zulu king Dingaan whereby they could settle in part of Natal. But Dingaan was suspicious and fearful of these Voortrekkers. He invited them to a farewell function during which he gave orders for Piet Retief and sixty of his companions to be killed. Other attacks followed and the whole area was plunged into conflict. The American Board advised its Natal missionaries to leave the colony, so Lindley moved again, this time to the Eastern Province of the Cape Colony.

In 1838 the power of Dingaan was broken at the Battle of Blood River and Lindley returned to live in the republic of Natalia and minister to the Boers. The republic was short-lived, but for the next seven years Lindley ministered to the largest parish any man ever had in South Africa. In his own words,

> I had for my parish all the country embraced in the district of Natal, the Free State and the Transvaal Republic. I was sole

minister for all the extended territory I have named and had the care of, I suppose, not less than 20,000 souls.⁹

During the seven years of Lindley's ministry to the Voortrekkers, five congregations were established. Thus he played a key role in the foundation of the Dutch Reformed Church in Natal, the Orange Free State and the Transvaal.

In 1847 Lindley resigned his post as minister to the Boers and returned to the American Board Mission and the work they were doing among the Zulus. At a time when many missionaries were inclined to take an overly strict view of many African customs and required converts to make a complete break with them in order to be received into the church, Lindley took a remarkably independent point of view. He vigorously defended those customs that in his view had social value and were not forbidden by God's Word. Such a custom was *lobola,* whereby a man would pay a certain number of cattle to his bride's father as part of the marriage contract. At a time when the custom was condemned by many other missionaries, Lindley declared:

> The *uku-lobola*, as it exists among the tribes of South East Africa, has been, on the whole, a great blessing to the people. If today one word from my mouth would instantly annihilate the custom, I would not speak that word."¹⁰

In these sentiments he was entirely supported by his wife, who claimed

> that their marriage custom of paying cattle is to the Zulu girls the greatest protection they have against the immorality of the nation, while it insures to the *women* good treatment and care which they would not otherwise receive. When a woman is married, the cattle are a surety in the father's hands of her good treatment . . . if the people are black, they have many better laws and customs than ours, white and civilized as we are.¹¹

For twenty-six years Lindley was associated with the mission at Inanda before he finally returned to the USA at the venerable age of 73. Lindley had the gift of being able to develop a deep understanding of and friendship with the people he served. At a time when relations between Boers, British and Zulu were marked by conflict, bloodshed and animosity, Lindley succeeded in gaining the respect and love of all three. To the Boers he became a Boer

---

9. Davies, *Great South African Christians,* 46.
10. Davies and Shepherd, *South African Missions,* 180.
11. Ibid., 181.

and to the Zulus a Zulu, understanding their peculiar customs and traditions with sympathy and insight. The little town of Lindley in the Free State was named after him.

The Formation of Two New Afrikaans Reformed Churches

The Voortrekkers established two republics, the South African Republic (SAR; also known as the ZAR or the Transvaal Republic) and the Orange Free State. After the resignation of Lindley in 1847, the few Dutch Reformed churches scattered throughout these two Boer republics struggled to obtain a minister. In 1849 Andrew Murray (junior) was inducted to the church in Bloemfontein. In the following years Murray made a number of preaching tours to the SAR. At least twice he was invited to be the minister of the Transvaal churches, but he felt unable to accept the calls.

During this time there were discussions concerning the incorporation of the Transvaal congregations in the Cape Synod of the DRC. With the arrival in the Transvaal in 1853 of Dirk van der Hoff, a minister from the Netherlands, a General Assembly consisting of both church and civil leaders decided against incorporation with the Cape Synod. The reasons for this decision included the following: First, the independent spirit of the Boers in the Transvaal Republic meant they did not like the idea of forming ecclesiastical ties with the British-ruled Cape Colony. Second, the Trekkers resented the fact that the Cape Synod had condemned the Great Trek in 1837 and had made no efforts to supply them with a minister. Third, the fact that they had obtained the services of van der Hoff meant that they were no longer dependent on the Cape Synod for the provision of a minister.

So it was that in 1853 a second Dutch Reformed Church came into being, known in Afrikaans as the *Nederduitsch Hervormde Kerk*. It became the official state church of the Transvaal Republic.

However, a group of earnest, strict Calvinist families in the Transvaal were not happy with the lack of confessional orthodoxy they perceived in van der Hoff and the Hervormde Kerk. The tensions came to a head over the issue of hymn singing. Traditionally, the book of Psalms had been the only hymn book for Dutch Reformed Christians. In 1807 a hymnal was introduced to the churches in the Netherlands. In 1814 it made its appearance at the Cape. But it was not welcomed by the "Dopper" element, as the strictly Reformed Christians were known. For them, no human hymns could compare with the inspired words of the sweet psalmist of Israel. They would use only the latter in public worship. This issue became the focal point of their desire for a fully confessional Reformed church.

In 1858 another minister from the Netherlands arrived in the Transvaal. Dirk Postma's theological convictions were similar to those of the Doppers. At a General Assembly of the Hervormde Church in 1859, the vexed question of hymns again arose. Van der Hoff proposed that it should be left to the minister to decide whether hymns should be sung. But this proposal was rejected and the use of the hymn book in public worship was insisted upon. Fifteen conscientious objectors approached Postma to help them form a separate church in which they could maintain their principles. Thus it was that in 1859 a third Dutch Reformed Church came into being, known in Afrikaans as the *Gereformeerde Kerk* and modelling itself on the doctrines, discipline and church order of the Synod of Dort, held in Holland in 1618–1619. Despite the small number of founders of this church, such was their dedication and the ability of Postma, their minister, that they put down deep roots and today number over 100,000 members in about 300 congregations.

After the death of Postma, the leading figure in the Gereformeerde Kerk was a remarkable Jewish Dutch poet, Jan Lion Cachet. He was born in 1838 in Amsterdam, a grandson of a Jewish immigrant from France who had been converted to the Christian faith by Isaac da Costa, also a Jewish Dutch poet and convert to Christ who played a leading role in the nineteenth-century *Réveil* (Awakening) in the Netherlands. In 1861 Cachet responded to a call by the Dutch Reformed Church for teachers and came to South Africa. Having worked in different parts of southern Africa as a teacher, he joined the Gereformeerde Church in 1865, deeply impressed by the convictions and integrity of the Doppers and their stand against the inroads of modernism threatening the state church. Cachet served as an assistant to Postma, who provided him with the necessary theological training before his ordination in 1868. Later, Cachet himself took a leading role in providing theological instruction to candidates for ministry in the Gereformeerde Church. He was a man of many parts. A lover of poetry and literature, he could recite from memory the works of many of his favourite Dutch poets. He was especially fond of the English author William Thackeray. Cachet wrote extensively in English, Dutch and Afrikaans, but his finest poetry and prose was written in Afrikaans. One of his most popular books, *The Seven Devils and What They Did*, ran into many editions.

Jan Lion Cachet had a brother, Frans, who also played an influential role in the spiritual life of the Boer republics. Dissatisfied with the state of affairs in the Hervormde Church, he travelled throughout the Transvaal in 1866 establishing Dutch Reformed (Nederduitse Gereformeerde) congregations in various places. These formed a synod and eventually linked up with the Cape Dutch Reformed synod.

By the year 1870, then, there were three separate bodies of Afrikaans Reformed churches in the Transvaal. The fact that their different names all translate into the English word "Reformed" causes endless confusion among English-speakers, but they can be differentiated as follows:

1. The Dutch Reformed Church (Nederduitsch Hervormde Kerk, NHK) was formed in 1853 as the established church of the Transvaal Republic.
2. The Reformed Church (Gereformeerde Kerk, GK) split off from the Hervormde Church in 1859 as a more strictly confessional Reformed body, popularly known as the "Doppers."
3. The Dutch Reformed Church (Nederduitse Gereformeerde Kerk, NGK) subsequently linked up with the Cape Synod.

These three denominations became known in South Africa as the three sister churches, although the GK and the NHK have always been much smaller than the NGK. Notwithstanding the considerable inroads made by the Pentecostal movements during the twentieth century, the three sister churches still encompass the great majority of Afrikaans-speaking Christians to this day.

Andrew Murray

The impact of Andrew Murray's ministry on the church in South Africa is probably unparalleled by any other single figure in its history. Today his name is honoured in Reformed, Anglican, Methodist, Baptist, Pentecostal and Charismatic circles. From his pen issued forth some 240 books and pamphlets, published in Dutch, English and Afrikaans. A few were published in up to fifteen languages and quite a number are still in print. He combined in himself a remarkable synthesis of his own Reformed/Presbyterian background with the Holiness, Revivalist and Evangelical movements current in his time. During his life he served four congregations, founded a number of influential educational institutions, and was six times elected moderator of his church. His influence extended far beyond his native country of South Africa and, through his books, continues to the present time. The story of this remarkable man cannot be omitted from any account of the church in South Africa.

Murray's father, also Andrew Murray, came to the Cape Colony in 1822 on the recommendation of George Thom, and became the minister of the Dutch Reformed congregation at Graaff-Reinet where he served for forty-five years. He married Maria Stegmann, who was of Huguenot and Lutheran ancestry, and they had ten children. Andrew Murray junior was born in Graaff-Reinet in 1828. Together with his elder brother, John, he was sent to Aberdeen in Scotland for his education. There they stayed with their uncle, a Presbyterian minister.

During their seven years in Aberdeen, the two young Murrays witnessed the struggle within the Church of Scotland between the Evangelicals and the Moderates over the issue of lay patronage. The Evangelicals stood strongly for the principle "that no pastor shall be intruded on any congregation contrary to the will of the people." The state, on the other hand, supported by the Moderates, upheld the right of a lay patron to appoint a minister to a congregation. When the issue went to the courts, judgment was made against the Evangelicals. This led to the Disruption of 1843 when more than a third of the ministers walked out of the General Assembly to form the Free Church of Scotland. Andrew Murray's uncle was a leader of the Free Church party, and the stirring events made a deep impression on the young Andrew, preparing him for the role he was to play in later years in the struggle between the church and the civil authorities.

Andrew and his brother both felt called to the ministry, so from Aberdeen they proceeded to Utrecht University in the Netherlands to learn Dutch and complete their theological training. In Holland, too, battles were raging in the church between advocates of a more rationalistic modern theology and upholders of traditional Calvinistic orthodoxy. The Murray boys joined a student society *Sechor Dabar* (Remember the Word), thus bearing witness to their essentially conservative convictions.

In 1848 both Andrew and John Murray were ordained at The Hague and returned to South Africa. Andrew was appointed to the Dutch Reformed congregation in Bloemfontein. At the age of twenty-one he found himself responsible for a parish covering an area of 130,000 square kilometres (50,000 square miles). Despite his youth, his earnest preaching and godly ways made a profound impression on the rough farmers who heard him. The comments made by an African who observed Murray preaching in the Transvaal give us a glimpse into his ministry:

I never thought that the white men stood in such fear of their chiefs. Look at the young chief yonder. He points his finger at the people: they sit quiet. He threatens them: they sit quite still. He storms and rages at them: they sit as quiet as death.[12]

Murray's facility in Dutch and English and his reconciling nature fitted him well to function as a mediator between the British government and the Boer leaders of the Transvaal. At the Sand River Convention of 1852, for example, at which the British guaranteed the independence of the SAR, Murray acted as a translator. In the following year he was one of two men nominated by a national convention held in Bloemfontein to go to England to dissuade the British government from abandoning the Orange River Sovereignty. At the same time, he was also commissioned by the Cape Synod to seek out ministers for the Colony in Scotland and Holland. The difficulties he experienced in this latter task made him an ardent advocate for the establishment of a theological seminary in the Cape to train indigenous ministers. This ideal was realized with the establishment of the Stellenbosch Theological Seminary in 1857.

In 1856 Murray married Emma Rutherford, the daughter of a Cape Town merchant. Four years later he accepted a call to the church in Worcester where he served for four years. While Murray was there, a number of congregations in the Cape, chiefly Dutch Reformed and Methodist, experienced a remarkable religious revival. This movement will be considered in greater detail in the next section. It can be noted here, however, that Andrew Murray was heir to a tradition of religious revivals. In Graaff-Reinet his father had prayed for many years for an outpouring of the Holy Spirit upon the churches of his adopted country. The younger Murrays never forgot that their father's study door was closed on Friday evenings as the faithful intercessor spent long hours in a time of fervent prayer for revival.[13]

The impact of the revival in Worcester was profound. Hundreds were received into membership of the church and about fifty men felt a call to full-time Christian ministry. Murray wrote his most famous book, *Abide in Christ*, to help and guide those converted in the revival. Many more books of a devotional, inspirational and teaching character were to flow from his pen. In 1862 he was elected Moderator of the Dutch Reformed synod. Although only thirty-four he was able to provide a spirited and mature leadership in the

---

12. Davies, *Great South African Christians*, 96.
13. Orr, *Evangelical Awakenings*, 53.

church's struggle against the inroads of rationalism and modernist theology. That story, too, is so full of interest that it will be covered in a later section.

After a seven-year stint as the minister of the Groote Kerk in Cape Town, the mother church of the Dutch Reformed denomination, Murray was called in 1871 to the congregation at Wellington where he served for the next thirty-four years. His interest in education and missions led to his founding the Huguenot Seminary (1874) and the Wellington Missionary Training Institute (1877). He had previously been involved in founding Grey College in Bloemfontein (later the University of the Orange Free State) and the Normal College in Cape Town.

While at Wellington, Murray embarked on a number of evangelistic tours around the country. So successful were these that he was also invited to preach at Northfield in the USA and at Keswick in England. While remaining firmly grounded in his inherited Reformed theology, Murray was deeply influenced by the holiness, revivalist and missionary movements of his time. He wrote a book, *Divine Healing* (1900), which paved the way for the Pentecostal movement in South Africa, although the tragic death of a close friend led him to modify his earlier views on healing. Perhaps the genius of Andrew Murray was that he was able to tap into many of the popular movements of spirituality and renewal in his day without yielding to sectarianism. For this reason he was held in high honour by many diverse strands of Christianity.

Not that he was without his critics, both then and now. He has been charged by some Reformed theologians with introducing "Methodism" and other unconventional doctrines into the Dutch Reformed Church. It is true that some of Murray's teachings on *The Second Blessing* (1891) and divine healing led a few of his followers to break with the DRC and establish new churches. It has also been alleged that Murray acquiesced in the decision of the 1857 Cape Synod to permit separate services for whites and blacks. Prior to that date all church members worshipped together, but pressure from the white members eventually led to the following resolution:

> The Synod considers it desirable and scriptural that our members from the Heathen be received and absorbed into our existing congregations wherever possible; but where this measure, as a result of the weakness of some, impedes the furtherance of the cause of Christ among the Heathen, the congregation from the

Heathen, already founded or still to be founded, shall enjoy its Christian privileges in a separate building or institution.[14]

It has been rightly observed that that synodical decision was one of the first steps on the road to the establishment of full-blown apartheid in 1948. Why then did Murray acquiesce in such a decision? It must be remembered that missiological thinking at that time stressed the importance of missionary work bearing fruit in indigenous churches within the culture of the people evangelized. The formation of separate churches for particular people groups was supported by many, including Murray, as a step that would enhance the process of evangelization. Only later was the danger of this separatism fully realized as it developed into a religio-political system of oppression.

Whatever mistakes Murray and others of his generation made, his basic interest in the welfare and development of Africans cannot be doubted. In one of his last books, *Religion and Politics*, he warned against the practice of Afrikaner Nationalist politicians promoting their political views in a way that led to the development of apartheid as "Christian politics."[15]

But we have no need to defend Murray. The best of Christ's servants have their weaknesses and inevitably share in some of the deficiencies of their age. The treasure of the gospel is always carried in earthen vessels. The impact of Murray's ministry continues to be felt, not least through his writings, which are still being published in many languages all around the world. Something of the spirit and burden of this man can be found in the following prayer, taken from his book *The Spirit of Christ*:

> O God! Thou didst send Thy Son to be the Saviour of the world. Thou didst give Him power over all flesh, that He should give eternal life to as many as Thou hast given Him. And Thou didst pour out Thy Spirit upon all flesh, commissioning as many as received Him to make known and pass on the wondrous blessing. In the Love and Power in which Thy Spirit was sent forth, He likewise sends forth those who yield themselves to Him, to be the instruments of His Power in glorifying Thy Son. We bless Thee for this Divine and most glorious salvation.
>
> O our God! we stand amazed, and abased, at the sloth and neglect of Thy Church in not fulfilling her Divine commission;

---

14. De Gruchy, *Church Struggle*, 8.
15. Hexham, "Andrew Murray," in Elwell, *Evangelical Dictionary of Theology*, 741.

we are humbled at our slowness of heart to perceive and believe what Thy Son did promise, to obey His will and finish His work. We cry to Thee, our God! visit Thy Church, and let Thy Spirit, the Spirit of the Divine Sending, fill all her children.

O my Father! I dedicate myself afresh to Thee, to live and labour, to pray and travail, to sacrifice and suffer for Thy Kingdom. I accept anew in faith the wonderful gift of the Holy Spirit, the very Spirit of Christ, and yield myself to His indwelling. I humbly plead with Thee, give me and all Thy children to be so mightily strengthened by the Holy Spirit that Christ may possess heart and life, and our one desire be that the whole earth may be filled with His glory. Amen.[16]

Revival

In 1857 and 1858 many of the Protestant churches in the USA were profoundly influenced by a movement of prayer and religious revival that apparently started in a noon-day prayer meeting in a Dutch Reformed Church in New York. Very soon the secular press was following with enthusiasm the spread of the movement from city to city as churches, halls and theatres were filled at noon for prayer. Prayer gave rise to testimony and preaching so effective that in a short time more than a million converts were added to the membership of the major denominations. It seemed to observers that the whole nation was turning to God in a movement singularly free of sectarian spirit.[17]

News of the revival leapt across the Atlantic to the British Isles where so many Americans originated, and very soon similar phenomena were being experienced there. So great was the impact in Northern Ireland in 1859 that approximately 10 percent of the population professed conversion. In Wales, Scotland and England the churches received about a million new members in the space of a few years in an extraordinary awakening of faith and religious conviction. Other parts of the world too, especially where there were peoples linked in some way to Britain or the USA, shared in this religious awakening.

In Cape Town, the journal of the Dutch Reformed Church carried regular news of the 1858 awakening in the USA and the 1859 Ulster Revival, promoting a rising tide of interest in and prayer around the subject. A

---

16. Murray, *Spirit of Christ*, 111–112.
17. Orr, *Evangelical Awakenings*, 47.

letter addressed to all South African Christians calling them to pray for a visitation of God's Spirit in the country was signed by leading churchmen and missionaries.[18] In April 1860 a conference of missionaries and ministers was held at Worcester to hear first-hand accounts of the awakening in the USA and Britain. The 374 delegates who attended were deeply moved and returned to their fields of labour full of great expectations. When the deputation from Montagu attending the conference at Worcester returned to their town, they instituted prayer meetings and soon a spiritual movement began in both the Wesleyan Methodist and the Dutch Reformed congregations there. A Wesleyan missionary reported:

> O, Sir, what can I write! The Lord is doing wonders here. The Spirit is amongst us . . . prayer meetings every day and every night in the week. People who never prayed publicly before are opening their mouth widely. Last Sunday evening, I spoke from "Behold, he prayeth." I asked the people to come up to the school room on Monday, Wednesday and Friday mornings early to pray the Lord for a spiritual blessing. They came in large numbers very early, three o'clock . . . On Thursday evening, at our prayer meeting, I felt downcast when we commenced, but soon had cause for rejoicing. A poor girl began for the first time to pray. What language! It was her mouth, but the words were of the Spirit. I cried out, "Pray, my child. Pray to the Lord. He is here!" and glory to His name, it was so! Young and old commenced crying for mercy, and I was kept till about twelve o'clock. The congregation of the Dutch Reformed Church came out of their prayer meeting; the place was crowded, while a great number had to remain outside.[19]

For many weeks the awakening at Montagu was marked by intense conviction of sin, with strong men crying out in anguish as in Ireland and Scotland. The whole town was profoundly affected.

One Sunday evening in nearby Worcester, sixty young people were gathered in a hall in a prayer meeting led by J. C. de Vries, an assistant to Andrew Murray. Several had risen to request the singing of a hymn and to offer prayer when a Fingo girl (from a branch of the Xhosa people) asked if

---

18. Ibid., 53.
19. Ibid., 56.

she might do the same. With some hesitation, permission was granted and the girl poured out a moving prayer. De Vries reported that while she was praying a sound like approaching thunder was heard, coming closer and closer until it enveloped the hall, shaking the place. The company burst into prayer, a majority audibly, a minority in murmuring tones.

Andrew Murray had just finished his evening services and, hearing that something unusual was happening, hurried over to the hall to investigate. Finding everyone engaged in simultaneous prayer, he tried without success to quiet them. Disturbed by the apparent confusion he departed, exclaiming "God is a God of order, and here everything is in confusion." It was some time before Murray was convinced of the divine nature of the visitation. But in the following week Murray himself was leading a prayer meeting in the school when the same mysterious roll of approaching thunder was heard followed by an outburst of simultaneous prayer. In a letter to her mother, his wife wrote:

> We are having many visitors from the surrounding places who come to see us on account of the revival meetings, and they go away blessed, saying that the half has never been told. It is a solemn thing to live in such a congregation at such a time. I feel sure that the Lord is going to bless us even more, and yet there are heavy trials before us; the work is deeply interesting and yet some things are painful.[20]

The revival quickly spread from Montagu and Worcester to Wellington, Tulbagh, Swellendam and Paarl. Even far-away Calvinia, 322 kilometres (200 miles) to the north, experienced a spiritual awakening that had a powerful impact on the entire community. Many other towns and villages throughout the Cape Colony witnessed remarkable conversions and spiritual awakenings. The Dutch Reformed synod of 1862 carefully investigated the awakening and concluded with gratitude that the work was of God. Professor N. J. Hofmeyr declared in a report that changes wrought by the revival were revolutionary. Fifty young men in the Worcester congregation alone offered themselves for the ministry, and within a decade the Dutch Reformed Church had a dozen mission stations in and beyond the Cape Colony and the Boer Republics.

Unknown to the Christians in the Cape Colony, a spiritual awakening had commenced in Natal a few months before that experienced in the Cape. As early as 1859 Aldin Grout, an American Board missionary working among the

---

20. Ibid., 59.

Zulus, reported that "now we are revived; and the reviving commenced a year and a half ago." In the same year a Wesleyan Methodist missionary recorded:

> I rose early this morning to preach to the people, but soon found by their sleepy countenances that they had but little rest during the night. After the service, I was informed that just as they had been about to separate, while singing the concluding hymn, the Spirit fell upon them in such an overpowering manner that they could not depart, but continued in prayer till break of day.[21]

A preacher whose ministry seemed to be the catalyst for a number of extraordinary spiritual movements was an American Methodist, William Taylor. His meetings among Xhosa, Zulu and Europeans were characterized by numerous conversions accompanied by deep conviction of sin and joyful assurance of salvation. Working closely with Taylor as his interpreter and playing an equally vital role in the revivals was a young Xhosa chief, Charles Pamla, who became the first African to be ordained to the Methodist ministry. His story will be told in the next section. Something of the impact of the Taylor/Pamla ministry can be glimpsed in the notes made by William Sargent of a meeting held at the Methodist mission station at Healdtown where a thousand people were crowded in the chapel:

> Tuesday – what a day! I know not how to record it. I have never witnessed anything that so reminded me of the scenes of Pentecost... The people were already in the chapel, engaged in a prayer meeting. Mr. Taylor took for his text "But ye shall receive power after that the Holy Ghost is come upon you." The truth told upon the congregation.
>
> At the close, after a season of silent prayer, seekers were invited to come forward, when I suppose that not less than 300 fell upon their knees and began to cry aloud for mercy, among them several Europeans. At first, all seemed confusion. Even the local preachers and leaders seemed petrified. Presently much of the noise subsided and little more than sighs and groans were heard. After a short time, one after another got into liberty... they generally rose to their feet, clasped their hands and with

---

21. Ibid., 65.

eyes sparkling and countenances beaming with joy unspeakable, they broke into a burst of praise.[22]

Such scenes were repeated at many other mission stations and churches throughout southern Africa. Pamla not only interpreted for Taylor but also held many meetings of his own with striking results. A missionary in the Grahamstown District of the Wesleyan field summed up the movement:

> The remarkable characteristic of the Revival is that the whole land is being blessed. In every place the Word of God is the power of God unto salvation to many that believe . . . At some of our native stations, as many as 300, 500 and, in one place, 800 conversions have taken place. More than two thousand of the native population have been saved, and certainly more than six hundred conversions have taken place among the English.[23]

In only two years of the revival the Methodists recorded a 40 percent increase in their membership. Of all Xhosa hymns, a third came from the revival of the 1860s. Something of the ethos of the revival is preserved in the original version of the Xhosa hymn *Nkosi Sikelel' iAfrika,* part of which has been incorporated into the national anthem of South Africa. Its refrain *Woza Moya*, which is repeated several times, means "Come Holy Spirit."

Charles Pamla

The first black South African to be ordained to the Methodist ministry, Charles Pamla, fully shared in the zeal and spiritual fervour of the other early Methodist pioneers. Born in Butterworth in the Eastern Cape in 1834 to parents who had only recently been baptized into Christ, Charles Pamla received a Christian education and seems to have been religious from his youth. While watching over his father's sheep, he studied his Bible and practised preaching to the trees. After coming to a full assurance of salvation and the baptism of the Holy Spirit, he became a class leader and lay preacher in his church.

In 1866 when William Taylor came to hold meetings at Annshaw where Pamla resided, he interpreted for the American evangelist. These meetings made a powerful impression on the hearers, with hundreds being converted.

---

22. Ibid., 68.
23. Ibid., 70.

Pamla then accompanied Taylor on a tour of the whole chain of Wesleyan mission stations in the Transkei. When they arrived in Natal, the young Xhosa evangelist held services on his own, with great effect. Encouraged by Taylor, Pamla enrolled as a candidate for the ministry at Healdtown, and after three years' training he was ordained in 1871.

For nineteen years Pamla laboured as a pioneer missionary at Etembeni where he experienced much resistance to his message. Nevertheless, the church grew in membership from 300 to 5,000. Some of the resistance he encountered probably resulted from his preaching against circumcision, *lobola*, dancing and beer drinking. Such prohibitions would be considered legalistic and overly restrictive today. Was Pamla influenced by white missionaries in these issues and their insensitivity to black culture? Perhaps to some extent. But it must be remembered that it is a common phenomenon among new converts from non-Christian societies to react strongly against practices perceived to be clearly associated with the old religion and the old ways. The danger of legalism is real, as it undermines the liberty of believers under grace. But so is the danger of syncretism, in which the purity of the gospel is compromised by idolatrous and immoral practices. Much of African Christianity has struggled between these two poles, and inevitably faithful and fruitful servants of Christ have erred one way or the other.

In 1909 Pamla was appointed connexional evangelist by the South African Conference of the Methodists. Later he became superintendent of the Clarkesbury circuit. When he retired in 1913, it was claimed that 25,000 people had been converted as a result of his preaching. In 1916 he wrote:

> Time would fail me to tell the wonders of God's grace which he has permitted me to see since the days when he called me to be a fellow worker with the reverend saint of God, Bishop Taylor. My own heart is full of wonder and thankfulness at the remembrance of all that my eyes have seen and my ears have heard. I am now a very old man, and in the quietness and in the peace of God, I am waiting for the coming of the chariots of my King, and I shall be caught up into heaven and see the face of His servant.[24]

In the following year, at the age of 83, he passed away quietly in the night after preaching at two services the previous day.

---

24. Crafford, *Trail-Blazers of the Gospel*, 55.

Although Pamla had been a leading figure in the early days of the revival, he was not the only one. Many other black evangelists and preachers initiated or continued to stimulate revivals in Methodist, Presbyterian and Congregational churches, and by far the largest number of the conversions which occurred during the revival could be attributed to black preachers rather than to white missionaries. In fact, according to Crafford, many of the missionaries were sceptical concerning the nature of these revivals. However, they may be regarded as the beginning of a process that was to lead to the conversion to Christianity of 70 percent of the black people of South Africa.[25]

Doctrinal Conflict in the Dutch Reformed Church

During the same period that the Dutch Reformed churches in the Cape were being stirred by an extraordinary revival, a profound struggle was taking place between defenders of traditional orthodoxy and proponents of a more modern rationalist theology. Before the establishment of a theological seminary at Stellenbosch, young Afrikaners desiring to enter the ministry studied in Holland, where they came under the influence of modern theological trends that were critical of traditional orthodoxy and sympathetic to the spirit of rationalism characteristic of the Enlightenment. A certain T. F. Burgers, for example, went to Holland to complete his theological studies at Utrecht in 1853. By the time he returned to take up the ministry in the Karoo town of Hanover he had moved away from his early pietism to a more modern theology, speaking out against revivalism in 1859. There were other ministers of like mind who hoped to steer the church in a new direction.

Things came to a head in the synod meetings of 1862, which one of its delegates, Frans Lion Cachet, described as "a struggle between faith and unfaith – a life and death struggle resulting from the unbelief which is proclaimed as truth in Holland and in the Dutch academies."[26] The liberals proposed that representatives of congregations outside the Cape Colony (all of whom were more orthodox-minded) should be excluded from the synod. The synodical rejection of this proposal was overruled by a Supreme Court decision. Thus the orthodox element in the synod was weakened. A charge was brought against T. F. Burgers that he denied the personal existence of the devil, the sinlessness of Christ, the resurrection of the dead and the survival

---

25. Ibid., 56.
26. Hofmeyr, Millard and Froneman, *History of the Church*, 133.

of the soul after death, and a commission was appointed to investigate the charge.

During another session of the synod it was proposed that ministers should positively defend the Heidelberg Catechism, one of the doctrinal standards of the DRC. To this J. J. Kotzé of Darling replied that he could not defend Question 60, where it was taught that the believer "still tends towards all kinds of evil." Kotzé was ordered to withdraw his statement, which he refused to do. When disciplinary steps were taken by the synod against Kotzé and Burgers, both took their cases to the civil courts, which found in their favour and revoked the actions of the synod. While the liberals prevailed against their orthodox opponents in the courts, the conservatives eventually won the battle for the church. By keeping close control over the seminary at Stellenbosch and by instituting carefully defined procedures for admitting candidates to the ministry, the conservatives were able to exclude modernist tendencies from the ministry and maintain an adherence to the traditional confessions of the church. Andrew Murray served as moderator of the DRC during this struggle and also personally undertook the defence of the church in the various court cases to which it was summoned.

Bishop Colenso

The Anglicans experienced a struggle against theological modernism very similar to that of the Dutch Reformed, and at about the same time. At the very centre of the Anglican conflict was the brilliant first bishop of Natal, John William Colenso, whose views and actions evoked admiration, exasperation and dismay from friend and foe alike.

Born in 1814 into a poor family, Colenso had to work hard to gain an education and finished his studies at Cambridge. Indicative of his ability, he compiled and published an *Arithmetic for Schools* that was successful enough to help him out of financial difficulties. At Cambridge, Colenso was strongly influenced by the universalist views of F. D. Maurice and Samuel Taylor Coleridge. After serving as the rector of a small country parish for a number of years, he was offered and accepted the bishopric of Natal in 1853. The following year he made a preliminary visit to his diocese, recording his impressions in a little book called *Ten Weeks in Natal*. Colenso did not hesitate to adopt and express clear views on controversial subjects. Concerning the African custom of polygamy, for example, he wrote:

> I feel very strongly that the usual practice of enforcing the separation of wives from their husbands, upon their conversion to Christianity, is quite unwarrantable, and opposed to the plain teaching of our Lord. It is placing a stumbling-block, which He has not set in the way of receiving the Gospel . . . If natives became Christians before their marriage, they would, of course, be allowed only one wife.[27]

When Colenso settled in Natal in 1855 he established his headquarters about eight kilometres (five miles) from Pietermaritzburg at Bishopstowe, or Ekukanyeni (The Place of Light) where he remained until his death. This place, he envisaged, would become a great mission centre from which a Christianizing impulse would radiate to the entire Zulu nation. It was planned on a grand scale and developed with tireless energy. It contained a forge, a carpenter's shop and a translation centre, as well as a printing office and a boarding school where the sons of chiefs would learn Christian leadership as well as grammar.

Colenso proved to be a gifted linguist. In a few years he not only learned the Zulu language but compiled a Zulu grammar, dictionary, readers, and manuals of instruction in Zulu on history, geography, astronomy, and other subjects. He also translated Genesis, Exodus, Samuel, and the entire New Testament into Zulu.[28]

Colenso needed considerable funds in the development of his mission and looked to the state to provide a portion thereof. Unashamedly imperial in his approach to evangelization, he regarded the British Empire in 1854 as superior to "the empire of ancient Rome in the days of its grandeur" and considered it as an instrument of "God's Providence working to Christianize the world."[29] He formed a close association with Theophilus Shepstone, Natal's Secretary for Native Affairs, who abandoned the Methodism of his missionary father and assumed a prominent position among Colenso's lay supporters.

But the bishop was soon embroiled in conflict with his fellow clergy. In 1858 he preached a series of sermons on the Eucharist that were offensive to the high-church views of his dean, James Green. Green accused Colenso of heresy and reported the matter to the bishop of Cape Town, Robert Gray, who

---

27. Hofmeyr, *Church History*, 208.
28. Ibid., 209.
29. Etherington, "Kingdoms of This World and the Next: Christian Beginnings among Zulu and Swazi," in Elphick and Davenport, *Christianity in South Africa*, 95.

took a conciliatory approach, stating that "the bishop's language, however unguarded and unsatisfactory, was capable of being construed consistently with the formularies of the Church."[30]

In 1861 Colenso caused an even greater stir when he printed at Ekukanyeni a commentary on Paul's letter to the Romans in which he attacked the teaching of penal substitution, denying not only that Christ had died to placate an angry Father but also that God has any righteous anger against sin at all. He also held that all are justified in Christ from their very birth; baptism is merely a recognition and proclamation of this fact. The gospel is preached to the heathen, not to convert them but to set before them a pattern of love so that they may follow it.[31] The influence of F. D. Maurice is clearly discernible here, but Colenso lacked his tact and was more impetuous and aggressive in advancing his views.

Gray was alarmed by the book and begged Colenso to keep it back for at least a year and consult his friends. Refusing to withdraw anything written in his commentary on Romans, Colenso proceeded to publish in 1862 the first part of a critical work on the Old Testament – *The Pentateuch and the Book of Joshua Critically Examined*. Convinced on the grounds of its bad arithmetic that the Old Testament could not be verbally inerrant, Colenso concluded that it was no more inspired than the words of "Cicero, Lactantius, and the Sikh Gooroos."[32]

By this time there was widespread outrage against the views of the bishop of Natal. On the basis of his works, nine charges of heresy were brought against him, and in 1863 he was deposed from his see by Gray, who presided over a court consisting of the other three South African bishops. This sentence was followed by one of solemn excommunication in 1866.

Colenso appealed to the courts against the sentence, claiming that Gray had no right to depose him as he was responsible to the British crown alone. This appeal was upheld by the Judicial Committee of the Privy Council in 1865, and so Colenso was reinstated as bishop of Natal. Furthermore, he was awarded for life the income from the endowment of the See of Natal, and the trusteeship of all diocesan property acquired since his consecration.

Despite his resounding victories in the courts, Colenso experienced increasing difficulty in maintaining his considerable projects and getting

---

30. Hofmeyr, *Church History*, 210.
31. Hinchliff, *Church in South Africa*, 67.
32. Ibid., 68.

suitable clergymen for his diocese. Gray consecrated an alternative bishop for Natal, and twenty years of schism followed. After the death of Colenso in 1883, nearly all the churches and clergy of Natal returned to unity with the archbishop of Cape Town.

It was the work of his twilight years, however, that gained for Colenso the greatest admiration, particularly among the black people of Natal. As noted, Colenso was unabashedly an imperialist, believing the British Empire to be a providential instrument of justice and righteousness. But when this same power became guilty of injustice, in Colenso's view, he was stirred to action. In 1873 Chief Langalibalele was arrested and sentenced to banishment for refusing to obey an order to disarm his tribe. Colenso believed the court was prejudiced and unfair. In the face of strong public hostility, the bishop succeeded in having Langalibalele moved to a more pleasant place of exile, and his protests were partly responsible for the retirement of the governor of Natal.

Colenso's final efforts were on behalf of the Zulu king Cetshwayo who, after having been defeated in the Anglo-Zulu War of 1878–1879, was captured and imprisoned in Cape Town. Colenso believed that the colonial authorities had deliberately created a picture of Zulu aggression in order to justify an attack on the independent Zulu state as part of a larger plan for a confederation of South Africa under British control. Working with his daughters, the bishop printed material providing evidence of the injustice of the British invasion. He was still working for the restoration of Cetshwayo to his kingdom when he died. His efforts cost him the friendship of Shepstone and earned him the hostility of the white settler community in Natal. But they also earned him the undying gratitude of the Zulu people who called him Sobantu (Father of the people). The little town of Colenso in KwaZulu-Natal is named after him.

Ethiopianism

The earliest African independent churches were often referred to collectively as "Ethiopian." The term is derived from Psalm 68:31 (AV): "Ethiopia shall soon stretch out her hands to God," a text greatly beloved by early African Christian leaders.

In 1872 about 150 members of the Paris Evangelical Missionary Society congregation at Mount Herman in Lesotho split off from the society to form an independent church. The schism did not last long, but it was a portent of things to come. Few, if any, at that time realized how significant the movement towards African independent churches would become in South Africa. With the benefit of hindsight, however, it is easy to see the inevitability of major departures from white instituted and controlled churches. The close association of the mainline and mission churches with the politically and economically dominant white community meant that resentment against the latter would unavoidably lead to the rejection of the former. Indeed, one of the very few areas where blacks could achieve independence from white control and dominance was church life. The trickle of African independent churches quickly swelled to a mighty torrent.

The division of Christians along racial, cultural and socio-political lines is not unique to South Africa but has afflicted the church from earliest times. The great division in the eleventh century between the Orthodox Church in the East and the Roman Catholic Church in the West was largely along cultural, ethnic and linguistic lines. The Greek-speaking Byzantines and the Latin-speaking Westerners could hardly understand one another, and the attempt of the West to assert its authority over the Eastern church only exacerbated the problem.

The great division of the western Catholic Church in the sixteenth century was again significantly influenced by cultural and political factors. The predominantly Germanic regions of northern Europe (Germany, England, Scandinavia, Holland) resented the interference of an Italian prince and Roman bishop in their affairs. Their rejection of the papacy arose in part from a nationalistic desire for autonomy in ecclesiastical matters. Southern Europe, where languages were more closely aligned with Latin (Italy, France, Spain, Portugal), retained its ties with the Roman church with which it had a closer cultural affinity.

We could examine the histories of many Christian divisions and find cultural factors at the root of many of them, in sad reversal of the apostolic ideal: "There is neither Jew nor Greek, slave nor free, male nor female, for you are all one in Christ Jesus" (Gal 3:28). South Africa has experienced this fragmentation of the Christian church to a peculiar degree. There are several possible reasons for this:

1. The relatively large number of Europeans who immigrated to the region and the subsequent loss of land, power and status by the black people led to deep, underlying resentment of whites by blacks.
2. The close association of Christianity, the church and missionaries with the white colonial community led to profound tensions within

the African soul, torn between a positive interest in the gospel and a negative reaction to the bearers of the gospel.

3. Paternalism and a lack of a positive appreciation of African culture were all too prevalent among missionaries, leading to frustration and discontent among many black members of missionary instituted churches.

4. Excessive caution hindered the development and ordination of indigenous leaders in the church.

5. Many Africans desired an African church that would fully reflect African culture and incorporate African traditional religious practices, a church initiated and governed by Africans.

6. The arrival in South Africa of many different missionary societies and denominations, not always working in close cooperation, provided the African people with a model of a divided Christianity.

7. African society itself had a tradition of aspiring leaders breaking away from established chiefs to form a new tribe. Such patterns easily transferred to the ecclesiastical realm.

The separatist groups experienced phenomenal growth in the twentieth century. In 1904 there were only three independent groups with about 25,000 adherents. By 1925 the number of separatist churches had increased to 130, which multiplied to 1,300 with more than a million adherents by 1946. In 1982 approximately three million adherents were gathered in about 3,000 groups, and by 1997 the numbers had swelled to more than ten million adherents gathered in an estimated 6,000 churches. In this chapter we will consider some of the early pioneers of these African Instituted Churches (AICs).

Nehemiah Tile and the National Thembu Church

In the Eastern Province of the Cape, near the former Great Place of the Thembu Paramount Chief, is a tombstone bearing the following inscription:

REV. NEHEMIAH X. TILE

Founder of the Ethiopian Church of Africa in 1884

Died 21 November 1891

Baptized and educated in Thembuland, Tile felt the call to ministry and served as a Methodist evangelist there and in Pondoland. At the first conference of the Wesleyan Methodist Church of South Africa in 1883, Tile and other black ministers complained about discrimination against them. They were not allowed to take part in discussions on issues such as the ordination of black ministers and the appropriation of funds. Tile was also refused ordination in spite of the fact that he had completed three years of theological training at Healdtown and his probationary period.

Tensions increased when Tile became the counsellor to Chief Ngangelizwe. Such political activity was unacceptable to the missionaries, and Tile was summoned to a disciplinary investigation. He was charged with stirring up agitation against the magistrate in Thembuland, addressing public meetings on the Sabbath, and donating an ox for the circumcision of Ngangelizwe's son, Dalindyebo. Tile did not answer the charges. Instead he left the church and in 1884 established the Thembu National Church with the Thembu Paramount Chief as its visible head. The parallel with the British situation is obvious and was probably intentional. If British sovereigns functioned as the visible heads of their national church, why could not the Thembu nation adopt the same system?

Tile did not live long, but the church he founded survived. Though it never grew to any significant size, it demonstrated that an African instituted church was possible and so became the forerunner of thousands more. For this reason Tile is widely regarded as the father of the independent church movement. It is interesting to note a reference to Tile made by another leader of a black independent church, L. M. Mzimba, who founded the Presbyterian Church of Africa:

> The first definite movement of the independent spirit started forty-two years ago. Rev. Nehemiah Tile separated himself from the Wesleyan Church, and founded a Church of his own organization. We are told that his movement began with Native assistants. Their position was a trying one. In many stations they did most of the work, but as they were not ordained, they could not celebrate marriages, baptize or dispense the Lord's Supper. They had also a lower salary and status than the White missionary. They felt much more isolated both from the blacks and whites. Being somewhat educated they wished to better their position, and the more ambitious wished to make a rapid ascent of the social ladder. They had also an awakening sense of power and racial responsibility. Social and political avenues were closed against them, but the Church seemed to offer a highway

to increased influence. They were no doubt also moved by the bearing of the white man, many of whom would not worship in the same building as them.[33]

Other Early "Ethiopian" Leaders

The first church to have the word "Ethiopian" in its name was the *Ibandla laseTiyopiya* (Ethiopian Church) established by Mangena Mokone in 1892. Mokone had been ordained into the ministry of the Methodist Church in 1887. A man of considerable gifts and abilities, he had helped translate a catechism into Sepedi and in 1892 was appointed as a teacher at the Kilnerton Institution in Pretoria, which had been founded as a school for the sons of chiefs and a theological training college for black ministers. In the same year he wrote a letter to the Conference of the Transvaal District of the Methodist Church accusing the church of racial discrimination in its treatment of its black ministers. Severing his link with the Methodists, he established the Ethiopian Church.

A number of other black ministers joined Mokone including James Dwane, a man of considerable intelligence and ability. Dwane had been educated and trained at the Healdtown Missionary Institution and had successfully ministered in a number of congregations. In 1888 he had served on a committee for the enlargement of the Xhosa hymn book, and in 1892 he was one of twenty-five ministers appointed to supervise the training of ministers. On a trip to England in 1894, Dwane was able to collect considerable funds for the work in South Africa. On his return home, however, there was conflict between him and the church authorities concerning the use of the funds. Dwane left the Methodist Church and went to join Mokone in the Transvaal, emerging as the leader of the Ethiopian Church by 1896.

In that same year the church sent Dwane to the USA to negotiate a union with the African Methodist Episcopal Church (AMEC). Dwane was ordained as vicar-bishop for South Africa, and the church grew rapidly to over 10,000 members. But Dwane remained unsatisfied, feeling that his American colleagues wanted too much control. Furthermore, a study of episcopacy led him to doubt the validity of his own orders. After lengthy negotiations with the Anglicans, in 1900 Dwane left the AMEC with about 3,000 of his followers to found the Order of Ethiopia as part of the Anglican Church (CPSA).

---

33. Crafford, *Trail-Blazers of the Gospel*, 61.

The majority of the AMEC members remained loyal to their church, even strengthening ties with the parent body in the USA. But in 1904 a further schism occurred in Pretoria when Samuel Brander, unhappy with the African-American missionaries, established the Ethiopian Catholic Church in Zion.[34]

Dwane's Order of Ethiopia has managed to maintain its existence within the Anglican Church, although not without a good deal of tension through the years between the clergy of the "Church" and those of the "Order."[35]

Elsewhere, the trickle of secessions from the mission instituted churches turned into a steady stream, and very few of the new AICs felt any need to affiliate themselves in any formal way with older European or American denominations. In 1897 two preachers from the American Board of Commissioners for Foreign Missions seceded to form the Zulu Congregational Church. In 1898 the Reverend P. J. Mzimba, who had been a student and personal friend of James Stewart of Lovedale and who had served the black congregation at Lovedale for twenty-two years, resigned to form the African Presbyterian Church. In 1899 the Cushites were founded by Johannes Zondi, in 1903 the Independent Methodist Church was begun by Joel Msimang, and in 1905 the African Native Baptist Church was launched by William Leshega. In 1917 Gardiner Mvuyana, one of the most capable of the American Board ministers, left the Board to found the African Congregational Church. With a certain flair for stage management, the Bantu Methodist Church was launched in 1933 using a donkey as the symbol of the church, hence the nickname "Donkey Church."[36] The ethos of this church and perhaps that of other "Ethiopian" churches is reflected in these lines by the church's historian:

An Exultant Song of the Donkey Church

We are children of black Africa,
We rise from all the lands south of Africa.
We are the black Wesleyans – we come from all nations.
We approach our God while offering our prayers.
We are children of black Africa.
We come to pray for the deliverance of the Blacks.[37]

---

34. Pretorius and Jafta, "Branch Springs Out," 215.
35. Hinchliff, *Church in South Africa*, 92.
36. Sundkler, *Bantu Prophets*, 172.
37. Pretorius and Jafta, "Branch Springs Out," 216.

By the first decade of the twentieth century, more than seventy AICs had been established with a total of some 25,000 followers. The stream was flowing strongly and showed no signs of diminishing. Indeed, it was soon to become a raging torrent, especially after missionaries from the USA arrived in South Africa representing the Holiness, Healing and Pentecostal movements. But that story must wait till a later chapter.

Lutherans

There is one last major Christian tradition which was firmly planted in South African soil during the course of the nineteenth century to which we have not yet given attention (apart from a reference to an early German-speaking congregation in the Cape) – the Lutherans. More than sixty million Lutherans in the world trace their spiritual descent from the life and work of the most famous of the sixteenth-century Reformers, Martin Luther, who once expressed dismay at the thought that anyone should ever be called a Lutheran. Out of the struggle of his own personal search for peace with God, Luther hammered out an evangelical theology proclaiming the good news of salvation as a free gift by the grace of God to all who believe in his Son, Jesus Christ. Over against the claims of traditions, councils and popes Luther affirmed the supreme authority of Holy Scripture and sought to reform the church by that criterion. Luther was a conservative Reformer, desiring to keep the essence of the Catholic tradition and changing only those abuses that obscured or undermined the gospel. He was little interested in details of the structure of church government and matters of rites and ceremonies, as long as the people could hear the good news of Christ and receive the sacraments according to the Word of God.

In the seventeenth and eighteenth centuries the Lutheran churches of northern Europe were stirred by movements of spiritual renewal that laid special emphasis on Bible study, prayer, personal faith in Christ, moral improvement, compassion for the needy and missions to the lost. It was among these "Pietists," as they were known, that the desire to spread the knowledge of Christ to foreign lands led to the formation of a score of missionary societies in the early decades of the nineteenth century. Representatives of nine of these societies arrived in South Africa, eager to bring the blessings of the gospel to the peoples of Africa. The first Lutheran missionaries were sent by the Rhenish Missionary Society (RMS) and arrived in the Cape in 1829, receiving encouragement and guidance from John Philip of the LMS.

From 1840 the RMS worked among the Nama, Damara and Herero and the people of the Rehoboth district in present-day Namibia. Together with the Finnish Mission Society, the RMS was so influential there that Lutherans are today the largest denomination in Namibia.[38] In the Cape Colony the RMS worked closely with the Dutch Reformed Church and turned a number of their stations over to them in the early decades of the twentieth century.

The Berlin Missionary Society (BMS), founded in 1824, sent the largest number of Lutheran missionaries to South Africa. They established stations among the Kora in the Orange River Sovereignty, among the Tswana in the Cape Colony, the Xhosa in British Kaffraria, the Zulu in Natal, and in the Transvaal, Mashonaland and Swaziland. Their largest field was the South African Republic (Transvaal), and their most important station was Botshabelo (City of Refuge). By 1955 the BMS was ministering to over 111,000 African Christians on 73 stations and 1,069 outstations.[39]

Another German Lutheran society that sent missionaries to South Africa was the Hermannsburg Mission Society (HMS), founded in 1849 by Ludwig Harms, whose preaching had brought about a revival of religion in the town of Hermannsburg near Hanover. Harms set up the HMS on strict Lutheran confessional principles, believing the people of Africa would be attracted by "the glory of our divine service, the pure teaching and divine sacraments of our church and the power of our singing."[40] By 1955 the HMS operated twenty-three stations among the Zulu and twenty-one among the Tswana.

The Norwegian Mission Society (NMS) was founded in 1842, drawing its inspiration in part from the work of Hans Nielsen Hauge, a farmer's son whose preaching had a profound impact on Norway. The first NMS missionary to South Africa, H. P. S. Schreuder, was able to heal the Zulu king Mpande of his rheumatism. Consequently he was granted land within the Zulu kingdom and served as the king's physician. Schreuder founded the first permanent mission stations in Zululand.

As was the case in other mission efforts, African converts played an important role in spreading the gospel. One woman, Paulina Dlamini, became known as the "Apostle of Northern Zululand." In her teenage years she had served the Zulu King, Cetshwayo. Later while working on a farm, she was visited twice in a dream by a figure in white robes who told her, "Paulina, arise

---

38. Scriba and Lislerud, "Lutheran Missions," 175.
39. Ibid., 176.
40. Ibid.

and accept this Bible. Go forth to where the sun rises and teach my people, the old and the young." After being persuaded by the farmer, Gert van Rooyen, that the figure in her dream was Jesus, she was baptized by Hermannsburg missionaries in 1887 and became an evangelist. She later recalled:

> I began with the work of the Lord while staying with the van Rooyens. I kindled a fire in the hearts of the people; this spread and grew in intensity. I then saw for myself that the Word of God is Truth. Yes, this fire from the Word of God spread and set many hearts alight.[41]

As a result of the multiplicity of Lutheran missionary societies working in South Africa, each distinct in terms of national origin and theological emphasis, there arose a number of separately organized Lutheran churches. Much energy has been expended in the twentieth century in trying to bring these together into one national body. To a large extent this was achieved with the formation in 1975 of the Evangelical Lutheran Church in Southern Africa. In the process, however, the Lutheran proportion of the population of the country has declined – down from 4.1 percent in 1960 to 2.1 percent in 1990 when there were about 842,000 Lutherans in South Africa.

Reflections on the British Period

Compared to the relatively slow pace of events during the Dutch period (1652–1800), there were rapid developments in the political, economic and religious arenas during the years of British rule (1800–1910). As a result of a series of military conflicts with the Xhosa, the Zulus and the Boers, British authority was extended from the Cape Colony to incorporate the whole of the Eastern Cape region, Natal, and ultimately the Transvaal and the Orange Free State. The economic development of the entire area was given a powerful boost by the discovery of diamonds in 1870 in the Kimberley area and the discovery of gold in the Transvaal in 1886. Mining brought about massive population relocations as multitudes, black and white, came to the diamond and gold fields in search of wealth.

On the religious front, the influx of English-speaking immigrants brought all the varieties of British Christianity to South Africa – Anglicans, Methodists, Presbyterians, Congregationalist, Roman Catholics and Baptists.

---

41. Ibid., 188.

The emigration of Dutch farmers from the Cape Colony and the establishment of two Boer republics to the north resulted in the extension of the Dutch Reformed Church to these parts, as well as the formation of two new Dutch Reformed denominations.

The arrival in South Africa of zealous missionaries representing scores of British, European and North American missionary societies heralded a large-scale attempt to bring the gospel of Christ to the indigenous peoples of southern Africa. Out of their labours black churches slowly began to emerge, not without many birth pangs and growing pains including tensions and conflicts between foreign missionaries and indigenous Christian leaders. In some cases these tensions led to a rupture of relations and the formation of new church bodies, instituted and governed by African leaders. And so a new type of church, categorized initially as "Ethiopian," appeared in the ecclesiastical spectrum. Many Christian leaders were dismayed and alarmed at the growing array of denominations arising out of the immigration of so many different people to South Africa, the work of so many different missionary societies and the secession of so many African leaders from missionary instituted churches. On the other hand, few would deny that the growing churches abounded with vitality and zeal. In the twentieth century both trends would continue – abounding vitality and growing fragmentation. Indeed, the greatest number of divisions occurred, more often than not, precisely in those sections of the church where growth and vitality were the most vigorous.

5

A South African Pentecost

Of the three major periods into which we have divided our story, the modern period (1910–2000), although the shortest, witnessed the most momentous events, the most rapid expansion of the church and the greatest proliferation of a bewildering variety of Christian movements.

As the twentieth century dawned, South Africans were locked in the bloodiest and most destructive war ever fought on South African soil – the Second Anglo-Boer War. At the same time as that conflict was drawing to its bitter close, many Protestant churches throughout the world were being stirred by movements of spiritual renewal. Missionaries arrived in South Africa with new angles on the old message of the gospel, placing a special emphasis on holiness, healing and the baptism of the Holy Spirit. A whole new breed of churches took root and began to grow vigorously – Pentecostal churches and a rapidly increasing number of AICs often referred to collectively as "amaZioni" (Zionist churches).

On the political front the twentieth century was dominated by the struggles of two powerful nationalist movements, white Afrikaner nationalism and black African nationalism. Rising out of the ashes of defeat by the British, Afrikaner nationalism organized itself to gain political power in order to promote the interests of the Afrikaner people and culture. This they achieved in 1948 when, after winning an election in which most of the voters were white, they instituted a policy of dividing the country into group areas in which the various races and cultures could achieve some measure of autonomy and self-rule.

African nationalist movements perceived and experienced this policy of *apartheid* (separation) as oppressive and unjust, and struggled against it until they finally achieved victory in the democratic elections of 1994. Inevitably all the churches became caught up, in one way or another, in these titanic struggles; even those churches claiming to eschew any political interest and involvement. Particularly in the older established churches much time and effort were expended in trying to determine proper Christian responses to the great social and political issues of the day.

If political life in South Africa was dominated by two powerful nationalist movements, the Christian world was strongly impacted by two spiritual movements that profoundly influenced Christian churches throughout the world in the twentieth century – Pentecostalism and Ecumenism. While the former gave birth to a whole new range of Christian denominations, the latter stimulated the formation of new institutions such as the South African Council of Churches (SACC), which sought to bring the disparate denominations into closer unity. These, then, are some of the themes we will be following as we conclude the story of the coming of Zion to South Africa and the many stories of those who have laboured to build the church of Jesus Christ here.

The Second Anglo-Boer War (1899–1902)

From the time of its inception the British government at the Cape was resented by the Dutch farmers who perceived it as prejudiced against them. This resentment eventually led to the Great Trek (1835–1840) in which approximately 15,000 people emigrated from the Cape Colony with the purpose of establishing independent states to the north. Even there the Boers had difficulty evading the long arm of British imperial interests. The first republic established by the Voortrekkers in Natal lasted only four years before being annexed by the British in 1842, prompting many Boers to trek again into the hinterland. Finally, after a further period of confusion, conflict and negotiation, the British authorities recognized the South African Republic (SAR), north of the Vaal River, and the Orange Free State. In 1877 the British annexed the SAR, but after a short, sharp conflict in 1880–1881 its independence was restored.

The discovery of exceptionally rich gold deposits on the Witwatersrand in 1886 led to the SAR soon becoming the biggest gold producer in the world. While this greatly strengthened the financial position of the SAR government (state revenue increased from £700,000 to £15 million in three years), it also sealed the fate of the independent Boer republic. From Britain, America, Australia and Europe, as well as from the Cape Colony and Natal, mine workers, businessmen and professionals flocked to the Rand. These

"Uitlanders" (foreigners) were resented by the Afrikaner burghers (citizens), especially as their number began to approximate the number of male Afrikaner voters, thus threatening the position of the Boer government. To keep the government in Boer hands, steps were taken to make it difficult for Uitlanders to obtain the vote. Tensions increased. Grievances were published. The Uitlanders accused the government of the SAR president, Paul Kruger, of oppression, injustice and incompetence. Cecil John Rhodes, the premier of the Cape Colony who dreamt of a chain of British colonies from Cape to Cairo, saw his opportunity to bring the Transvaal and its gold under British control. A string of political intrigues and inflammatory incidents led to the outbreak of war between Britain and the two Boer republics in 1899.

By seizing the initiative, the Boer commandos were able to score a number of victories at the outset of the war, but the outcome was inevitable. The massive military and economic superiority of the British war machine meant that by June 1900 the Boer capitals of Bloemfontein and Pretoria were in British hands. It looked like the war was over, but the Boer generals resorted to guerrilla tactics which the British forces found frustratingly difficult to oppose. This prolonged the war another two bitter years. In order to cut off all sources of supplies to the guerrillas, the British initiated a policy of destroying Boer farmsteads and forcing the women and children into concentration camps. More than 100,000 were gathered in these camps where nearly a third died as a result of unhygienic conditions and disease.

Hostilities finally ceased in 1902. The war proved to be the longest, costliest, bloodiest (at least 22,000 British, 34,000 Boer and 15,000 black lives were lost) and most humiliating for Britain between 1815 and 1915. But the cost to South Africa was more than lives and property. It left a legacy of bitterness that was to stoke the fires of Afrikaner nationalism and sow the seeds of further racial strife. Its long shadow was to reach to the end of the twentieth century.

One of the disastrous outcomes of the war was Clause 8 of the Peace Treaty signed at Vereeniging in which any decision to grant the franchise to blacks was postponed until after the introduction of self-government. And postponed it was – for ninety-two years! Despite the protest of black leaders, this concession was made by the British in the interests of bringing the *bittereinders* (those who wanted to fight to the bitter end) to the peace table and of promoting a spirit of reconciliation between Boer and Brit in order to repair the ravages of war and lay a foundation for a united and prosperous South Africa. The motive was good, but the foundation was tragically flawed.

Prisoner-of-War Camp Revivals

While trying to mop up the remaining pockets of Boer guerrilla resistance, the British transported large numbers of prisoners of war to camps scattered throughout the British Empire in places such as Bermuda, St Helena, India and Sri Lanka (Ceylon). Together with these prisoners went ministers of the Dutch Reformed churches, sharing their imprisonment and ministering with the goodwill of the British military authorities. Remarkable religious awakenings occurred in these camps that deeply influenced the lives of many individual prisoners and had an impact on the subsequent religious and social history of South Africa.

On the island of St Helena, a Reverend Louw led 6:30 a.m. prayer meetings attended daily by a hundred prisoners. Many conversions were reported. A stirring revival of religion was experienced among the prisoners on the island of Bermuda. In India, a thousand men were detained in Fort Ahmednagar. There Rev Viljoen began holding services among them. These were poorly attended at first but after a few weeks there was increased interest in the services with a number of conversions reported. In his carefully researched account of evangelical awakenings in Africa, Edwin Orr writes:

> Fort Ahmednagar became a place of praise and prayer, singing sweeping the camp in daytime and the voice of prayer muting the murmurs of the night. The Christians were impressed by the needs of the Hindus around them and eighteen of them became missionaries to African tribesmen on their release. The awakening continued in camp till war's end.[1]

It was the same in Boer camps in other parts of India. Rev Burger from the Transvaal was taken prisoner and went with 2,000 others to a prison camp at Shahjahanpur, Uttar Pradesh. He began regular worship services and taught school classes every day. The pattern of revival was repeated. At night, the Muslims and Hindus nearby listened to the hearty singing of 500 or more prisoners. There were similar reports from Boer chaplains in Sialkot, in the Punjab (now Pakistan).[2] In Ceylon (now Sri Lanka), there were 5,000 Afrikaner prisoners at Diatalawa under close guard. These prisoners suffered from boredom and sickness, and a typhoid epidemic killed many, but a little

---

1. Orr, *Evangelical Awakenings*, 122.
2. Ibid., 122.

prayer group grew into hundreds and then into thousands. Hundreds were converted, and many received missionary vocations.[3]

The fact that so many prisoners returned home in 1902 with renewed faith and hope in their hearts contributed to the spirit of reconciliation which enabled post-war South African society to engage in successful reconstruction. Two vanquished Boer generals, Louis Botha and Jan Smuts, played leading and constructive roles in the post-war governments of South Africa.

Another result of the widespread revival of religious feeling was an openness to new movements of Christian spirituality entering South Africa from the USA in the first decade of the twentieth century. These movements were to result in the establishment of a whole new genre of Christian churches on South African soil.

Zion and Pentecostal Beginnings

More than ten million South Africans belong to Pentecostal or Zionist type churches. The two are closely related, as we shall see. These churches have experienced the most rapid growth throughout the twentieth century and play an influential role in the spiritual life of the country. Yet surprisingly little attention has been given to them in many historical accounts. Peter Hinchliff's excellent history, *The Church in South Africa*, first published in 1968, barely mentions them. Later surveys devote more space to Pentecostals and Zionists but not in proportion to their size and growth. These churches have grown chiefly among the poor, the dispossessed, the oppressed and the illiterate. Such communities are not, of course, known for their scholarly and literary interests, and thus there is a scarcity of primary documents with which scholars can work. Also, from the perspective of the mainline churches, Pentecostals and Zionists have often been regarded as sectarian and heretical in their beliefs and practices. Consequently, the story of their churches has not usually been accorded the same sympathetic and serious attention given to other longer established churches.

In the eighteenth century, John Wesley, the father of Methodism, taught a doctrine of Christian perfection, or perfect love, which was seen as an instantaneous work of grace in the lives of believers, appropriated by faith and imparting holiness and power for Christian living. This teaching was the chief inspiration behind the nineteenth-century Holiness movement in Great

---

3. Ibid., 123.

Britain and North America that stressed "second blessing" sanctification and the baptism of the Holy Spirit endowing one for service. In the twentieth century the Pentecostal movement was born when the charismatic gift of glossolalia, or speaking in tongues, was taught to be the initial and necessary evidence of the baptism in the Holy Spirit.

John Alexander Dowie, one of the more eccentric products of the Holiness movement, was destined to have an unusual influence on South Africa. When Dowie was thirteen his family emigrated from Scotland to Australia. At the age of twenty he decided to enter the ministry and left Australia in 1868 for the University of Edinburgh, where he studied at the Free Church School. After three years Dowie returned to Australia where he served in several Congregational churches. He became convinced of the practical message of divine healing and in 1874 started a publication, *Leaves of Healing*. Leaving the Congregational Church in 1878, Dowie launched an independent ministry. In 1888 he moved to the USA where he eventually established Zion City just north of Chicago.[4] This model community, in which pork, alcohol, tobacco and drugs were strictly prohibited, became the headquarters of Dowie's Christian Catholic Church in Zion (CCCZ), over which he ruled as "Elijah III, the Restorer."

In South Africa, Dowie's *Leaves of Healing* was eagerly read by those interested in its message of divine healing. These included Pieter L. le Roux, a Dutch Reformed missionary and disciple of Andrew Murray; Johannes Büchler, a Congregationalist pastor; and Edgar Mahon, a Salvation Army officer. In 1895 Büchler left the Congregationalists to found his own congregation, which he called the Zion Church, and in 1897 he sought affiliation with the CCCZ. Edgar Mahon was healed after prayer by Büchler, who also developed a close friendship with Le Roux. In 1901 the DRC missionary commission found Le Roux guilty of rejecting doctors and medicines, pork, tobacco, and infant baptism.[5] He and his wife resigned from the DRC in 1903 and continued as missionaries of the Zion Church in Wakkerstroom.

In 1904 Dowie sent Daniel Bryant to South Africa, having commissioned him as overseer of the CCCZ congregations there. Le Roux met him in Durban. Shortly thereafter, Le Roux, his wife, and about 140 black Zionists were baptized by threefold immersion in a river outside Wakkerstroom.

---

4. Blumhofer, "John Alexander Dowie," in Burgess and McGee, *Dictionary of Pentecostal*, 249.

5. Hofmeyr and Pillay, *History of Christianity*, 188.

From the Wakkerstroom congregation came many future leaders of Zionist churches in South Africa, so Wakkerstroom can be called the "Jerusalem" of the *AmaZioni* of South Africa. Bryant ordained Le Roux as overseer of the CCCZ in Pretoria.

In 1901 a former Methodist preacher, Charles Parham, principal of the Bethel Bible School in Topeka, Kansas, came to the conviction that speaking in tongues was the evidence of the baptism in the Holy Spirit. The new Pentecostal movement received its greatest impetus from the Azusa Street revival in Los Angeles (1906–1909) led by William J. Seymour, a black Holiness preacher and former student of Parham. From Azusa Street, the movement rapidly spread throughout the world by means of the mission's newspaper, *Apostolic Faith*, and the witness of pilgrims who flocked to Los Angeles to experience glossolalia.[6]

In 1908 two American Pentecostal missionaries, Thomas Hezmalhalch and John G. Lake, arrived in South Africa. Lake was formerly an elder in Dowie's Zion City and was acquainted with Seymour. A photograph taken at Azusa Street in 1907 shows Lake and Hezmalhalch together with Seymour and other early Pentecostal leaders.[7] The two missionaries began to hold services in a black (Zion) church in Doornfontein, Johannesburg. Many members of the CCCZ attended these meetings, where they learned that "Zion taught immersion and divine healing, but *not* Pentecost."[8] Most of the CCCZ people accepted the Pentecostal message and they soon offered their Zion Tabernacle in Bree Street for these services. This became the headquarters of the Apostolic Faith Mission (AFM), as the new Pentecostal church was called – the same name as that of Seymour's church in Azusa Street.

Attracted to the church were many poor and socially uprooted whites, a large number of them Afrikaners who had flocked to the city after the devastation of the Second Anglo-Boer War.[9] Le Roux also attended Lake's meetings but was initially repelled by the noise of the Pentecostal preaching and worship. After becoming convinced, however, of their message, he joined the AFM. When Le Roux went back to Wakkerstroom to explain this step to his flock, they were dismayed, because they did not want to lose their identity as Zionists. A period of confusion ensued. Some of his members went with

---

6. Robeck Jr. "Classical Pentecostalism," in Burgess and McGee, *Dictionary of Pentecostal*, 220.
7. Anderson, "African Pentecostalism," 118.
8. Sundkler, *Bantu Prophets*, 48.
9. Hofmeyr and Pillay, *History of Christianity*, 191.

him, but several others seceded to form their own African-led Zion churches. Those who followed Le Roux remained the Zion branch of the AFM. Later there were secessions from this church as well. It is from this point that the paths of the classical Pentecostal churches and the *amaZioni* begin to diverge, and we shall be obliged to consider their stories separately. But it is important to remember that South African Pentecostals and Zionists share the same common sources – John Alexander Dowie's Zion City and William Seymour's Azusa Street revival.

The Apostolic Faith Mission (AFM)

The church that grew out of the Pentecostal preaching of Lake and Hezmalhalch was registered with the government in 1910 as the AFM of South Africa. Hezmelhalch was its first president, and he was succeeded in 1915 by Le Roux, who held this position until his death in 1943. In its early days the services of the church were racially integrated so that, in the words of pioneer Pentecostal missionary William Burton, "all shades of colour and all degrees of the social scale mingled freely in their hunger after God."[10] But soon social realities and the power of racial feelings prevailed, and an entry for 6 November 1908 in the minute book of the AFM reads: "It has been decided that in future the baptism of Blacks will take place after the baptism of Whites." And on 30 July 1909 we find: "In future the baptism of Whites, Coloured and Blacks will be separate."[11]

Notwithstanding the good personal relations between P. L. le Roux and many of his black fellow Christians, the pattern and attitude of white leadership in general in the AFM alienated many black Christians and resulted in numerous schisms. In 1932 the general secretary of the AFM stated that "112 of 400 Zionists groups could be shown to be offshoots of the Apostolic Faith Mission."[12]

One of the most outstanding black leaders who stayed with the AFM was Elias Letwaba. Born in the northern Transvaal in 1870, he joined the Berlin Lutheran Mission in 1889 to train as a preacher. It seems that in 1890 he joined the newly formed Bapedi Lutheran Church (an independent "Ethiopian"

---

10. Anderson, "African Pentecostalism," 118.
11. Hofmeyr, *Church History*, 153.
12. Anderson, "African Pentecostalism," 121.

church) in which he worked for nineteen years.[13] At the beginning of 1909 Letwaba met John G. Lake and was so impressed by the miracles of God's power that he decided to stay with Lake in his home to learn from him. Soon Letwaba received the Pentecostal "baptism" and became one of the first black preachers in the AFM. Embarking on an evangelistic tour of the northern Transvaal, his home country, he walked many hundreds of kilometres, preaching the gospel of salvation, healing and baptism in the Holy Spirit. Despite considerable persecution, he was able to build up a strong following.[14]

One of the highlights of Letwaba's achievements was the establishment in 1930 of the Patmos Bible School without financial help from the white church. According to the Pentecostal leader and author Gordon Lindsay, "thousands" graduated from this institution to preach the gospel throughout Africa. Letwaba declined to get involved in socio-political issues, quietly and humbly accepting many of the indignities placed on black people as a result of the harsh realities of South African racism. Towards the end of his life, he wrote the following in the AFM magazine *Comforter/Trooster*:

> I pray for our benefactors, the white people, who have brought the Eternal Light to us. My nation must learn to love our benefactors . . . and be obedient to them, because there would be no heaven for us poor Blacks if it were not for the white man.[15]

Letwaba's ministry was characterized by reported healings and miracles. Lake described one of the latter in the *Comforter/Trooster* in 1912:

> A great drought had rested for a number of months over that section of the country . . . While preaching to a large concourse of native people the Lord caused him to prophesy that before the next morning there should be abundance of rain. He continued in prayer all night, apparently submerged in the Spirit, and was only aroused by the rain falling upon him . . . the Chiefs called a thanksgiving meeting. The Holy Ghost fell mightily upon the people, with pungent conviction for sin. In writing of this Bro Letwaba says "and hundreds were saved."[16]

---

13. Ibid., 125.
14. Ibid., 126.
15. Ibid., 127.
16. Quoted in Anderson, "African Pentecostalism," 127.

Elias Letwaba died in 1959 and was buried in the Waterberg district in the northern Transvaal where he had spent most of his life. Lindsay wrote that "no other man . . . carried on the great work started by John G. Lake in Africa."[17]

Other outstanding black AFM leaders such as Edward Motaung were contemporaries of Letwaba. Because they broke away to form their own churches, however, they will be considered later when we look at the other AICs.

An early member of the AFM, David du Plessis, achieved international renown as "Mr. Pentecost." Born in 1905, he came from a most unlikely background – that of conservative Afrikanerdom. His parents became believers under the ministry of Andrew Murray and became Pentecostals through the influence of Lake and Hezmalhalch. The use of medicine was forbidden in the du Plessis household, and when young David went to Grey University College in Bloemfontein, his father, disturbed over his son's involvement with education, voluntarily surrendered his lay preacher's license out of a sense of paternal failure. At the age of thirty, however, David du Plessis was ordained to the ministry of the AFM. For many years he played a leading role in his denomination, editing the AFM magazine *Comforter/Trooster* and serving as general secretary from 1936 until 1947.[18]

In 1936 visiting British Pentecostal evangelist Smith Wigglesworth prophesied that du Plessis would bear witness to the Pentecostal message in remote parts of the world and to representatives of mainline denominations, a prophecy that was remarkably fulfilled in the following decades. In 1947 du Plessis left South Africa and was subsequently involved as organizing secretary of the Pentecostal World Conference for nearly a decade. From 1948 on du Plessis resided in the USA where contact with the president of Princeton Theological Seminary, John Mackay, led to his being introduced to the ecumenical movement. Du Plessis was to attend all six assemblies of the World Council of Churches from Amsterdam (1948) to Vancouver (1983). During this time he became known as "Mr Pentecost" and lectured at many major theological centres – Princeton, Yale, Union, Colgate, Bossey and others. Du Plessis was also received by three popes – John XXIII, Paul VI and John Paul II. Indeed, the crown of his ecumenical achievements probably lay in the development of the Roman Catholic–Pentecostal dialogue.

---

17. Anderson, "African Pentecostalism," 128.
18. Spittler, "David Johannes du Plessis," 251.

While pre-eminently a man of peace and reconciliation, du Plessis was unafraid to take a bold stand on controversial issues. Widely condemned by his Pentecostal brethren for his ecumenical contacts (the Assemblies of God in the USA asked him to surrender the ministerial credentials they had granted him), he remained outspokenly and solidly Pentecostal in his doctrinal convictions to the end. If conservatives protested against his ecumenical sympathies, liberals were aghast at his opinion that South African apartheid was a workable scheme, given the social realities. And both liberals and conservatives were puzzled by his favourable comment on the reported appearances of Mary at Medjugorje in Yugoslovia, a place he had visited.[19] Whether they agreed with all his views or not, those who met du Plessis came to respect his honesty, transparency, love and courage. No one in the twentieth century so effectively linked three of the major Christian movements of the time – the Pentecostal movement, the ecumenical movement, and the charismatic movement.[20]

The Full Gospel Church of God

Although the largest, the AFM was not the only Pentecostal church to emerge in South Africa in the early decades of the twentieth century. Two other major bodies of the classical Pentecostal type were formed, namely, the Full Gospel Church (FCG) and the Assemblies of God.

Archibald Cooper visited the Cape as a sailor in 1901 and decided to stay. Converted at a Gypsy Smith meeting, he joined a Presbyterian church for a while. He received the *Apostolic Papers* from Azusa Street, and a Pentecostal experience in 1907 led him to join Lake and the AFM in 1908. But after about a year, tensions with other AFM leaders resulted in Cooper leaving that body.

In 1909 George Bowie, a Scottish immigrant to the USA, was sent by the Bethel Pentecostal Assembly of Newark, New Jersey, to South Africa, where he founded the Pentecostal Mission. In 1910 Bowie and his colleague Eleazer Jenkins invited Cooper to join the Pentecostal Mission, which was registered as a company in 1913, a pragmatic act as it was not easy for a Pentecostal body to obtain official recognition as a church in the early days.[21] This registration, however, brought about a schism when the congregation in

---

19. Ibid., 253.
20. Ibid.
21. Du Plessis, *'n Pentekostalisties*, 7.

Pretoria, unhappy at being a "company" rather than a "church," broke away and called themselves the Church of God. The schism was healed in 1921 when the Pentecostal Mission and the Church of God reunited, adopting the name Full Gospel Church (FGC). In 1951 the FGC united with the Church of God (Cleveland, Tennessee) in the USA and took the name Full Gospel Church of God in Southern Africa. Various attempts were made over the years to unite the FGC and the AFM, but their differences with regard to baptism and church government could not be overcome. The FGC practised single immersion compared with the triple immersion of the AFM, and FGC congregations enjoyed greater local autonomy than those in the more centrally organized AFM.

The FGC has the distinction of being the largest Christian denomination among the Indian population of South Africa. This is largely due to the work of one of South Africa's more remarkable Pentecostal pioneers and evangelists, John Francis Rowlands. In 1925 the United Pentecostal Mission was established in Pietermaritzburg by Rowlands's father and a Methodist Indian friend, Ebenezer Theophilus. In 1928 J. F. Rowlands took over the work, which grew slowly by means of open air services, cottage meetings and evangelistic campaigns. A major breakthrough occurred with a Revival and Healing Campaign in 1931. In the first three weeks of the campaign, over one thousand new converts were baptized in the Umzinduzi River.[22] Rowlands's strongly revivalist stance made affiliation with any of the established churches difficult, and when some Baptists, Anglicans and Methodists joined his church, his ministry was denounced as divisive. Thereupon, Rowlands and his congregation joined the FGC. In October 1931 Rowlands moved to Durban, where he established the Bethesda Temple in Carlisle Street. This became the headquarters for the Full Gospel Indian work in South Africa, with all branches being daughter churches of "mother Bethesda" in order to encourage a family atmosphere.[23]

For the next few decades the Bethesda movement, as the work of Rowlands became known, grew rapidly. His younger brother, Alec, assisted him in the work. The two brothers remained bachelors, committed wholly to the work of Bethesda. Rowlands achieved a level of acceptance among Indians unprecedented for a white person in South Africa. He lived with an Indian family for a while and later shared a room with his first Indian co-

---

22. Hofmeyr and Pillay, *History of Christianity*, 235.
23. Oosthuizen, *Pentecostal Penetration*, 73.

worker, F. Victor, the first of more than forty Indians to be ordained as pastors in Bethesda by 1980.[24]

In the earlier part of his ministry, Rowlands experienced considerable opposition from incensed Hindus who resented the conversion of their co-religionists. There were threats of attack; there was a case of food poisoning and an attempt to burn down the church.[25] But the manifest love that Rowlands bore not only to his own flock but also to the wider Indian community, eventually gained him widespread respect. He was able to combine in his ministry a unique balance of Pentecostal enthusiasm, sound common sense, and an enlightened social conscience. "Bethesda stands 100% for Pentecost!" wrote Rowlands in his annual report of 1963. "A sane, solid Pentecost that works! Much fanaticism in Pentecost throughout the world today! Bethesda will continue to reprove and rebuke all demonstrations in the flesh!"[26] "The backbone of Bethesda's ministry," he stated on another occasion, "is the Cross of Calvary, not preached with the enticing words of man's wisdom, but in demonstration of the Spirit and Power."[27]

As might be expected, Bethesda held to conservative moral principles with regard to personal life. Women were instructed to cover their heads in God's house. Ministers were urged to be properly dressed. "Ties are essential," Rowlands insisted. "An open-necked shirt is an insult to the pulpit."[28] Dancing was denounced, and rock and roll music condemned. Yet Rowlands did not confine himself to personal ethics and was among the few Pentecostals who publicly criticized social injustices. In 1946, when the Indian community was reacting against restrictions on land tenure and franchise, Rowlands wrote in his annual report:

> The church is not a political caucus; but the Body of Christ. But everyone of us was vitally concerned. We turned to God and publicly announced special Prayer Meetings twice daily, at 9 a.m. and 6 p.m. We did what nobody else had the courage to do! We put God's point of view to the public. Forty-three advertisements in the local paper. This took courage which was rewarded.[29]

---

24. Pillay, "Community Service and Conversion," 292.
25. Oosthuizen, *Pentecostal Penetration*, 74.
26. Ibid., 87.
27. Hofmeyr and Pillay, *History of Christianity*, 236.
28. Oosthuizen, *Pentecostal Penetration*, 79.
29. Ibid., 78.

Rowlands and other Bethesda people also supported the fasts for the freedom of Gandhi in India, which had been called for by the Natal Indian Congress. In 1949, one year after the Nationalist Party came to power, he wrote:

> It is our firm conviction that the policy of the present South African Government in trying to introduce "apartheid" into the country has no sanction whatever in the teachings of the New Testament . . . We rejoice because our citizenship is in heaven and there is no "apartheid" there . . . There is also no "apartheid" at Bethesda where we are all one in Christ . . . irrespective of race or colour.[30]

Rowlands was, however, also concerned that political agitation should not distract his people from their spiritual calling. "We have no room in Bethesda for agitators!" he wrote in 1948. "We are Pentecostal! And we must be united. 1 Cor. 1:10. No room for a 'left wing' in that Scripture." Again in 1964 he stated that "some would like Bethesda to participate in Politics! The Bible tells us to pray for them that are in authority! . . . and to render unto Caesar that which belongs to Caesar. Jesus took no part in the politics of His day! We have been commissioned to preach the Gospel."[31]

Rowlands possessed a ready pen and in 1954 alone, according to Oosthuizen,[32] he wrote 10,000 letters, although the claim hardly seems credible. The Bethesda monthly magazine which Rowlands edited, *Moving Waters*, proved to be a valuable instrument for the extension and consolidation of the work.

The heavy labour of shepherding and guiding a rapidly growing movement took its toll. Often Rowlands referred to his weighty responsibilities. "Responsibility is crushing!" he wrote in 1972. "Continually fighting against TIME! AR [his brother] and JFR about worn out! Now obliged to leave Durban and set up house again in a suburb. Slowly and surely being killed."[33]

Rowlands was popularly known as "JF." One of his concerns in later years was the proliferation of new Pentecostal movements that did not hesitate to proselytize Bethesda members. "Many strange doctrines abounding," he complained in 1963.

---

30. Pillay, "Community Service and Conversion," 293.
31. Oosthuizen, *Pentecostal Penetration*, 79.
32. Ibid., 81.
33. Ibid., 85.

Many of our members are being "kidnapped!" Why do people leave Bethesda? . . . How many other churches manned by ex-Bethesda members! They criticize Bethesda left and right . . . but jump to get hold of our members!! *Bethesda is Unmoved*. We shall continue to stand for the highest principles.

In his 1966 annual report, Rowlands referred to "many new denominations . . . herded by self-appointed pastors . . . I have never known such a day for sheep stealing!"[34]

When J. F. Rowlands was finally laid to rest in 1980, he left behind him a Christian community of more than 23,000 souls, the largest single Christian denomination among the Indian population of South Africa. At his death, control of Bethesda effectively passed to the FGC, with which Bethesda had affiliated forty-seven years earlier.

Assemblies of God (AG)

Together with the AFM and the FGC, the AG is one of the oldest Pentecostal churches in South Africa. It came into being through the work of several Pentecostal missionaries from Britain and North America. One of these was William Chawner who was sent to South Africa by the Canadian Pentecostal Mission in 1907. Another was R. M. Turney who arrived in 1908 to conduct a Pentecostal mission in South Africa. When the AG was formed in the USA in 1914, Turney and his wife affiliated with them. They were soon joined by other Pentecostal missionaries.

From the beginning the AG was primarily a black church. In fact, until 1935 there were no white AG congregations in South Africa. As AG churches were established among the various peoples of South Africa, three AG "groups" emerged which were united in a common General Executive. For much of its history the General Executive has had a majority black leadership. Associated with the AG of South Africa was a man who, on account of his extraordinary gifts of evangelism and leadership, became famous throughout Africa and was described in the November 1959 issue of *Time* magazine as the "black Billy Graham," Nicholas Bhengu.

---

34. Ibid., 83.

Nicholas Bhengu

Born in 1909 in KwaZulu-Natal where his father was an evangelist at the Norwegian Lutheran mission church at Eshowe, Bhengu was attracted to Marxism as a youth and became an active worker in the Communist Party in Kimberley. In 1929 he attended a Full Gospel evangelistic crusade held in Kimberley by two American evangelists. There he surrendered his life to Christ. From 1934 until 1936 he attended the South African General Mission Bible Training School in Dumisa, Natal. After graduating, his proficiency in several languages helped him procure work as a court interpreter. Feeling the call to full-time ministry, however, he resigned his secular employment to work as an evangelist and in 1937 was ordained by the AG of God with whom he had affiliated. While Bhengu retained this affiliation until his death, his work was of an independent nature and at no time was he under any sort of white supervision. In 1940 he became a member of the first multiracial executive council of the AG.

From 1945 Bhengu began holding meetings in Port Elizabeth which were marked by "changed lives, outstanding miracles of healing and the overflowing joy of the people."[35] Out of these meetings a local church began to grow, and in 1950 Bhengu opened the Pilgrim Bible School. In the same year he launched the Back to God Crusade in East London. The results "far exceeded what had happened in Port Elizabeth. Thousands attended the services which were characterized by extraordinary power both in preaching and in healing. The whole of East London was moved."[36]

Bhengu's Back to God Crusade began as a non-denominational ministry, but soon he began to gather his converts into a church which grew to 1,500 active members within a year and was probably the largest Pentecostal church in the country at the time. In April 1952 a mass baptism of 1,300 converts was held under Bhengu's direction. Five years later a church building seating four to five thousand people was dedicated in East London. This became the headquarters of his evangelistic and church planting ministry.[37] By 1959 at least fifty churches with about 15,000 members had been established. The churches planted by Bhengu and his workers soon became the biggest group within the AG. The impact of his preaching was astonishing. In some areas where he ministered, the crime rate dropped by as much as a third, and it was

---

35. Anderson, "African Pentecostalism," 132.
36. Ibid.
37. Ibid.

not unusual for people to respond to his messages by leaving their weapons and stolen goods in piles at his feet.[38]

Bhengu's refusal to become involved in political issues brought considerable criticism, both during his life and since his death. He was described as a "sell-out" by some African nationalists and even received death threats. He believed national redemption would come "through non-violence, good relations with Whites, obedience to the laws of the land and, above all, through faith in God rather than in political action."[39] He forbade his members having any political affiliation. Yet his was no spirit of subservience. He possessed a strong independence of mind, a sense of dignity, and self-confidence. C. P. Watt, the historian of the AG in South Africa, even went so far as to suggest that "Bhengu was motivated philosophically by his understanding of Black Consciousness. He taught the people by word and example not to be ashamed of their blackness."[40] Bhengu's commitment to building black self-reliance led him to entertain, for a while, a certain sympathy for the ideology of apartheid, with its emphasis on the separate development of black people within their own cultural context and under their own forms of government. Later, however, he changed his views as the injustice and unworkability of the apartheid system became increasingly apparent.

In matters political Bhengu was certainly influenced by the views prevalent among most Pentecostals at that time. But in one thing he remained constant: from the time of his conversion to Christ, he had a passionate desire to see people of all races, cultures and classes come to an experience of salvation, peace and unity in Christ. Several weeks before his death in 1986 he wrote in a *Farewell Message to the Church*:

> Build the Church of God. The names of our Churches are our own inventions and not God's! Let the Christians come together as God's children. Build the nation where you are remembering that you are part of that nation and you are in it for a specific purpose for God. Pray for all leaders in Africa, support leaders of your nation and present Christ to them by all means. The Church is the light of the world. The Church is the salt of the

---

38. McGee, "Nicholas Bhekinkosi Hepworth Bhengu," 57.
39. As quoted in Anderson, "African Pentecostalism," 134.
40. Anderson, "African Pentecostalism," 133.

earth and the Church should lead the nation to peace, unity and prosperity.[41]

Further Pentecostal Movements and Churches

From its first beginnings at Azusa Street in Los Angeles, the Pentecostal movement has been characterized by schisms and the formation of new groups. The hundreds and thousands of separate African independent churches that will be considered in the next section have their roots, to a large extent, in the Pentecostal movement. But before looking at them, we shall examine a few of the new groups that emerged from the classical Pentecostal churches, particularly from the AFM.

In the industrial town of Benoni, just east of Johannesburg, Maria Fraser began to express criticisms of the AFM. Sin, she felt, was creeping increasingly into the movement. In 1927 she prophesied a new outpouring of the Holy Spirit within the AFM. Over the following nine months, Fraser's followers experienced times of heavenly ecstasy with singing in tongues, holy dancing, laughing in the Spirit and visions of angels.[42] After the completion of nine months (an allusion to pregnancy), a "latter rain" movement was born. Following divine instructions given through a heavenly vision, Fraser instructed all the women to wear blue dresses with long sleeves and a high collar, and black shoes and stockings. On Sundays they had to wear white dresses. Men's dress was also prescribed. The distinctive weekly dress of the women gave rise to the "Latter Rain" people becoming known as the *Blourokkies* (Blue dresses). The AFM leadership reacted strongly to what they regarded as the strange behaviour and unfair criticism levelled at them by Maria Fraser and her followers, who were eventually expelled from the church. The headquarters of the Latter Rain Assemblies in Benoni has become a remarkable instance of Christian communal living, similar in many ways to that of the nineteenth-century Shakers in the USA and characterized by discipline, industry, high-quality craftsmanship and orderliness.

By the mid-twentieth century the South African government was attempting to draw rigid lines between the various racial groups. Within the "white" community, the AFM had its greatest growth among Afrikaans-speaking people. In 1955 G. R. Wessels, a senior pastor in the AFM and its

---

41. McGee, "Nicholas Bhekinkosi Hepworth Bhengu," 57.
42. Hofmeyr, *Church History*, 154.

vice-president, became a senator in the ruling National Party government. Many AFM members were unhappy with his political involvement. Further discontent was aroused when the AFM leadership, in an attempt to improve the image of their church within the Afrikaner community, began to tone down some of the more exuberant Pentecostal liturgical practices and to encourage higher standards of education and training for their pastors. In reaction to these developments, a group led by J. H. Snyman protested that the fire of God was no longer burning brightly in the AFM and organized a conference in Benoni, summoning the Pentecostal people to fan into flame again the fire from heaven. Out of this protest was formed in 1958 the Pentecostal Protestant Church. Since then it has grown rapidly throughout South Africa so that it has become the largest of the classical Pentecostal churches after the AFM, the FGC and the AG.

The African Instituted (or Independent) Churches

P. L. le Roux's acceptance of the Pentecostal message and his association with the AFM did not immediately lead to a split in his Zion congregation at Wakkerstroom. His black colleagues indicated a strong desire to retain the name "Zion," so the church at Wakkerstroom was at first called the Zion Apostolic Church. For many years the AFM regarded this congregation as its "Zion branch." Le Roux focused his attention on his work with the AFM, however, and gradually the Pentecostals and the Zionists became estranged.

Probably the earliest definite secession took place in 1917 when Elias Mahlangu founded the Zion Apostolic Church of South Africa. Sometime between 1912 and 1920 Daniel Nkonyane, the most impressive of the early Zion leaders in the opinion of Sundkler, founded the Christian Catholic Apostolic Holy Spirit Church in Zion. It was Nkonyane who, as a leader in the Christian Catholic Apostolic Church in Zion (Dowie's church) had introduced certain elements in worship that have remained visible hallmarks of Zionism to this day: white robes, bare feet, holy sticks, and Old Testament symbolism.[43] Le Roux and other white Pentecostals objected to the use of such symbols.

One of the best educated of the early Zionist leaders was Paulo Mabilitsa, who founded the Christian Apostolic Church in Zion in 1920. Of him Sundkler wrote, "He gave one the impression of being a fine, almost

---

43. Pretorius and Jafta, "Branch Springs Out," 218.

distinguished personality. He was certainly much respected on the Rand and in the Reserves, and was widely known. He took an active part in the building up of a solid school work in Alexandra, Johannesburg."[44] Another early Zionist leader associated with Le Roux and his former congregation at Wakkerstroom was J. G. Phillips, a Malawian who founded the Holy Catholic Apostolic Church in Zion.

From these early beginnings and by a process of fragmentation grew the multitudes of Zionist churches. The dozens became hundreds, and the hundreds became thousands. With this expansion grew a wide diversity of teachings and practices. Yet certain features have continued to characterize the great majority of Zionist churches. These include threefold baptism by immersion; belief in divine healing and the rejection of medicine and doctors; taboos against alcohol, pork and tobacco; the wearing of white robes with green and blue cloaks, cords, and turbans; holy sticks; Sabbath observance; holy dances; purification rites and various degrees of accommodation with traditional African customs.

In 1945 a Swedish missionary and scholar, Bengt Sundkler, compiled a list of about 900 "Native Separatist Churches." It makes fascinating reading. Most of the church names consist of permutations of a selection from the following key words: African, Apostolic, Bantu, Baptist, Catholic, Christian, Church, Ethiopian, Faith, Gospel, Holy, Holy Spirit, Independent, Jerusalem, National, Native, New, South Africa, United, Zion. Some of the churches have long titles such as the Christian Catholic Apostolic African Church in Zion of South Africa or the Apostolic First Assembly of Holy Spirit Catholic Church in Zion. Such titles indicate their theology and pedigree.

Among so many churches there are such curiosities as the African Casteroil Dead Church, the Afro-Athlican Constructive Gaathly, the Catholic Church of South Africa King George Win the War, and the True (Truth) Zion Church of God. But these oddities are exceptions. The vast majority of church names bear witness to the desire to remain faithful to traditions of Zionism and Pentecostalism brought by the emissaries from Zion City and Azusa Street and mediated by divinely called and anointed African leaders.

It would be impossible even to attempt to follow the history of all the Zionist churches. We shall therefore focus on a few outstanding leaders and the churches they brought into existence.

---

44. Sundkler, *Bantu Prophets*, 49.

Edward Motaung and the Zion AFM

Edward Motaung (Sotho for "lion person"), also known as Edward Lion and Edward of Basutoland, was one of Edgar Mahon's first converts. How he became a Pentecostal is not clear, but it appears that he met up with the AFM (and possibly with John G. Lake) in 1910. Motaung joined the AFM in 1912 and was given oversight of its work in Lesotho. Sundkler described him as "the most spectacular of the Sotho Zionists of an earlier generation" and referred to his baptism of 130 converts in the Caledon River as "the first mass baptism in that Sotho Jordan."[45] There are many reports of Motaung's extraordinary ministry. Lake, for example, wrote that

> on one occasion when a multitude of sick folk had been brought into a valley, the power of God came upon him and he went upon the mountainside, stretched out his hands over the sick below, and poured out his heart to God. In a minute, hundreds were healed! Healing power fell upon them.[46]

Anderson, drawing on Gordon Lindsay's biography of Lake, writes of Edward Motaung:

> Crowds of five and six thousand used to gather to hear him preach, and sometimes he would preach the whole day. He had a remarkable healing ministry, and thousands were reported healed as a result of his prayers. He used to spend whole nights praying for the sick until his strength was gone. He would then ask his assistants to direct the long line of sick people to the stone on which he had sat that they might also sit there and be healed in the name of Jesus Christ.[47]

Independent confirmation of such reports is difficult to obtain, but by all accounts Motaung made a powerful impact on his generation, although the precise evolution of his church affiliation is difficult to establish. As late as 1921 the AFM still regarded him as the leader of its work in Lesotho, but some time before that he had seceded to form the Zion Apostolic Faith Mission (ZAFM). Other evidence suggests that Motaung's ZAFM seceded from the

---

45. Anderson, "African Pentecostalism," 128.
46. Quoted in Anderson, "African Pentecostalism," 128.
47. Anderson, "African Pentecostalism," 129.

Zion Apostolic Church of Elias Mahlangu in 1920.[48] In seeking to understand these contradictions, it must be remembered that the lines between different Pentecostal and Zionist bodies were very fluid during the first two decades of the twentieth century. It seems that Mahlangu's Zion Apostolic Church and Motaung's ZAFM were both considered part of the AFM at an earlier stage. One person whom Motaung deeply impressed and who joined him for a while was Engenas Lekganyane, the founder of what was to become the largest African instituted church (if not the largest Christian body of any kind) in South Africa.

Job Chiliza and the African Gospel Church

The term AIC is a broad umbrella covering a wide range of churches, from those very close to mainline or Pentecostal denominations to those more deeply influenced by African traditional religious customs. Chiliza's church is an example of the former. Raised in the church established by the American Board of Commissioners for Foreign Missions, Chiliza served as one of its preachers for six years before joining the Zion Church of Ezra Mbonambi. His Zionist phase was transitional. "They [Zionists] are just like wind," he later commented. "They do not stand on the foundation of Christ."[49] In 1926 he joined the FGC of Archibald Cooper, who baptized him in the Umhlatuze River together with a number of his followers. Chiliza remained with the FGC for sixteen years and was the leader of the black section of its work. When his request in 1942 for greater autonomy for the black congregations was turned down, Chiliza, with about 7,000 followers, reacted by leaving the FGC. For a few years he formed an association with the Pentecostal Holiness Church, but in 1947 he left them to form the African Gospel Church. In the estimation of Sundkler, who knew him personally, Chiliza was "one of the most outstanding church leaders in South Africa in this century, and, as was to be expected, altogether unknown to Whites or Blacks outside his chapel in narrow Fountain Lane, in what was then the African slum in the centre of Durban."[50]

---

48. Ibid., 120.
49. Quoted in Anderson, "African Pentecostalism," 130.
50. Ibid., 131.

Engenas Lekganyane and the Zion Christian Church

The Zion Christian Church has become one of South Africa's largest churches, yet information on the early life of its founder is very sketchy. Engenas Lekganyane was born sometime between 1880 and 1885 in the Northern Transvaal of Northern Sotho (Pedi) stock. Anderson mentions that he became an evangelist in the Free Church of Scotland,[51] while Paul Makhubu claims that he began as a preacher of the Bantu Baptist Church.[52] Both assertions could be right.

For many years Lekganyane suffered from a serious eye disease. Then he had a vision in which a voice told him that if he went to Johannesburg and joined the church that baptized by threefold immersion, he would find healing. After arriving in that city in 1912, he joined the Zion Apostolic Church (ZAC) of Elias Mahlangu, who baptized him. His eyes were healed.[53]

At this early stage there was no difference between the ZAC and the AFM, as Mahlangu did not break with the white Pentecostals until about 1917. Even before his baptism by Mahlangu, Lekganyane might have met P. L. le Roux, but later he came to know him well and received his preaching credentials from him.

Lekganyane developed into a powerful preacher in the ZAC, but soon differences began to emerge between him and Mahlangu, who was promoting customs which Lekganyane found objectionable. These included the wearing of white robes, the growing of beards and the removal of shoes before services. It was about this time that Lekganyane interpreted an incident involving his hat to be a divine revelation that he would found a large church. While he was at prayer, a whirlwind blew his hat off his head. The hat settled under a tree where falling leaves filled it. The leaves symbolized, he believed, the many members he would gather together. His prophecy in 1917 of the defeat of Germany by Britain also helped to enhance his prestige as a prophet and a man of God.

Leaving the ZAC, Lekganyane went to Lesotho in 1920, joined up with Edward Motaung's Zion AFM, and was ordained as a bishop of the ZAFM for the Transvaal. Once again differences arose, chiefly over administrative matters, and at the end of 1924 or the beginning of 1925 Lekganyane founded his own church, the Zion Christian Church (ZCC). His marriage to a second

---

51. Anderson, "African Pentecostalism," 140.
52. Makhubu, *Who Are the Independent Churches?* 15.
53. Anderson, "African Pentecostalism," 141.

wife was a further reason for the break with Motaung, who opposed polygamy. Lekganyane, however, remained a strong admirer of Motaung and named his second son, Edward, after him.[54]

In 1930 Lekganyane moved the centre of his operations to a farm he purchased about fifty kilometres (thirty miles) east of Pietersburg. This became Moriah, the headquarters and spiritual centre of the ZCC, the place where the faithful come together to celebrate and to which they bring their gifts and offerings every Easter.

The ZCC grew rapidly. Its 926 adherents in 1925 became 2,000 by 1935 and 8,500 by 1940. In the next two years, membership of the ZCC trebled to 27,487 and the church spread to Zimbabwe, Botswana and the Northern Cape Province. Lekganyane's ability to keep his followers together resulted in the ZCC becoming one of the largest indigenous churches in Africa by 1974, with about 45,000 members. Like other Pentecostal and Zionist leaders, Lekganyane laid a strong emphasis on divine healing. At first he used to heal by laying on of hands, but as the church grew he would bless various objects such as strips of cloth, strings, papers, needles, walking sticks and water to be used for healing and protective purposes.[55] Such practices contributed to the increasing distance between the ZCC and the classical Pentecostal churches.

Lekganyane's death in 1948 led to a dispute between his two sons, Edward and Joseph, over who should lead the ZCC. Such crises are common in African independent churches and often lead to schisms. The ZCC did split, but by far the larger section continued as the ZCC under the leadership of Edward and continued to grow rapidly. By 1954 membership had reached 80,000.

In 1963 Edward enrolled at the Dutch Reformed Church's Stoffberg Theological College for a three-year course in theology. It appears that at the end of his life he sought to steer the ZCC in a more biblical direction and away from the elements that tended to view Lekganyane as an African Messiah. Not all were happy with these new developments, and some felt that the ZCC had lost spiritual power. Nevertheless, Edward Lekganyane was an effective leader, and the church continued to grow under his episcopal rule. After his death in 1967 his son Barnabas succeeded him as bishop.

Membership of the ZCC in the closing years of the second millennium is estimated to have surpassed one million. The annual Easter gatherings at Moriah, near Pietersburg, cause major traffic congestion on the 300 kilometre

---

54. Ibid., 141.
55. Ibid., 142.

(185 mile) road from Gauteng to Pietersburg as up to a million adherents make their pilgrimage to their holy Zion in the north.

Ma Nku and the Saint John Apostolic Faith Mission

One of the largest and most prominent independent churches in the Gauteng region was founded by a woman, Christina Nku, known to her followers as Ma (Mother) Nku. Born in 1894, she grew up as a member of the Dutch Reformed Church. As a young girl she experienced various visions and dreams. At the age of thirty, she had a vision while ill and saw a large church with twelve doors (inspired, perhaps, by the vision of St John in Rev 21). She was told to follow the baptism of John and Jesus. She felt called by God to build the church of her vision. In that same year Christina and her husband were baptized in the AFM and became acquainted with P. L. le Roux.[56] Le Roux objected to some of her more elaborate displays of prophetic rapture, however, and soon Ma Nku left the AFM to establish the St John AFM. The name of her church, like that of Edward Motaung's, implied continuity with the AFM and the Pentecostal movement in general.

In another vision she was shown the exact place to build her twelve-door church in Evaton, south of Johannesburg. Ma Nku began to visit this site and pray and eventually she was able to buy the site. The building which she erected there in the 1950s became known as the Temple and was for many years the largest independent church building in the Gauteng urban area.

Ma Nku, who took the title "Founder and Life General President" of the St John AFM, became well known as a person of prayer with healing power. She gathered thousands into her church. It was particularly her healing practices, however, that brought increasing distance between the St John AFM and the Pentecostal movement. She prayed over thousands of bottles and buckets of water, which were then used by the faithful to bring healing.[57]

In her old age Ma Nku was troubled by a conflict over who would succeed her in leadership of the St John AFM. She wished her son to succeed her, but at an official meeting of the church a certain Petros Masango was chosen as her successor. This led to a serious and protracted wrangle and the matter was eventually taken to the Supreme Court in Pretoria, which ruled that Masango was the lawfully-elected archbishop of the church. He served in this

---

56. Ibid., 144.
57. Ibid.

capacity until his death in 1982, when conflict again arose as to who should succeed him. The tendency in church to practise hereditary leadership and the inevitable tussles that arise after the death of a leader are probably a major reason for the fragmentation within these communities.

Isaiah Shembe and the Ama-Nazaretha

The ama-Nazaretha of Isaiah Shembe represents one of those AICs that have wandered so far from their Zion (Dowie) and Pentecostal roots that it is unlikely that any Holiness or Pentecostal church would be able to recognize them. Thunder and lightning, dreams and visions and heavenly voices all played a part in Shembe's stormy spiritual pilgrimage. Born in 1870, he was a young boy when he received his first revelation while he was praying in the cattle kraal. Sundkler, drawing on a short biography of Shembe written by Dr John L. Dube, relates:

> During a thunderstorm the Word was brought to him by lightning: "Cease from immorality (*ukuhlobonga*)!" Later, as a young man and husband of four wives, he had another vision, also brought by lightning: he saw a multitude of people, or angels, and they pointed to something lying on earth. He saw his own corpse, in a rotten state, evil-smelling. The word reminded him of his first vision, and the command to cease from immorality. "And that day, though he was an industrious man, he did not work, and he ceased working until Sunday, because he said: I have seen Jehovah." In a third vision it was revealed to him that he should leave his four wives, and though this was so hard that he almost committed suicide, yet he finally followed the divine command.[58]

The decisive, final call to be a prophet was also conveyed by a terrifying storm in which lightning killed his best ox and burned Shembe. He was ill for three weeks after that and came to the conviction that "Jehovah has revealed to me that I must not be healed by medicine, only through His Word."[59] Shembe then travelled around Natal, preaching and driving out demons. When he was baptized in 1906 by W. M. Leshaga of the African Native

---

58. Sundkler, *Bantu Prophets*, 110.
59. Ibid., 110.

Baptist Church (an offshoot of an African-American Baptist mission to Natal begun in 1899), he was already famous as a healer. Immediately following his baptism Shembe was ordained a minister, and soon thereafter he led his followers to be baptized in the sea near Durban. In 1911 he broke with his Baptist church over the Sabbath issue and started his own church, the *amaNazaretha* (Nazarites).

Mountains and holy high places have often played a special role in AICs (e.g. Lekganyane's Moriah near Pietersburg). In 1916 Shembe established his Ekuphakameni (High Place) some thirty kilometres (19 miles) from Durban. This became the spiritual centre of the ama-Nazaretha, their own Mount Zion, to which all the faithful come for a great annual festival in July. The Nazarites have their own printed hymn book, unusual among AICs, containing many verses composed by their founding prophet, Isaiah Shembe. These hymns are a valuable source of information concerning the ethos, theology and aspirations of the church. The extraordinary role of Shembe as the one who revealed the power and grace of God emerges clearly in these hymns. He is seen as more than a prophet; he is the Servant, the Promised One, sent as a Liberator to the Zulu people. Thus Hymn 60 reads

> Praise Jehovah,
> Because he is righteous,
> Because he is benevolent for evermore.
> He remembered his people,
> He sent them Isaiah, his Servant,
> Because he is righteous.[60]

The "Isaiah" referred to in Hymn 60 is identified in Hymn 134: "Shembe, the Servant of the Lord, will wipe the tears of his people."[61] It becomes clear that just as Moses was sent to the Jews, so Shembe was sent to the Zulus.

> Our Liberator,
> We Dingaan's people,
> We have heard him,
> He has come.
> The Liberator has arrived,
> You, Zulus, we have heard him. (Hymn 214)[62]

---

60. Ibid., 282.
61. Ibid.
62. Ibid.

There is a strong Old Testament and Zulu nationalistic ethos among the Nazarites. Just as the Jews are the children of Abraham to whom God sent his prophets, so the Zulus are the children of Shaka, the great king who established them as a mighty nation, and Shembe is the Zulu prophet. Following the Zulu custom of *inhlonipho* (language of respect), no direct mention is ever made of the name of Shaka. Instead the reference is always to those close to him, such as Senzangakhona, his father, or Dingaan, his successor.

> From time immemorial,
> We used to drink
> from the spring,
> Senzangakhona's spring,
> Yes, my King. (Hymn 216)[63]

Was Shembe merely a prophet in the eyes of his people, or was he seen as a Messiah? In the official doctrines of the church, he is a prophet. His son and successor, Johannes Galilee Shembe, stated in a sermon in 1958: "Shembe is nothing. He is nothing but dust in the hands of God. Shembe is not God, but the vessel of God. He was just like Moses, but our Moses is among us. Shembe brought him from overseas among us."[64]

In the experience of the faithful, however, Shembe assumes quasi-divine status. Bengt Sundkler was once told by a Nazarite woman, "Jesus? Him we have only seen in photos! But I know Shembe, and I believe in him. He is the one who created heaven and earth; he is God for us black people."[65] Another Nazarite put it this way: "Jesus came first as a white man. But now he has come as a black man, in the flesh, through Shembe."[66] In the Nazarite hymn book there is a photo of Isaiah Shembe, by which the sick, merely by looking at it, can find healing. The same hymn book also contains three hymns written by Shembe "after his resurrection from the dead."[67] This was explained by his son as meaning that the hymns had been revealed in visions and auditions to some women.

The tendency to attribute Messianic status to Shembe is further enhanced by the very few references to "Jesu Kristu" in the hymn book. In Hymn

---

63. Ibid., 288.
64. Ibid., 330.
65. Ibid., 281.
66. Ibid., 285.
67. Ibid., 284.

154, which provides a Nazarite *credo*, the omission of any reference to him is conspicuous:

> I believe in the Father
> and in the Holy Spirit
> and in the communion of saints
> of the Nazarites.[68]

The Nazarites do not deny the person of Jesus, but he is somehow too "white" and distant. More central and real in their faith are the Jehovah of the Old Testament and Shembe, his servant and messenger to the Zulus.

In keeping with the Old Testament ethos of the church, Shembe introduced circumcision, Sabbath-keeping and a prohibition of eating pork. Nazarites often refuse to shake hands with other people, as "they cannot be friends with the unclean and the uncircumcised."[69] Polygamy is sanctioned by the example of the Old Testament saints, and Shembe even declared that European monogamy was the Apostle Paul's invention. "It was Paul's legislation, but not God's. Had not God said: *Zalani nande* (Be fruitful and multiply)?"[70]

Together with most other amaZioni, the ama-Nazaretha strongly opposed the use of medicines. This included vaccination, which many regarded as "the mark of the Beast." Shembe's attitude was that "they had taken a sacred oath not to resort to medicine in any shape or form nor submit their bodies to be cut."[71] This rule was later relaxed by Shembe's son, Johannes Galilee, who had a BA degree from Fort Hare Native College (later the University of Fort Hare).

We close this account of the Nazarites with Sundkler's description of a typical July festival service at Ekuphakameni:

> The climax of the festival is from Thursday to Sunday in the last week. On Thursday evening there is the Washing of the Feet and the Passover. On Friday and Sunday dances are held. On Saturday all congregate in the "Paradise," an open space in the centre of Ekuphakameni. The Paradise is divided into two parts, the upper for men and the lower for women. All are dressed in white, only a few of the priests wear long blue vestments. When "The Servant"

---

68. Ibid., 283.
69. Ibid., 163.
70. Ibid., 277.
71. Ibid.

himself – Johannes Galilee Shembe – arrives in the middle of the service he is all in black, wearing his father's black veil round his head. There reigns a dignified quietness throughout the service, contrasting with the vivid gaiety of the dancing on Friday and Sunday. The Sabbath service – with its lengthy exhortations on the keeping of the Sabbath and the observance of the *hlonipha* (rules of the Zulus) – is read by priests and congregation. Free prayer follows with all taking part at the same time, but there is no hysterical shouting.

Then come testimonies by various people. The first man starts off by posing a rhetorical question:

> Who is going to open the Gate? There is only one who can open the Gate for us Zulus. Therefore, ye Senzangakhona's people, come to Ekuphakameni. There is nobody whom the Lord of Ekuphakameni loves as much as you, Nazarites. Do not waste your money on medicines. Come here and you will be healed for nothing.[72]

On 20 July 1981, in the presence of 40,000 followers, Isaiah Shembe was officially canonized. The church he founded was reckoned to have half a million members in 1986, making it the largest African instituted church in South Africa after the ZCC.

Enoch Mgijima and the Bulhoek Massacre

Enoch Mgijima and his followers, known as "Israelites," achieved prominence not because of the size of their movement, but because of the dramatic and tragic circumstances of a violent clash with government forces that left about 180 Israelites dead.

Born in the Eastern Cape Province in 1868, Mgijima was serving as a Wesleyan preacher when he joined the Church of God and Saints in Christ, a church of African-American origin that strongly emphasized aspects of Mosaic law such as Sabbath-keeping and the Passover. In 1913 he became a bishop of this church and gained renown as a forceful preacher.

---

72. Ibid., 187.

A South African Pentecost 143

Visions and dreams played a central role in Mgijima's preaching, and after the appearance of Halley's Comet in 1910 these visions became increasingly apocalyptic and violent. In one of them, as reported by Sundkler, Mgijima saw

> a battle between two white Governments. In his vision he had seen a baboon crush these Governments and destroy them. The interpretation he put upon this was that the white Governments represented the Dutch and the English, the baboon the Africans. This meant that the white people would be crushed by the Natives.[73]

In the light of the acute tensions between Afrikaans and English communities during the First World War and the ultimate triumph of the African nationalist movement over white rule, Mgijima's prophecies were remarkably accurate. But their violent tone and visions of black and white conflict and bloodshed disturbed his American-based church, and he was excommunicated in 1919. Those who remained loyal to Mgijima, the Israelites, believed themselves to be the chosen people of Jehovah, who would deliver them from bondage. Mosaic law and ceremonies were enjoined, and the New Testament was regarded as a fiction of the whites.

In 1919, the same year in which he was excommunicated, Mgijima assembled his disciples at Ntabelanga or Bulhoek, his ancestral home, to celebrate the Passover and await the imminent coming of the Lord. The Israelites built a village of some three hundred houses at Bulhoek (near Queenstown). Warned by the authorities that they were illegally occupying crown land, Mgijima agreed to vacate the land after he and his followers had celebrated Passover in April 1920. But the Israelites did not vacate and gave no indication that they intended to. Police action on 24 May 1921 to remove them forcibly turned violent, and about 180 Israelites were killed.

As with many other massacres, there are conflicting views of exactly what happened and who was at fault. In the eyes of many African nationalists, it was simply a case of detachments of the army and police, armed with artillery, machine guns and rifles, opening fire on unarmed Africans.[74] Sundkler's opinion was that

> the Government handled the case with perfect patience, a generosity which was interpreted by Enoch and his followers as

---

73. Ibid., 72.
74. Pretorius and Jafta, "Branch Springs Out," 219.

weakness and fear on the part of the authorities. When in the end military force was dispatched to the place, the prophet told his people that the bullets of the white men would turn to water.[75]

In the *Dictionary of South African Biography*, V. M. Martins writes:

> The prophet's followers, on orders from him, charged the police like religious fanatics, using assegais and home-made weapons. The police opened fire at close range with rifles and a machine-gun, mowing down the attackers, while others were at prayer in their church.[76]

The shooting at Bulhoek caused a political outcry against the prime minister, General J. C. Smuts, who was vehemently attacked in parliament by opposition leaders for the massacre of Christians by fellow Christians.[77] The clash between the Israelites and the political authorities was, however, quite exceptional. AICs have been generally apolitical, some of them even subservient in their attitude to government.

Some Concluding Reflections on the AIC Movement

In the case of the AICs of South Africa, questions are often asked as to the theological standing of these groups with doctrines and practices so different from those of most Christians in other parts of the world. Professor M. L. Daneel, a South African scholar with decades of intimate experience with independent churches in Africa, has described the difficulty of such reflection:

> A theological reflection on the independent churches in Africa and an evaluation of the different trends are by no means easy matters. The incredible wealth of nuances, contradictions within one and the same church, data that are not always reliable, one's reliance on observers who are themselves outsiders and can only partially fathom what is going on in these churches, the lack of documentation for analysis, etc. combine to make this an extremely delicate and complex undertaking.[78]

---

75. Sundkler, *Bantu Prophets*, 73.
76. De Kock, *Dictionary of South African Biography*, 540.
77. Ibid.
78. Daneel et al., *Missiology*, 410.

A wide range of opinions exists among reputable scholars. Some such as G. C. Oosthuizen of South Africa and P. Beyerhaus of Germany have adopted a condemnatory approach. Oosthuizen refers to the AICs as "post-Christian." Their main characteristic, he feels, is the upholding of the traditional cult rather than the Word of God. Because of their ethnocentric features, they cannot claim to be churches of Christ.[79] Beyerhaus maintains that the Zionists are in a state of self-deception because they fail to realize that their concept of God is confined to the human dimension and bears no relation to the holy and mighty God. He maintains that all biblical concepts have been sacrificed and replaced with heathen ones and that no Zionist rites can be regarded as a faithful rendering of Christian worship.[80] Beyerhaus evaluates the black prophets as an extension of pagandom, controlled by demon forces hat need to be expelled through exorcism.

Daneel questions how much time Beyerhaus has actually spent with Zionists and observes that those researchers, such as Sundkler and M. W. Turner, who have had prolonged contact with the independent churches tend to evaluate them much more positively, without disregarding their less favourable tendencies. Sundkler himself came to change his evaluation of Zionists. In a second edition (1961) of his classic *Bantu Prophets in South Africa*, he wrote:

> The Bantu Separatist Church – a bridge to a religion of the past, a bridge leading people back to "African spiritism," was our concluding note when writing on the subject in 1945–46. Looking at the situation some fifteen years later, we have had to ask ourselves whether this viewpoint was not, in fact, too foreign, too Western, perhaps.[81]

Daneel, after many years of research among the Shona independent churches in Zimbabwe, which show many of the same characteristics as South African AICs, concluded that "the indications are sufficiently positive to allow us to speak of Christian churches. Owing to defects and forms of syncretism a partial *degeneracy* may be discerned, but this is not so pronounced as to warrant calling them 'post-Christian' or 'neo-pagan.'"[82]

---

79. Ibid., 411.
80. Ibid.
81. Sundkler, *Bantu Prophets,* 302.
82. Daneel et al., *Missiology,* 420.

To AIC leaders, such discussion by outsiders are insulting. In the following comments by Paul Makhubu, his references to the divided nature of the church that came to South Africa are specially pertinent:

> The most insulting argument is that some of us are not Christian churches, just because our beliefs and actions do not match what they believe and do.
>
> . . . It is true that there are AICs which claim to be Christians even though they may not fully understand and know Christ and His redeeming work. But are they not like all of us growing in the grace and knowledge of Him? . . .
>
> We of the independent churches find it difficult to understand why we are criticized for forming different churches. Missionaries came to us divided. They came from different parts of the world, under different names, some came from the same countries and towns, believing the same doctrines and practices. But each one wanted converts for his own mission and doctrinal emphasis. Even today the mainline churches are poles apart, and will not agree or compromise. Those who are seeking unity are having problems. They do not agree on a number of issues . . . People can call us what they want, judge us, put us in pigeon holes if they wish. We exist and are growing very fast. They may ignore us now in some quarters but they cannot dismiss us. We are a thorn in the flesh of some mainline churches for various reasons.[83]

In South Africa some 10,000,000 people have found their spiritual homes in about 6,000 AICs that span a wide theological spectrum. Any broad generalization or evaluation of these groups is really impossible, and there is not even a uniform self-evaluation emerging from within the movement. The triumph of the African National Congress (ANC) in the 1994 elections, bringing to an end more than three centuries of white political and social domination, has surely removed at least one of the factors that gave rise to the AIC movement. Perhaps in the future the process of fragmentation may be replaced by a growing spirit of reconciliation and unity. The present author, however, claims no special prophetic insights in such matters, only *pia desideria*.

---

83. Makhubu, *Who Are the Independent Churches?* 1–3.

6

The Growing Church Struggle

We have considered the birth and rapid growth of the Pentecostal and Zionist churches which represent new manifestations of Christian faith in the twentieth century. The traditional or mainline Christian denominations have also continued to grow, albeit at a slower pace, and still hold within their folds the great majority of Christians in South Africa. These churches were drawn closer together by the worldwide ecumenical movement but divided again by political developments. They were plunged into a tremendous struggle as they sought to respond to the massive social and political problems of the twentieth century, particularly the rise of Afrikaner nationalism and the ideology of apartheid. But before we proceed with these stories, it is necessary to fill in some background information.

The Ecumenical Movement

Only in the nineteenth century did the Protestant churches of Europe and North America become engaged in worldwide missions on a scale comparable to the great work being done by Roman Catholic missionaries. The work of William Carey, the well-known Baptist missionary to India, is often considered to have been the catalyst that brought about a change of attitude from scepticism and indifference to enthusiastic involvement.

In the closing decade of the eighteenth century and in the opening decades of the nineteenth, numerous Protestant missionary societies were founded in Britain, Germany, France, the USA, the Netherlands, Switzerland, and the Scandinavian countries. Thousands of Methodists, Anglicans, Baptists, Lutherans, Moravians, Reformed, Presbyterians and Congregationalists were sent out to the four corners of the earth to preach the good news of the kingdom of God and gather believers into the church of Christ. The idealism of many of these missionaries was severely tested by the hardships and rigours of the mission field. It was there, too, that many became convinced of the importance of cooperation and mutual support in order to carry out the task of evangelization more effectively. Denominational differences that kept Christians apart in their home countries often seemed less relevant on the mission field in the light of the immensity of the task before them. So the modern ecumenical movement was conceived in the mission field as Christian workers reached out to one another in mutual support and encouragement and discovered in the process bonds of faith and love that transcended their differences.

To facilitate and promote cooperation between the various missionary societies, a number of missionary conferences were organized at local, regional and national levels. The culmination of these conferences was the great International Missionary Conference in Edinburgh, Scotland, in 1910 under the leadership of an American Methodist, John R. Mott. About a thousand delegates from all over the world attended.

If the ecumenical movement was conceived in the mission field, then its birth was in Edinburgh in 1910. A spirit of confidence and optimism prevailed, captured in the watch phrase: "The evangelization of the world in this generation." The experience of cooperation between Christians from so many different denominations and nationalities made a deep impression on the delegates and ignited a vision for united Christian action in other areas as well. Three organizations were born out of the Edinburgh conference: the International Missionary Council, to advance the cause of missions worldwide; the Conference on Life and Work, to seek Christian answers to urgent social and political problems; and the Conference on Faith and Order, to promote consensus in doctrine. Each met at regular intervals. In 1937 both the Conference on Life and Work and the Conference on Faith and Order agreed that a new, more inclusive organization was needed and proposed the establishment of a World Council of Churches (WCC).

Delayed by the outbreak of World War II, this council finally came into being in 1948 when 351 delegates representing 147 denominations from 44 countries gathered in Amsterdam and formed the World Council. Present in Amsterdam were South African delegates representing the Transvaal synod of the Dutch Reformed Church, the Hervormde Church, the Church of the Province, the Methodist and the Presbyterian churches – all founding members of the WCC.

The strong evangelistic and missionary emphasis of the ecumenical movement in its early days was increasingly replaced by concerns for social and political justice. This change of emphasis alienated a number of conservative Evangelicals and led to a new polarization in the Christian world, between "evangelicals" and "ecumenicals." This tension has been felt in an acute way in South Africa.

The Rise of Apartheid

Like the words "Pharisee," "inquisition," "propaganda," "fascism" and "fundamentalism," the word "apartheid" has acquired an essentially negative connotation. This makes it all the more difficult to understand how many Christian people and a few churches actually supported the policy of apartheid and proclaimed it just and Christian. Yet the effort to obtain such an understanding is necessary for insight into one of the saddest and most complex eras in the story of the church in South Africa.

The defeat of the two Boer republics in the Second Anglo-Boer War left a legacy of bitterness in the hearts of many Afrikaners, who felt that a great imperial power, enticed by its desire to gain control of the richest gold fields in the world, had ruthlessly crushed two small and peaceful countries. In their efforts to round up Boer guerrillas in the last period of the war, the British destroyed Boer farms and gathered the women and children into concentration camps where thousands died of disease. This only enhanced the bitter feelings that a great injustice had been perpetrated, and many Afrikaners prayed and longed for the restoration of the Boer republics.

In order to promote a spirit of reconciliation and bring embittered Afrikaners to peace talks, the British made the fateful decision to postpone indefinitely the question of African voting rights. Thus the Union of South Africa came into being in 1910 with political power effectively in white hands.

The centenary of the Great Trek in 1938 stimulated a powerful wave of Afrikaner nationalistic feeling, and on its crest the National Party rode to power in 1948. At once, the new government began to put into effect a lasting solution to the vexed "race problem." How could the principles of democracy and Afrikaner self-rule both be maintained? The answer was clear – a radical separation of the people of South Africa into discrete "nations," each to govern itself in its own territory (just as the peoples of Europe, it was argued, were divided into autonomous national states). The fact that this separation (apartheid means "separateness") was unilaterally decided on by one "nation" without consultation with all the other parties, and the fact that the black nations received only 13 percent of the country meant that the policy of apartheid was doomed from the beginning. But in 1948 and for many years thereafter, it seemed to many to be the only way in which a people who had struggled and suffered so much in history could maintain control over their own destiny. Therefore they believed passionately and blindly that it must work.

The preceding lines do not adequately convey the total socio-political picture of twentieth-century South Africa; all they offer is a very rough sketch of the political background against which the various churches sought to carry out their God-given mission as they understood it.

The Development of the Christian Council of South Africa (CCSA) and the Growing Rift between Afrikaans and English Churches

The desire for closer cooperation between missionaries and their societies so that there might be a more effective fulfilment of their evangelistic task led to the formation in 1904 of the General Missionary Conference (GMC). Eighty delegates from twenty-one societies and churches met in Johannesburg and formulated the aims of the GMC as follows:

> To promote cooperation and brotherly feeling between different Missionary Societies.
> To labour for the most speedy and effective evangelization of the Native races of South Africa.
> To enlighten public opinion on Christian Missions.
> To watch over the interests of the native races, and where necessary to influence legislation on their behalf.
> To keep ever in view the goal of establishing self-supporting and self-propagating Native Churches in South Africa.[1]

Membership of the GMC was on an individual basis, and Dr James Stewart of Lovedale was elected as its first president. In a letter to the 1904 conference a French missionary to Lesotho, François Coillard, expressed the hope

> that the Conference is only the first one inaugurating a new era in African Missions. It is time for us also, as in China, Japan

---

1. Strassberger, *Ecumenism in South Africa*, 135.

and elsewhere to uproot the hedges and pull down the barriers of denominations as far as possible, and blend all our energies into one mighty effort to extend the boundaries of our Lord's Kingdom.²

Between 1904 and 1932 a total of eight conferences were held under the auspices of the GMC, and the experience of fellowship and cooperation was valued by many participants. Bridges were built between missionaries of the most diverse denominations and societies, and thus missions were drawn into closer contact with one another. But because the GMC was composed of individuals who had joined on their own initiative, mission societies and churches as such were not directly represented and felt no obligation to carry out any resolutions. This lack of authority was felt to be a defect and caused much frustration. This feeling is summed up in the following statement made by J. Dexter Taylor at the 1925 Conference:

> One is grieved to admit that in the twenty-one years that this conference has been in existence it has brought us no further forward in cooperation than the passing of joint resolutions and the occasional sending of joint deputations to the Government. Our Commission on Survey and Occupation has brought about no strategic readjustments of forces, or divisions of territory. Our commission on uniformity of discipline has left us each going our own denominational way. Even in the cooperative production of vernacular literature and music we are still marking time.³

The need was felt for a more authoritative council, and so in 1929 Dr John R. Mott was invited to visit South Africa in connection with the establishment of a national Christian council. Mott had been the moving spirit behind the International Missionary Conference at Edinburgh in 1910. He had also planned a series of conferences in Asia in 1912 and 1913 which, in India, China and Japan, brought into being national missionary councils. These later became national Christian Councils. Mott's visit to South Africa in 1934 paved the way for the Christian Council of South Africa, which was formally constituted in Bloemfontein on 24 June 1936 for "the closer co-ordination of the Christian forces of South Africa, with a view to the more

---

2. Ibid., 136.
3. Ibid., 137.

effective propagation of the Gospel."[4] Thirty different churches and missionary societies representing the whole spectrum of traditional Protestant churches affiliated themselves to the council. One Dutch Reformed minister, W. Nicol, was unanimously elected first president of the CCSA, while another, J. Murray du Toit, was appointed general secretary. On the acceptance of this appointment du Toit remarked:

> The world has invented many machines, some very cruel. Perhaps the most complicated of all is the mechanism of organized Christianity. In spite of this I have taken on the secretaryship of the Christian Council of South Africa because I believe it will be used by God to bring souls to his Kingdom. I wish, however, to state my clear conviction that Christ has called us to change lives, hence life-changing will ever be my primary concern.[5]

At an early meeting in Johannesburg, Nicol pointed out some of the problems facing the council. One was linguistic. Afrikaans and English were the official languages of the Union of South Africa, and the council had accepted the principle of bilingualism. But Afrikaans speakers felt that their language was not given its rightful place in council deliberations, thus putting them at a disadvantage. Nicol appealed to the Afrikaans churches and societies not to draw aside because of the language situation. "The great task before us demands that nothing of a temporary nature, not even tongues which will pass away, should prevent our cooperation," he pleaded.[6]

Another difficulty arose from the different views which were held by the various groups in the council on almost all questions affecting the African population. In commenting on this problem Nicol observed: "All this must sound very depressing and hopeless to people who do not appreciate the genius of South Africa and do not know that all our best things have been born out of conflict and strife."[7] One of the main reasons for the existence of the Christian Council was precisely the united study of such problems. "Some Council of this kind," he concluded, "was necessary in South Africa, if the Christian churches were to give our nation a true picture of Christ."[8]

---

4. Ibid., 142.
5. Ibid., 143.
6. Ibid., 144.
7. Ibid., 145.
8. Ibid.

At a public meeting in 1937, Z. R. Mahabane expressed gratitude for the establishment of the CCSA and spoke on "What an African expects of the Christian Council." He said that Africans were on the verge of despair and were giving up hope that their welfare would be attended to, but "the coming into being of the Council had revived their hopes and inspired them with a feeling of confidence and high expectations." He further expressed the hope that the council would promote the educational, economic and political advancement of the African people.[9]

Tensions between Afrikaans- and English-speaking members of the council made its work difficult and nearly led to its dissolution in 1941. Only the Transvaal Synod of the DRC participated in the council; repeated invitations to the Cape DRC Synod to join were in vain. In 1939 Nicol expressed his disappointment that the differences of opinion between churches over racial and language policies were driving them apart. "There is now very little hope," he lamented, "of the other seven Dutch Churches (or any one of them) joining the council. I have held on during the past few years in the hope that the breach would be narrow enough for them to be drawn in. It is, however, clear that we are drifting apart." Nicol concluded that "the Council, under whatever name it may operate in future, will have to be satisfied to represent the opinion of the English-speaking churches through the English medium, and leave it to the Afrikaans churches to make their own arrangements for co-operating as is now envisaged."[10] Nicol was referring to the formation of the Federal Mission Council of Afrikaans-oriented churches.

The withdrawal of the DRC from the CCSA led to the departure of the Church of the Province of South Africa, as well. The Anglican bishops felt that the absence of the DRC, the largest denomination in South Africa, from the CCSA undermined the very purpose of its existence. At a meeting of the CCSA in 1941, deep concern was expressed in anticipation of the possible dissolution of the Christian Council. After thorough discussion it was resolved that the CCSA should continue to exist. Letters were sent to the Church of the Province of South Africa with the result that the Synod of Bishops decided to re-affiliate the CPSA with the CCSA. For the next fifty years relations between the CCSA (or the SACC, which replaced it in 1960) and the Afrikaans churches were characterized by tension and conflict.

---

9. Ibid.
10. Ibid., 161.

The Federal Mission Council (FMC) of the DRC and Its Efforts to Devise a Just Racial Policy

In 1926 a conference was held at Bloemfontein at which representatives of the Anglican, Presbyterian, Methodist, Baptist, Congregationalist and Dutch Reformed churches consulted together in order to come to a better understanding of one another's approaches to the "Native Question." Having agreed that "no solution to the Native problem can create an expectation of permanency, unless it be based on Christian principles," the Conference resolved that:

> It is contrary to Christian principles to limit the progress of nations.
> It is not necessarily contrary to Christian principles to seek the progress of the native people separately from the whites.
> It is the duty of Christians to keep a watchful eye with regard to discrimination so as to make sure that all sections of society receive equal treatment.[11]

The second decision concerning "separate development" was to become a central plank of DRC policy.

In 1942 the FMC was constituted with the purpose of putting the declared DRC mission policy into practice and advancing cooperation and unity in mission work. Nine Dutch Reformed synods, including those of the younger black churches, were represented on this newly formed council, and one of its tasks was "to organise mission conferences on a Union-wide basis and on a Regional basis."[12]

In 1948 the National Party, representing the interests of Afrikaner nationalism, came to power. D. F. Malan, the new prime minister, had previously played an influential role as a dominee in the DRC, to which most of his cabinet ministers also belonged. To Malan and many of his followers, it seemed as if a God-given opportunity had been given to the Afrikaner to order the affairs of the country according to Christian, national and Protestant principles. "Our history is the great masterpiece of the centuries," declared Malan.

---

11. Ibid., 184.
12. Ibid., 186.

We hold this nationhood as our due for it was given to us by the Architect of the universe. [His] aim was the formation of a new nation among the nations of the world.... The last hundred years have witnessed a miracle behind which must lie a divine plan. Indeed, the history of the Afrikaner reveals a will and a determination which makes one feel that Afrikanerdom is not the work of men but the creation of God.[13]

Fired by feelings of a divine mission and manifest destiny, leaders of the Federal Mission Council organized a number of conferences during the 1950s with the aim of forging solutions to the unique social problems of South Africa along Christian lines and in accordance with traditional Afrikaner feelings. The conviction emerged that "the only Christian way to safeguard every culture and to avoid friction and abuse was to separate the nations, thus providing room for the organic development of each according to its special needs."[14] Such ideas were not new. In 1939 Professor Lategan of the DRC seminary at Stellenbosch had stated:

The policy of segregation as advocated by the Afrikaner and his Church is the holy calling of the Church to see to the thousands of poor-whites in the cities who fight a losing battle in the present economic world. This policy will entail the removal of unhealthy slums, the creation of healthy suburbs where a sound Christian family can be developed. The application of segregation will furthermore lead to the creation of separate healthy cities for the non-whites where they will be in a position to develop along their own lines, establish their own institutions and later on govern themselves under the guardianship of the whites.[15]

In 1949 the chairman of the Federal Council of the DRC expressed the conviction that "[The aim of apartheid is not] oppression but development, growth, upliftment, more privileges and rights according to one's abilities, talent and potential."[16] The separation envisaged by the 1950 Bloemfontein conference was a total one in which white South Africans would have to be willing to pay the price: no cheap black labour to do menial tasks and

---

13. De Gruchy, *Church Struggle*, 31.
14. Kinghorn, "Modernization and Apartheid," 145.
15. Ibid., 141.
16. Ibid., 145.

heavy labour. Whites would have to be willing to clean their own homes, till their own soil and dig their own mines. Dr G. B. A. Gerdener, a principal organizer of the 1950 Bloemfontein conference and an advocate of apartheid as total separation, saw no hope in a multiracial society. Such a society, he felt, could only lead to exploitation of the blacks or a vengeance wreaked upon the whites.

When the implications of such a radical territorial separation and segregation were realized, the ruling National Party quickly repudiated the proposals of the church conference. Soon after the conference, the prime minister, D. F. Malan, made it quite clear that while total separation might be the ideal of the church, it was not the policy of his party or the intention of the government. He stated:

> What they resolved was that we should have a total or complete territorial apartheid. Well, if one should attain total territorial apartheid, if it were practical, everybody would admit that it would be an ideal state of affairs. It would be an ideal state, but that is not the policy of our party... impracticable under present circumstances in South Africa, where our whole economic structure is to a large extent based on Native labour.[17]

The desire to promote the FMC mission vision formulated at Bloemfontein in 1950 and the desire to interact with people of various racial groups and ecclesiastical denominations led to a number of conferences during the 1950s. A conference for Sotho-speaking people was organized in 1951. In 1952 a similar conference for Xhosa-speaking people was held in Uitenhage, and a conference for Zulu-speaking people was held in Vryheid, Natal. In December 1952 approximately one hundred African leaders of the Zulu, Xhosa and Sotho groups, representing four synods of the Dutch Reformed "Daughter churches," conferred with thirty representatives of the Dutch Reformed "Mother Church" in Bloemfontein. A positive attitude and a cordial spirit were reported to characterize all these conferences.[18]

In order to bring English and Afrikaans-speaking leaders of the various churches together, a conference on Christian Principles in Multiracial South Africa was held in 1953. Among the delegates were Dr Norman Goodall, Secretary of the International Missionary Council, and missionaries of many

---

17. Strassberger, *Ecumenism in South Africa*, 203.
18. Ibid., 206.

nationalities. The conference was characterized by frank and open discussion which did not seek to hide the radical differences between the points of view of Afrikaans- and English-speaking South Africans. Yet there was a willingness to listen to differing viewpoints and a mood in favour of dialogue prevailed.

An even larger conference of church leaders was held in Johannesburg in 1954 and attended by 160 delegates, a third of whom were black. Outstanding speakers from the African, Afrikaans and English churches participated in this conference. The following resolutions were passed:

> Realising the call that we have as ministers of the Church of Christ, to avow and demonstrate our unity to the world, we, the delegates of the various denominations, thereby declare: that we recognise and accept one another as brothers in Christ and avow our unity in Him;
>
> That we, recognising that our common history and the circumstances in which we find ourselves account for the existence of our various denominations, acknowledge that each seeks to expand and serve the Kingdom of God sincerely and devoutly;
>
> That we undertake to strive for and to use opportunity to practise the fellowship of believers to which we are called.[19]

A Continuation Committee was appointed and mandated to arrange further consultations between the churches. In 1956 this committee organized a conference in Johannesburg on "Christian Literature for the Bantu of Southern Africa." But the greatest achievement of this committee was a conference held in Johannesburg in December 1959 to consider "Christian Responsibility towards Areas of Rapid Social Change." This important gathering was attended by 140 persons representing a wide variety of churches and organizations from both within and without South Africa.[20] This conference made a great impression on the delegates from different races and denominations who came together in a spirit of Christian fellowship and acceptance of one another to discuss some of the basic problems peculiar to South Africa. It seemed that a turning point in church and race relations had been reached. A committee was appointed for the purpose of working towards a Council of Churches in South Africa that would be inclusive of

---

19. Ibid., 211.
20. Ibid., 218.

the churches with the CCSA and those within the FMC. The air was full of hopeful expectation that something new would be born out of the labours of a decade of conferences and of deepening ecumenical contacts.

Then came the tragedy of Sharpeville in 1960, which was followed by a series of events that wiped out the ecumenical gains of the previous decade and ushered in a period of growing conflict, crisis, struggle and division between Christians and churches that was to last thirty years. But before we relate the story of those dark years, certain parts of the ecclesiastical picture prior to 1960 that must be filled in.

The decade of the 1950s saw not only a series of conferences struggling with the socio-political implications of the gospel but also an explosion of missionary zeal within the DRC. That denomination established mission stations in many rural areas of South Africa, and the various DRC synods appointed full-time mission secretaries. Financial support for missions increased dramatically so that by 1974 the DRC spent nearly seven million rand a year on internal missions, an amount equal to three percent of the average gross monthly income of all its members.[21] A number of pastors resigned from their comfortable suburban congregations to serve as missionaries. In the five years after 1957, DRC missionaries in the Transkei increased from 30 to 180, and mission expenditure was raised from R40,000 to R480,000. In the Transvaal the number of DRC missionaries increased from 44 to 80 within two years of 1957. In the 1950s the number of DRC mission hospitals mushroomed, and scores of young medical doctors and nurses spent the first part of their careers in them. In 1978 the missionary arm of the DRC had (inside and outside South Africa) forty hospitals, six schools for the deaf and six for the blind, nine old-age homes, seven homes for victims of chronic diseases, eight orphanages, eight reformatories, four youth hostels, and assorted other institutions.[22] The black churches born of all this missionary work had grown in membership to 1,892,000 by 1978.

Despite all this sacrificial missionary effort, the overall mission vision of the Dutch Reformed Church, which included separate development as an intrinsic element of its policy, began to encounter increasing opposition. When the National Party proposed legislation in 1948 that would deprive Africans of their already limited parliamentary representation, there were protests from many churches. "Our sincere prayer is that white South Africans

---

21. Kinghorn, "Modernization and Apartheid," 147.
22. Ibid.

may be saved from the contempt in the eyes of the world that such action is bound to produce," declared the Presbyterian General Assembly. "No person of any race should be deprived of constitutional rights or privileges merely on the grounds of race," noted the Methodist Conference. "It is our sincere conviction that the Government's policy of apartheid has no sanction in the New Testament Scriptures," stated the Congregational General Assembly. The Baptist Union condemned "any tampering with the accepted constitutional understanding of the franchise rights of non-Europeans." "Discrimination between men on the grounds of race alone is inconsistent with the principles of the Christian religion," declared the Anglican bishops.[23]

The reaction of black leaders went further. On 6 April 1952 the ANC and the South African Indian Congress jointly launched the Defiance Campaign. They rejected segregation and the pass system and called on the authorities to stop introducing apartheid legislation. One of the leaders of the Defiance Campaign, Albert Luthuli, was dismissed by the government from his position as chief of his tribe. The guiding influence of Luthuli's personal Christian faith is displayed in his response: "I try . . . in a spirit of trust and surrender to God's will as I see it, to say: 'God will provide.' It is inevitable that in working for freedom some individuals and some families must take the lead and suffer. The Road to Freedom is via the Cross."[24]

Even in Afrikaans-speaking and Dutch Reformed circles there were voices that questioned the FMC policy of segregation and the social separation of the races. In 1952 Ben Marais, Professor of Church History at the University of Pretoria, published *Die Kleurkrisis in die Weste* (*Colour: The Unsolved Problem of the West*) in which he rejected arguments based on Scripture as support for the policy of segregation. Only on pragmatic grounds, Marais argued, can separate churches for different racial groups be justified. He pointed out that in seeking a scriptural basis for racial separation the DRC was completely isolated in the Christian world. Neither was there any support in the early church for a separation of believers on the grounds of race or colour.

Another early Afrikaans critic of separate development was B. B. Keet, evangelical theologian and Professor of Systematic Theology at the University Stellenbosch. In his 1955 book *Whither South Africa?* he criticized the existing racial structure and questioned the viability of the policy of separate development or apartheid. The protests of Keet and Marais influenced Beyers

---

23. Hofmeyr and Pillay, *History of Christianity*, 270.
24. Ibid., 271.

Naudé, who emerged in 1960 as the leading Afrikaans witness against the policy of apartheid.

Sharpeville and Cottesloe

The goodwill between English and Afrikaans churches that had been built up during the 1950s and the bright hope that South African Christians of all races would be able to forge a common consensus concerning the sociopolitical implications of the gospel were dashed on the rocks of violent and tragic political events.

By the end of the 1950s serious tensions had developed within the African National Congress (ANC), the largest African political organization in South Africa. The ANC, which had been founded in 1912, was inclusivist in its policy with the goal of establishing a future democracy in which the contributions of non-Africans would also be welcomed. A more radical faction led by Robert Sobukwe criticized the ANC for allowing itself to be dominated by "liberal-left multi-racialists." Sobukwe ardently believed in an "Africanist" future for South Africa, rejecting the idea of working with whites.[25] In 1959 this faction broke away from the ANC to form the Pan Africanist Congress (PAC) under the leadership of Sobukwe.

The ANC had been planning a campaign against the passes Africans were required by law to carry at all times. When the ANC announced the date of 31 March 1960 for the commencement of their campaign, Sobukwe proposed that the PAC launch "a sustained disciplined, non-violent campaign" against the pass laws on 21 March. On the morning of 21 March a crowd estimated at between 3,000 and 5,000 gathered to protest outside the police station at Sharpeville, a black township near Vereeniging, south of Johannesburg. When a portion of the fence surrounding the police station was broken and some stones thrown, the police panicked and opened fire. Sixty-nine people, mainly women, were killed and about 180 wounded. The incident provoked outrage throughout the country and the world. The government declared a state of emergency. The ANC and the PAC were banned. Albert Luthuli, Nelson Mandela and Robert Sobukwe, along with thousands of their supporters, were arrested.

While the English-speaking churches strongly criticized the actions of the government, the Afrikaans churches defended the government's right

---

25. Saunders, *Illustrated History*, 400.

to take whatever steps were necessary to prevent chaos and revolution. The Anglican archbishop of Cape Town, Joost de Blank, demanded that the WCC expel the Dutch Reformed synods that were then members. In a letter to the WCC, he stated: "The future of Christianity in this country demands our complete dissociation from the Dutch Reformed attitude . . . Either they must be expelled or we shall be compelled to withdraw."[26]

The WCC did not accede to the demands of de Blank but called rather for a "consultation on Christian race relations and social problems in South Africa." This consultation took place in Cottesloe, a suburb of Johannesburg, from 7 to 14 December 1960. It was attended by ten delegates from each of the eight South African member churches (Bantu Presbyterian Church of South Africa; CPSA; Congregational Union of South Africa; Methodist Church of South Africa; DRC, Cape Synod; DRC, Transvaal Synod; Hervormde Church; Presbyterian Church of Southern Africa), and five representatives of the WCC. There were eighteen black participants, including Bishop Alphaeus Zulu and Professor Z. K. Matthews.

Each of the eight participating churches had submitted previously prepared memoranda, which formed the basis of the discussions. Although the conferring churches came to Cottesloe with differing points of view, especially with regard to the racial issue, an amazing atmosphere of trust, acceptance and Christian fellowship developed during the consultation. An honest sharing of deepest convictions took place, something seldom experienced in a conference with such different participants. Misunderstandings were cleared up, especially between the DRC and the CPSA. De Blank, the Anglican archbishop, personally asked the delegates of the DRC for forgiveness, and one of the delegates of the DRC said that they too had failed and accepted the hand stretched out in reconciliation with thankfulness. Only the Hervormde (NHK) delegates, it seemed, did not share in the spirit of trust and reconciliation. One of them leaked information to the press, notwithstanding a prior unanimous agreement that no statements would be issued or interviews granted to any newspaper before the end of the conference.

The Cottesloe Declaration caused a storm when it was published. Its statements and proposals were very moderate, or even conservative, by today's standards, but in the context of 1960 with Hendrik Verwoerd as prime minister of a government determined to implement the policy of apartheid,

---

26. De Gruchy, *Church Struggle*, 163.

its provisions were a challenge to the status quo. Some excerpts from the Declaration follow:

PART I

. . . The general theme of our seven days together has been the Christian attitude towards race relations. We are united in rejecting all unjust discrimination. Nevertheless, widely divergent convictions have been expressed on the basic issues of *apartheid*. They range on the one hand from the judgment that it is unacceptable in principle, contrary to the Christian calling and unworkable in practice, to the conviction on the other hand that a policy of differentiation can be defended from the Christian point of view, that it provides the only realistic solution of the problems of race relations and is therefore in the best interests of the various population groups. . . .

PART II

6. No one who believes in Jesus Christ may be excluded from any church on the grounds of his colour or race. The spiritual unity among all men who are in Christ must find visible expression in acts of common worship and witness, and in fellowship and consultation on matters of common concern.

9. Our discussions have revealed that there is not sufficient consultation and communication between the various racial groups which make up our population. There is a special need that a more effective consultation between the Government and leaders accepted by the non-White people of South Africa should be devised. The segregation of racial groups carried through without effective consultation and involving discrimination leads to hardship for members of the groups affected.

10. There are no Scriptural grounds for the prohibition of mixed marriages. The well-being of the community and pastoral responsibility require, however, that due consideration should be given to certain factors which may make such marriages inadvisable.

15. It is our conviction that the right to own land wherever he is domiciled, and to participate in the government of his country, is

part of the dignity of the adult man, and for this reason a policy which permanently denies to non-White people the right of collaboration in the government of the country of which they are citizens cannot be justified.

PART III

... We give thanks to Almighty God for bringing us together for fellowship and prayer and consultation. We resolve to continue in this fellowship, and we have therefore made specific plans to enable us to join in common witness in our country.

We acknowledge before God the feebleness of our often divided witness to our Lord Jesus Christ and our lack of compassion for one another.

We therefore dedicate ourselves afresh to the ministry of reconciliation in Christ.[27]

The delegates of the Hervormde Church made a statement to the effect that they were convinced that separate development was the only just solution to the South African racial problem and that they rejected integration in any form as a solution to that problem.

The Cottesloe Declaration alarmed Verwoerd, who perceived it as an attempt to undermine the support of the DRC for the National Party government. "Any form of political multi-racialism or so-called partnership," declared Verwoerd, "would ultimately deprive the white man of his rightful heritage."[28] Conservatives within the DRC played upon the fears and prejudices of its white members. As a result Cottesloe and its conclusions were rejected by the various DRC synods which, together with the Hervormde Church, withdrew from the WCC.

The year 1960 was truly a watershed in the history of South Africa. The opportunity for a negotiated settlement of the country's problems through a process of dialogue and consensus was rejected by a government determined to enforce an unworkable ideology at all costs. Major African political movements that had hitherto been legal and committed to a policy of non-violent resistance and protest were now banned and thus adopted a policy of armed struggle against the ruling regime. Churches that shared

---

27. Hofmeyr, Millard and Froneman, *History of the Church*, 230–235.
28. Hofmeyr and Pillay, *History of Christianity*, 274.

common membership in ecumenical forums and that were engaged in fruitful dialogue with one another were now separated into hostile camps. The decades following Sharpeville and Cottesloe were to see growing conflict, violence, repression and hostility. Outstanding Christian leaders such as Albert Luthuli, Beyers Naudé and Z. K. Matthews found themselves in the wilderness and sometimes in jail or in exile. We shall now turn our attention to the stories of some of these leaders.

Albert Luthuli

The son of a Zulu Seventh-day Adventist evangelist working in Zimbabwe, Albert Luthuli was born in 1899. Six months later his father died. About ten years later his widowed mother returned with her children to Natal. Albert was sent to live with his uncle, Martin Luthuli, a tribal chief living near Groutville. There Albert attended a school run by Congregationalist missionaries. Luthuli later became a lay preacher in the Congregationalist Church. Throughout his life his Christian faith played a decisive role in guiding his convictions and actions.

After furthering his education at a Methodist institution in Edenvale and at Adams College, Luthuli joined the staff of Adams and for thirteen years was involved in the training of teachers. He developed a close friendship with Z. K. Matthews, the principal of the high school at Adams. These two became the outstanding figures in the struggle for African rights. Luthuli was the more powerful orator and charismatic leader, Matthews the scholar and adviser.

In 1936 Luthuli was elected chief of his people at Groutville. To take up this post, he left his teaching vocation. His duties as a chief brought him into closer contact with the social needs of his people and into increasing conflict with the government. In 1945 he joined the ANC. Soon Luthuli became president of the Natal branch of the ANC, and in 1952 the Native Affairs Department demanded that he resign from the ANC or from the Groutville chieftainship. When he refused to do either, the government deprived him of the latter office. In December 1952 the National Conference of the ANC elected him its President-General by a huge majority.[29]

Despite his policy of moderation and non-violence, Luthuli was restricted in 1952 to the Lower Tugela district for two years. In 1954 this banning order

---

29. De Kock, *Dictionary of South African Biography*, 330.

was extended for a further two years. In 1956 he was arrested with 155 others and charged with high treason. His response at that time expressed his faith in the essential rightness of the cause he had espoused and the course he had taken:

> What the future has in store for me I do not know; I only pray to the Almighty to strengthen my resolve so that nothing may deter me from striving, for the sake of the good name of our beloved country, to make it a true democracy and true union of all the communities in the land.[30]

After Luthuli had spent a year in detention awaiting trial, the charges against him were withdrawn. In 1959 he was banned for five years under the Suppression of Communism Act, despite his strongly anti-communist convictions.

Luthuli's policies of non-violence and collaboration with people of all races also brought him into disfavour with the more radical Africanist faction of the ANC, which eventually broke away under the leadership of Robert Sobukwe to form the PAC.

After the Sharpeville shootings in 1960 Luthuli was arrested when he called for a one-day protest strike. His words of warning at that time were:

> The churches have simply submitted to the secular state for far too long; some have even supported apartheid. While it is not too late for white Christians to look at the Gospels and redefine their allegiance, I warn those who care for Christianity, who care to go to all the world and preach the Gospel, that in South Africa the opportunity is three hundred years old. It will not last forever. The time is running out.[31]

Luthuli was banned again in 1962 and forbidden to speak on any topic. He remained under some or other ban until his death in 1967. The only time this restriction was relaxed was when the government grudgingly permitted him to travel to Oslo to receive the Nobel Peace Prize in 1961.

---

30. Briggs and Wing, *Harvest and the Hope*, 291.
31. Walshe, "Christianity and the Anti-Apartheid Struggle," 385.

Z. K. Matthews

If the dream of some early Christian missionary educationalists (e.g. William Govan of Lovedale) was to provide an education that would equip Africans to hold their own anywhere in the world, then Zachariah Keodirelang Matthews, often referred to as ZK by his friends, was a fulfilment of that dream. Born in 1901 in humble circumstances in the diamond mining town of Kimberley, he showed early promise at the missionary schools he attended and won a bursary to Lovedale. The intense idealism with which education was viewed at that time in the African community as well as the sacrifice it entailed is expressed in ZK's description of the event:

> At home, when I arrived with the tidings [of the bursary], the light leaped into my mother's face . . . When my father came home he clasped my hand with joy and pride. He and mother and my brother John, then in his final year of teacher-training at Perseverance School, talked the whole thing over as I listened in dazed delight and wonder. "We must see him through," my father said, and my brother John unhesitatingly assented. It meant that some of his small hard-earned income would, for years to come, be spent on giving me the chance of a high school education. I never knew in detail how my family managed, how much of my father's meagre savings and meagre salary, how much of John's hopes and efforts, went into giving me my start. I know only that it was an offering of the spirit that is forever beyond repayment.[32]

After successfully completing his studies at Lovedale, Matthews enrolled at the South African Native College (later University of Fort Hare). In 1924 he became the first African to obtain a Bachelor of Arts from the University of South Africa. In 1925 he was appointed as the first African principal of Adams College in Amanzimtoti, Natal. In his spare time Matthews studied law by correspondence, and in 1930 he became the first African to obtain a Bachelor of Laws from the University of South Africa. Matthews subsequently travelled to the United States of America and in 1934 was awarded a Master of Arts from Yale University. After that he did a postgraduate course in social anthropology at the London School of Economics where he studied under Bronislaw Malinowski.[33]

---

32. Matthews, *Freedom for My People*, 28–29.
33. Pobee, "Zachariah Keodirelang Matthews," 665.

Matthews returned to South Africa in 1935, initially to Adams College. The following year he became a lecturer in social anthropology and native law at the South African Native College at Fort Hare. Teaching was his first love and primary vocation, as he himself testified:

> I was determined upon a career in teaching. It was the way I knew I could fulfil my need to serve my own people and discharge my enormous obligation. . . . Teaching in a society like that of South Africa was not like teaching elsewhere. It was not merely a profession. It was more like a mission than a way of earning a living, a vocation, a call to help satisfy the great hunger for education that existed among the millions of our people, a hunger which so few had done so little up to now to appease.[34]

His wife Frieda, whom he married in 1928, soon realized that she "would always have to share Zac with all of Africa and our people, the black man throughout the world."[35]

An internationally respected educationalist, Matthews was called upon to serve on many committees, including the Royal Commission to investigate higher education for Africans in the British territories of Uganda, Kenya, Tanganyika and Anglo-Egyptian Sudan.

It was inevitable that he would be drawn into the political struggle for African rights. Matthews joined the ANC in 1940 and soon assumed a prominent part in it. He was also elected to the Native Representative Council (NRC) in 1942 and played a leading role in the disagreement between the government and the NRC until 1950, when he resigned in protest against government policy. In the 1940s, Matthews could still say:

> My own belief is that the African has such a good case for justice and fair play in this country that there is no need for him to be either extreme or crude in the presentation of his case . . . I shall do all in my power to state the African case as fully as possible, without fear or favour, but I shall not work against the Department or the Government. It is to them that we must look for justice and fair play, and no good purpose will be served by antagonising them.[36]

---

34. Matthews, *Freedom for My People*, 82.
35. Ibid., 91.
36. Saayman, *Man with a Shadow*, 69.

Later events gave him reason to doubt the value of looking to the government for "justice and fair play." After the banning of the ANC in 1960 and its adoption of a policy of armed struggle, Matthews gave an address in 1964 entitled "The Road from Non-Violence to Violence." Visser t'Hooft, at that time general secretary of the WCC, commented as follows on this speech:

> ZK Matthews moved us profoundly because in telling this story he showed the anguish of his own mind. He had himself always thought in terms of non-violence and cooperation. To him, as to his friends Luthuli and Xuma, this had seemed the Christian way. But what could one say to the younger generation who retorted: "What have you achieved?" Could one simply go on urging them to stand by the methods of persuasion and discussion in the face of increasing and relentless force? At no time did ZK Matthews advocate the use of force. But he did show that we would have to consider again what the Christian attitude would be with regard to violence.[37]

In 1952 Matthews was involved in the preparations for the Defiance Campaign. During it, however, he was visiting professor at the Union Theological Seminary in New York giving lectures on Christian missions in Africa. Shortly after his return to South Africa in 1953, he addressed the Cradock Congress of the ANC and proposed "a national convention, a congress of the people, representing all the people of this country, irrespective of race or colour, to draw up a Freedom Charter for the democratic South Africa of the future."[38] His proposal was approved by the ANC and several other organizations and resulted in the Congress of the People in June 1955, during which the Freedom Charter was adopted. Matthews himself did not attend this meeting. Nevertheless, he was arrested in 1956 as one of the 156 accused in the Treason Trial which lasted until 1961, when he was acquitted.

During the state of emergency that followed the Sharpeville shootings in 1960, Matthews was detained for six months. He was also one of the nineteen black delegates invited to participate at the Cottesloe Conference. His contribution to that consultation was described as follows by Professor Leslie Hewson, editor of the official Consultation report:

---

37. Ibid., 86.
38. Pobee, "Zachariah Keodirelang Matthews," 666.

ZK put the African case quietly, consistently, logically, and said: "In planning for Africans you must consult African leaders." "But we have done so," said the pro-apartheid men. "You chose the leaders you wished to consult." By the end of the week the Afrikaners were asking ZK: "What is your opinion on this?" He made an enormous impression by his quiet logic and his firmness. He brought a continental – almost a world vision – to the group.[39]

Very likely as a result of his outstanding contribution to that conference, Matthews was appointed by the WCC as Africa secretary of the Division of Inter-Church Aid, Refugee and World Services. He left South Africa and worked from Geneva, Switzerland. In 1965 he indicated his intention to retire to Botswana. The following year he was appointed as Botswana's first ambassador to the USA and its envoy to the United Nations. Two years later he died in Washington.

Despite many disappointments at the hands of fellow Christians, he retained a positive evaluation of Christian missions in South Africa. If missionaries had made mistakes in education, he once observed, it was because they were the only ones providing education. He acknowledged that the church "has achieved a nobler aim . . . it has recognized and fostered in the African that dignity, and self-respect, that essential humanity which others with less lofty motives have sought to deny or destroy."[40] In a lecture given at Union Theological Seminary, he mentioned three challenges facing the mission of the church in Africa: greater personal and human contact between missionaries and Africans; recapturing the universality of the gospel in terms of all people and all of life; and the greatest challenge (and his greatest wish) the unity of the church, a "United Church of Africa" in the second half of the twentieth century.[41] As the church moves into the twenty-first century, those challenges remain.

Beyers Naudé

In the closing days of the Second Anglo-Boer War, as the cause of the commandos became increasingly hopeless, some sixty Boer representatives

---

39. Matthews, *Freedom for My People*, 203.
40. Saayman, *Man with a Shadow*, 85.
41. Ibid.

gathered at Vereeniging in the Transvaal in May 1902 to choose between unconditional surrender and continuing the war. For three days the arguments raged, until eventually most of the delegates became persuaded that the continued existence of the Boers as a people depended on the cessation of war. A few *bittereinders* vowed never to surrender their arms, among them Jozua Naudé, the DRC minister who later became the father of Beyers Naudé. General Jan Smuts himself pleaded in vain with the influential pastor to accept the peace and, for ever after, Jozua regarded Jan Smuts as a traitor to the Afrikaner cause. It was in this environment of intense Afrikaner nationalism that Beyers Naudé spent his formative years. Few could have guessed that he would one day embrace the cause of African liberation with all the intensity of commitment that had characterized his father's Afrikaner nationalism.

It has been a tradition in the DRC, since the time of the great revivals of the 1860s, to devote the ten days between Ascension Day and Pentecost Sunday to a series of special meetings, often with an evangelistic emphasis. Beyers was deeply moved by the Pentecostal sermons his father preached in 1930 and decided to give his life to Christ. He was then sixteen years old. Two years later he enrolled at the University of Stellenbosch to study theology, more on account of the theological bursary he qualified for than from any strong sense of call to the ministry.[42] At Stellenbosch he met Ilse, his future wife, the daughter of German Moravian missionaries. He also met many with whom he would later cross swords, including John Vorster, the future prime minister, and Hendrik Verwoerd, his sociology professor and also a future prime minister. Naudé took little interest in his theological studies, doing the bare minimum just in order to pass examinations. He entered the theological library twice, and then only to deliver messages.[43]

In 1940, while serving as an assistant minister in Wellington, Naudé accepted an invitation to join the Broederbond, a secret society of elite Afrikaner leaders committed to the promotion of Afrikaner culture, language and power. Following the Broederbond line, Naudé voted for the National Party in 1948, even though he had reservations about the policy of apartheid. In that same year, at the Transvaal Synod of the DRC, Ben Marais had stood virtually alone in opposing a church report in favour of apartheid. Although he said nothing, Naudé, together with twelve other ministers, asked that the record reflect that they did not support the report.

---

42. Ryan, *Beyers Naudé*, 19.
43. Ibid., 27.

Beyer's vote for the NP certainly pleased his aged father, Jozua, who, rejoicing in the victory of the NP at the polls, wrote in a letter to his sons:

> It is now 6 in the morning. We have drunk coffee and read the old chapter, Lamentations 5, which I have been reading for the last 46 years on this day [31 May, anniversary of the surrender of the Boers at the Treaty of Vereeniging] . . . The sun of freedom which went down at Vereeniging, has after 46 years risen more magnificently and more wonderfully than when it disappeared.[44]

But Beyers Naudé was beginning to entertain serious doubts about the apartheid policy of his government and his church. In 1952 Ben Marais was senior minister to Naudé in a Pretoria congregation when Marais's book *Die Kleur Krisis en die Weste* (*Colour: The Unsolved Problem of the West*) was published. Marais argued that the concept of forced segregation was foreign to the experience of the early church and rejected by all leading Protestant theologians in the contemporary world. Although Marais was vigorously supported by Professor Bennie Keet of Stellenbosch, the overall reaction of Afrikaners to his book was negative. Naudé, however, was disturbed by the book, which challenged him to re-examine crucial questions about the biblical basis for his understanding of race, human dignity and the unity of the church. He was also troubled by what he felt to be the excessive power of the secretive Broederbond in influencing church and society, especially when that power was used to try and suppress dissident voices like that of Ben Marais.

By the time Naudé was the minister of the Aasvoëlkop Dutch Reformed congregation in an affluent suburb of Johannesburg, he had become involved with a small group of DRC ministers who hoped to lead their church away from apartheid. Bible study groups were established to consider the social and political implications of the gospel. When the Cottesloe Conference was called to help the churches deal with the crisis that followed the Sharpeville shootings in 1960, Beyers Naudé was one of the representatives of the Transvaal Synod of the DRC. He was excited by the depth of fellowship and unity experienced by the delegates at Cottesloe, and the memorandum brought by his church made a significant contribution to the final document produced by Cottesloe.

---

44. Ibid., 35.

Prime Minister Hendrik Verwoerd realized that the DRC delegates at Cottesloe represented the cream of the church leadership with the potential to sway many Afrikaners. In his New Year's message in 1962 he called upon the church to reject Cottesloe and support the policies of the National Party. At a special meeting held in Pretoria the Broederbond executive council rejected the Cottesloe decisions. Naudé, who was chairman of the Broederbond cell in his area, was deeply upset by this interference. But the triumph of the conservatives was complete. As the various synods of the DRC met, Cottesloe was rejected and all ties with the WCC were broken. Determined not to give up the struggle to lead the church away from its support of apartheid, Naudé launched a new monthly journal, *Pro Veritate*. He experienced increasing hostility, even from members of his own congregation. In a sermon in May 1962, Beyers shared his convictions with his flock:

> Because I don't want a single one of you to be unsure of what I believe, I want to now spell out the following . . . I believe that the Bible is the only true Word of God. . . . Every believer must accept and be obedient to the authority of the Word, as the authority which is higher than any human authority . . .
>
> Nobody can be excluded from the Church of Christ on grounds of race or colour . . . All people are called to love one another . . . the outcome of this love is that I should allow other people to have the same rights and opportunities as my group demands . . . All laws which hinder love and justice between people are against the will of God . . .
>
> I do not regard these issues that I've raised as being political ones, but I speak of them as deep Christian convictions which have grown in me over a long period and which are the basis of a serious study of the Word of God. I am not saying these things to bring the government into disrepute, to intimidate any group or to indoctrinate you. . . . I am also not saying this to give support to the enemies of our church. No! There is just one motive, one goal in me: to proclaim nothing other than Jesus Christ, Jesus Christ who was crucified.[45]

In 1963 Naudé decided to resign from the Broederbond. In that same year an extraordinary development took place which illustrates something

---

45. Ibid., 70.

of the ambiguities of Afrikaner politics and the struggles within the soul of Afrikanerdom at the time. Beyers Naudé was elected as moderator of the Southern Transvaal Synod of the DRC. This was the very same synod that gave its approval of the Broederbond and condemned *Pro Veritate*. It was as if the Afrikaner establishment was appealing to Naudé to stay within its ranks and work for reform there, rather than establish alternative organs and institutions which might come into conflict with church and state. Naudé chose the latter course. In 1963 the Christian Institute (CI) was launched with the aim of pursuing the ecumenical dialogue which had been started by Cottesloe. When Naudé was forced to choose between the post of director of the CI and retaining his ministerial status in the church, he chose the former. He announced his decision to his congregation in a deeply emotional service in which he preached on the words of Peter in Acts 5:27, "We must obey God, rather than men."

> . . . although the synod has not in so many words prohibited pronouncements which are not in accordance with church policy and the traditions of the past, in spirit and practice these decisions come to this: that the God-given right and freedom of the minister and member to witness to the truth of God's Word in the spirit of the prophets and the Reformers is so restricted that the minister of the gospel in principle no longer enjoys the freedom to declare his deepest Christian convictions.[46]

In the years to come, the rift between Naudé and the Afrikaner establishment became wider. An exposé of Broederbond secrets in the public press was traced back to documents in the possession of Naudé. Thereafter the organization pursued him as a traitor. The editor of the official DRC newspaper *Die Kerkbode*, Andries Treurnicht, repeatedly attacked Naudé and the CI in its pages. Treurnicht later entered politics, but finding the NP too liberal, led a right-wing breakaway faction to form the Conservative Party in 1982.

As the political situation in the country deteriorated, *Pro Veritate* and the CI moved in a more radical direction. Even some friends of Naudé and the CI wondered about the course his ministry had taken. One CI member wrote in a letter to *Pro Veritate*:

---

46. Ibid., 81.

the Institute has lost patience with the churches so that the tone of voice it now uses has become strident and thus counter-productive. . . . Do you really still love the racialist sinner while hating his sin or do you hate and ultimately condemn him too now? Are you speaking the truth in love? Or in condemnation? We know our problem and so it doesn't really help to rub our noses in it.[47]

After the Soweto riots of 1976 the political situation deteriorated even further, and in 1977 the government banned the CI, *Pro Veritate* and Beyers Naudé, along with other persons, organs and institutions. Naudé had failed in his attempt to lead his fellow Afrikaners and his church away from apartheid. It could be argued that those who worked for reform *within* the church, like Ben Marais and Bennie Keet during the 1950s, and later David Bosch and Johan Heyns, were ultimately more successful in persuading the DRC to abandon its support of apartheid. But the life of Beyers Naudé remains a remarkable testimony to the power of the Christian faith in enabling one man to strike out on a course of action totally at variance with that for which his culture, background and history had prepared him.

After his banning order was lifted in 1984, Naudé accepted the post of caretaker General Secretary of the South African Council of Churches between 1985 and 1987, a time of escalating violence and conflict. He himself never changed his view that violence was wrong and counter-productive. He threw his considerable influence behind a drive for negotiations and meetings with the ANC. When finally the ANC was unbanned in 1990 and the government entered into serious talks about democratic elections, Naudé was asked by the ANC to be one of its representatives. After the successful completion of the first fully democratic elections in 1994, Naudé retired from of the public gaze to enjoy a last few years of rest.

A Non-Political Interlude

Visitors to South Africa have often been struck by the depth and intensity of political feelings in South Africa. Wherever a conversation begins, be it with sport, religion, the economy, medical care, education or the price of potatoes, it often ends in politics. The intensity of the political struggle in the latter half of the twentieth century has subsumed all other interests and

---

47. Ibid.

activities. Accounts of Christianity and theology are also often dominated by the relation of Christianity and churches to the great political questions of the day. Yet it is important to remember that great spiritual contributions have been made by some with very little political awareness, and even by some with mistaken political convictions. Their story is also important as their lives have profoundly touched many people.

William Duma

One of the glories of the Christian church is the extraordinary variety of people and diversity of gifts and ministries contained within its fold. This variety is so great that often Christians have difficulty in recognizing certain fellow believers as their brothers and sisters in Christ. And sometimes the particular gifts and ministries of a Christian are so strange and unusual that they stretch the credulity of those who hear or read of them. The ministry of William Duma falls into this last-named category. The author himself felt the need to consult one who was well-acquainted with both Duma and his biographer, Mary Garnett, in order to ascertain the reliability of her account of the life of this Zulu Baptist pastor. The quotations attributed to Duma below come from Garnett's interviews with him. While the thoughts expressed are Duma's; the English phrases are Garnett's. The Zulu pastor's education would not have enabled him to express himself in the polished English phrases found in Garnett's biography.

Outwardly there was nothing remarkable about Duma's life. He founded no new denomination. His theological training was rudimentary and his command of English limited. He spent most of his life as the humble pastor of one congregation. But there was a spiritual depth to this simple Zulu pastor that singled him out as an extraordinary servant of Christ.

Born in 1907, Duma received his earliest instruction in the Christian faith from his mother, who on her deathbed expressed her desire that Duma should become an *umfundisi* (minister). From his earliest years, Duma evinced a deep seriousness concerning the things of God. He was troubled with continual ill health, and at the age of twenty he decided to fast and pray for seven days. During these days his dominant desire to be healed was replaced by a greater longing – that God himself should be the utmost fullness of his desire. At midnight on the seventh day of the fast, unhealed, he arose to pray. Some time later he felt a touch on his head and knew it as the finger of

God. An experience of heat caused him to sweat profusely. He collapsed, felt a surge of cold follow the heat, and realized that his pain had gone.

> Although I knew God had touched me, I was afraid that the pain would stealthily return. I placed my hands on regions where pain had ridden me for years. I tested and retested myself, then gathered my courage to see if I could walk without pain. I walked, walked faster, then stopped in a joy anchored in certainty – I was healed! Dumb with gratitude I knelt, knowing my healing was His charter for my life's work. In His good time, I had arrived. Solemnly I made a covenant with God that each midnight, throughout my life, I would, as far as possible, keep tryst with HIM in prayer – a vow which I have kept by His grace.[48]

Prayer and fasting became hallmarks of Duma's personal spiritual life. After his healing, Duma went to Durban where he became a cook in the boarding house of a Christian woman, Mrs Stewart. She arranged for him to attend Bible classes. During this time he had his first opportunity for ministry in a small American Board Mission church.

One night a man and his nephew from Duma's home district lodged with him. They were on their way to hospital for the removal of a needle that had entered the boy's leg. In the middle of the night they were wakened by the cries of the boy, whose leg was in a violent spasm. Duma asked if he could lay hands on the boy and pray that he might be released from pain.

> As I prayed he began screaming, his body stiffened; pulling the blankets aside he exposed the site at which the needle had entered. As I continued in prayer, the body ceased its spasm and there shot out of the leg, as if expelled by a powerful force, the needle and the cotton! Aghast with surprise we looked at each other speechless, then fell to praising God. It was the very first time God used me as His instrument in healing.[49]

Not long after this incident, Mrs Stewart asked Duma to pray for her daughter who had tuberculosis. After prayer he had assurance that recovery would follow – an assurance that was often to be repeated throughout his ministry. The girl recovered, and Mrs Stewart encouraged Duma to believe that God had given him the gift of healing through prayer.

---

48. Garnett, *Take Your Glory Lord*, 13–14.
49. Ibid., 15.

In 1939 Duma was inducted to the pastorate of the Umgeni Road Baptist Church. After a year's hard work, he was despondent at the lack of progress in the tiny congregation. He decided to fast and pray for twenty-one days. During the days of his fast, his first experience was that of the pervasiveness of sin. "I knew I was commissioned never to dally and parley with sin in my ministry. I was rather to expose it in all its hideous cruelty."[50] He received the following assurance from God: "My servant, as the tall cluster of white lilies growing in profusion out of the black earth in the valley below, so your dead church will become a witness to me. You will see humanity transformed from darkness to light."[51]

On returning from his hilltop retreat, Duma commenced a five-day campaign. On the very first night, extraordinary things occurred in the packed church. Five women who began screaming and behaving in a wild manner were exorcized of demons by Duma. Exorcism became a significant part of his ministry. Indeed, for the rest of his life, Duma's ministry was characterized by powerful encounters with sin, sickness and Satan in the realm of the supernatural. Only the briefest account of some of these confrontations can be given here.

A Jewish lady who had suffered five miscarriages was deeply distraught over her inability to have a child. When her domestic helper, a member of the Umgeni Road Baptist Church, suggested that she send for Duma to pray to Jesus, she responded angrily, "Who is this Jesus? Even a white Gentile minister can't come here to talk about Jesus and you want a black one to come!" Not long afterwards, however, she personally phoned Duma in desperation and pleaded with him to visit her. After he had arrived and listened to her story, Duma told her, "Madam, I cannot pray for you except in the name of Jesus Christ of Nazareth . . . you want me to ask God to give you a child of your own. I must ask God through Jesus Christ his Son."[52] Again the woman reacted in anger and scorn. "Do you believe God has a wife that brought a child Jesus? That is insulting God. You're stupid, I want you to go." She ordered him out. "All right," responded Duma, "Let us put it off, but I am sorry to leave you because this Name is my medicine to cure you. I give you ten minutes. Go upstairs, I'll remain here, then give me your decision." The woman returned with a change of heart and accepted Duma's prayer.

---

50. Ibid., 17.
51. Ibid., 18.
52. Ibid., 20.

Some time later, Duma noticed two white people squeezed into the back of his church during a service. It was the Jewish lady and her husband come to announce the imminent birth of their child. Duma was summoned to the hospital to bless the boy and choose a name for him. Later he attended the synagogue service on the day Peter Reuben was circumcized.[53]

Some of the healings associated with Duma sound bizarre, although they are not without apostolic precedent. A Canadian woman who heard about Duma from a visiting South African preacher sent the following letter:

> I am a very ill woman. For eighteen months I have suffered from cancer of the breast. Medical treatment has failed, I am a teacher unable to work. I believe God urges me to write to you to pray for my healing. I send a snap of myself and a blouse of mine, over which please pray and return to me. I believe I shall be healed while wearing it.

The garment was duly prayed over, posted back, and the healing received.

The most extraordinary healing attributed to Duma was the raising to life and health of a young woman who had died and whose death certificate had been issued by the police. She was Litta, the seventeen-year-old daughter of Bhengu, a Baptist evangelist in a rural area of Zululand. When Duma was informed of her death by phone, he left Durban immediately by taxi. He was dropped off short of his destination and, as he trudged the last eight kilometres (five miles), faith began to rise in his heart that he must pray for Litta's restoration. What followed is reminiscent of scenes from the Acts of the Apostles and from the life of Elisha. After Duma's prayer for the stone-cold corpse, he describes his experience as follows, as related by his biographer:

> I turned to look at Litta. There was a slight movement. We watched, scarcely breathing, for an agonizing timelessness during which, unaware that we were watching, she raised, or rather the slow movement was that of one being very slowly raised, inch by inch, until she lay upright against the wall, her startled eyes unrecognizing, unmoving, unknowing. I tried to stand. I longed with unutterable craving to run from that house, from that room, away, away from the Power of the Presence of God which was too "rich." It overpowered me. But I could only crawl on my knees. I could not stand. I was sweating profusely. Someone picked me

---

53. Ibid., 21–22.

up, carried me to a bed, gave me a change of apparel. For three days I could not lift my hands, nor walk. My only sustenance was pawpaw or amasi. I was carried to a car for home where, for two weeks, I lay in bed, my son, Enoch, feeding me. For three weeks I saw people in duplicate and was totally powerless.[54]

The experience of feeling exhausted and drained after an extraordinary manifestation of divine power occurred quite often in Duma's ministry.

Duma did not always presume he could pray for the healing of those who came to him. In fact, he would never pray definitely for healing unless he received an inward assurance that God would heal the person prayed for. On one occasion he anointed a man for death, after helping the man's wife to become reconciled to her husband's departure.

News of Duma's extraordinary ministry spread abroad. He received invitations to minister in Britain, India, the Congo, Zambia, Zimbabwe and Swaziland. In 1966 he attended the World Congress on Evangelism in Germany. But the main thrust of his ministry remained in the simple building of the Umgeni Road Baptist Church, especially in the Wednesday prayer meeting there, which became the focus of his healing ministry. Over the years he developed a prayer circle of those he had invited to share with him in this special ministry. One member of the prayer circle who became very close to Duma was an Indian Anglican priest, Father Francis, whose wife had been healed through Duma after a long and debilitating disease for which no medical cure could be found. Father Francis bore witness that his own ministry in the parish of St Aidans was revitalized through his association with the Wednesday Prayer Circle at Umgeni Road.

Concerned about the poverty of many of his flock, Duma began to encourage some of them to start their own businesses. In time more than eight developed successful businesses in Durban and elsewhere. Four times a year they met in Durban for prayer and thanksgiving. Soon other Christian businessmen from Swaziland, Transvaal and Natal were attending these retreats under the "Angel of the Shops," Pastor Duma.

Duma was not without his times of failure, one of the most serious of which nearly cost him his life. A white friend wished to obtain some photos of a Zulu traditional healer, or *sangoma,* and asked Duma to take him to one. The pastor later related:

---

54. Ibid., 41.

> The morning I had unexpectedly been asked to take Mr Mason to a witchdoctor, I had not prepared myself in prayer for holy coverage in contact with demons. I was vulnerable, I was off guard and walked into the situation unknowingly. The witchdoctor had given himself in totality to Satan and was one of his super-powerful agents. The visit was to have been for a momentary snapshot with which Rev Mr Mason would illustrate his story . . . that was all . . . so I thought."[55]

The visit to the *sangoma* was prolonged and Duma came under the influence of demonic powers. He returned home with darkness in his soul. In the middle of the night he awoke and, still in his pyjamas, began to follow two or three people who summoned him. When he began to walk into the sea, "Someone I did not see took hold of me, turned me to face where I had come from and shook me powerfully by taking hold of my arms. The unknown and unseen led me out of the sea." Dazed and lost, Duma found his way to the home of his brother, who took him back to his own house. It took him a few days to achieve spiritual restoration. There was no doubt in his mind that the ones leading him down to the sea were ambassadors of Satan and that the one who turned him around was an angel of God.[56]

It was this close proximity to the supernatural world in which Duma seemed to live that makes his life such an enigma to most of us lesser mortals. His biography is little more than a string of testimonies of remarkable events and healings. Yet the evidence for the trustworthiness of these accounts is compelling. On returning from the Congress on Evangelism in Berlin, Duma stayed in Glasgow with Dr J. Kelly, a cardiologist, whose own eleven-year-old son was so ill with a heart condition that he could not walk. Duma prayed for him one morning during a church service and the next day, "early, the little lad, Howard, brought coffee to my room, scarcely able to believe he was walking." The next year Duma received the following letter from Mrs Kelly, "Howard is really wonderful; to see him walking around, playing with other boys! The Lord has really done a miracle for which we constantly praise Him."[57]

---

55. Ibid., 112.
56. Ibid., 111.
57. Ibid., 102.

One of those who also came to share in the ministry of the prayer circle at Umgeni Road was a qualified nursing sister in charge of a ward in Clairwood Hospital, Durban. She described her own healing from a serious illness:

> I felt ill for months. Frequent medical overhauls and tests failed to account for my condition. Entering the ward one day I collapsed and had a fit which was followed by intermittent fits all through the day. Doctors and specialists having failed to arrive at a diagnosis, I was transferred to a larger hospital, King Edward VIII, Durban where white specialists took routine tests, but the fits continued and the physicians were baffled. I was fed through a nasal tube. Because it was feared that the fits would damage the brain, there was brain scanning by angiogram. An electro-encephalogram was taken which revealed an incurable cyst on a part of the brain. I was returned to Clairwood Hospital and the doctors kindly allocated a nurse to special me until death inexorably intervened. My husband was summoned to be informed of my condition. The prognosis of my life limit was three months.[58]

Elizabeth's husband decided to take her home, where she could die in the presence of her family. She continues her story:

> Because periods of consciousness were brief, with no one to tube-feed me, I rapidly deteriorated. It was then I developed rheumatoid arthritis. My fingers curled right over into my palms, my toes curled inwards, my knees bent and my neck joints ached. In snatches of consciousness, I suffered fearful pains."[59]

At the urging of a black Lutheran minister, Elizabeth was taken to the Wednesday morning prayer meeting at Umgeni Road. The Rev A. Spann of the Central Baptist Church was the speaker that morning and was accompanied by his wife. When Duma came to pray for Elizabeth, he offered a very short prayer and then commanded her to stand in the name of Jesus. "As she stood up," related Duma himself afterwards, "every arthritic bone clicked, clicked, echoing throughout the keyed-up silence of the church." Mrs Magwaza testified:

---

58. Ibid., 155.
59. Ibid.,

Each deformed bone had straightened to normality, pain was no more and Pastor said, "Walk back to your seat." Amazed at the outrageous suggestion I stood rooted to the floor. He repeated, "I say walk, walk in the Name of Jesus." – *and I walked unfalteringly to the seat at the back of the church . . .*

Mrs Spann, radiant with joy, wanted to drive me home, but I insisted that she take me only to the city bus rank. When I alighted near home the neighbours were terrified. They cried, "Is she now a spook?" When they realized the truth, they were frantic with excitement.[60]

After her healing, Mrs Magwaza confessed that she had secretly consulted sangomas and izinyangas many times. She destroyed all the costly potions and talismans received from them and was exorcized of eleven demons by Duma. When asked how he knew there were demons at all, Duma replied, "That is simple. One of the classic symptoms is bestial-like sounds, beginning as a rumbling in the throat, which deepen with threatening intensity when in the Presence of the Holy Spirit." When further asked how he knew there were eleven demons, Duma responded, "Because after each evil spirit had been exorcized, there remained an alien voice until she was free."[61]

These were the characteristics of Duma's ministry: fasting and prayer, exorcism, assurance of God's gift of healing for those he prayed for, and an experience of exhaustion after unusual manifestations of healing. And in this kind of ministry he continued until the end. A heart attack in 1976 slowed him down temporarily, but soon he was back in his pulpit with renewed zeal. After a baptismal service at Umgeni Road he was taken ill and died on 8 October 1977.

Hans von Staden and the Dorothea Mission

Although churches and their leaders have been the primary focus of this book, no account of Christianity in South Africa would be complete without some mention of the many parachurch organizations that have sought to promote the cause of Christ. As with the number of churches in South Africa, the number of parachurch organizations is too large to mention them all. But a short list would include organizations such as Campus Crusade for

---

60. Ibid., 156.
61. Ibid., 157.

Christ, Youth for Christ, Africa Enterprise, Africa Evangelistic Band, Christ for All Nations, Crusade for Christ, Great Commission Ministries, Hope for Southern Africa, Jesus for School Ministries, Revival Challenge Ministry, Child Evangelism, Dorothea Mission, Jews for Jesus, Kwa Sizabantu, Operation Mobilization, Scripture Union, Students Christian Association, Youth Alive, Youth With a Mission, and Frontline Fellowship. The list could easily be extended a hundredfold, and every one of these organizations has its own unique story, vision, and conviction of a special calling to extend the kingdom of God in southern Africa.

We will focus only on one representative of these parachurch organizations, the Dorothea Mission. Though not the largest, best known, or most enlightened, it is nevertheless typical of an indigenous South African parachurch organization founded with a vision to bring Christ to the needy of the land.

Hans von Staden, founder of the Dorothea Mission, was born of German parents in 1905 in Winburg in the Orange Free State. Influenced by the devout faith of his mother, Hans had religious impressions from a young age. At the age of eight he dreamt that his soul left his body for a long journey that reached the gates of hell. At Stellenbosch, where the family moved in 1920, he developed a close friendship with Andrew Murray, a grandson of the well-known Dr Andrew Murray whose writings were later to have a profound influence on von Staden.

A brilliant student, Hans studied science at the University of Stellenbosch and seemed destined for a successful career in that field. His scientific studies raised doubts in his mind about the existence of God, but in a series of three experiences over a period of a few years he came to a conviction of the reality of God, a commitment to Jesus Christ and experienced the infilling of the Holy Spirit. For the rest of his life, von Staden was a firm protagonist of the classical Holiness teaching that after justification by faith the believer should seek and experience a subsequent empowerment by the Holy Spirit for effective and fruitful service. His favourite authors, by whom he was guided in his theological convictions, were Andrew Murray, Oswald Chambers, A. B. Simpson, Charles Finney and R. A. Torrey.

Desiring to engage in some kind of Christian ministry, von Staden joined the Africa Evangelistic Band (AEB), a parachurch evangelistic organization in the Holiness tradition. In 1927 he travelled to Edinburgh, Scotland, to study at the Bible School of the Faith Mission. Before his studies were through, however, von Staden returned to South Africa to begin service as a pilgrim in the AEB. His ministry took him to countries beyond the borders of the South Africa, including Rhodesia (now Zimbabwe), the Congo, Uganda and Kenya.

While serving as superintendent of the AEB in the Transvaal in 1942, von Staden experienced God's call to what was to be his life work:

> One morning, while communing with God beside the river and reading His Word, I became intensely aware of His presence. Deep in my heart I discerned His commission: we were to dedicate our lives to the evangelization of the people in the dark city townships of South Africa. It was a sudden and unexpected command. If anyone were to ask me how I knew it to be the Lord's call, I would not be able to explain or prove it. But to me it was a matter of absolute certainty.[62]

To provide a base for training African workers for this new mission, von Staden purchased a farm at Rosslyn, north of Pretoria. This purchase was made possible by an unexpected gift from von Staden's mother, Dorothea. Hence the name Dorothea ("gift of God" in Greek) Mission. Some of the neighbours in the district, men of influence, objected to the prospect of blacks being trained on the farm and their efforts to obtain an eviction order from the government seemed likely to be successful. Von Staden was interviewed by the Minister of Bantu Affairs. When the matter was referred to parliament, Prime Minister Jan Smuts decided that the permit that had been granted should be irrevocable.[63]

Soon there was a small band of evangelists. Their method of operation was to pitch a tent in the sprawling shantytowns that were mushrooming all around the major South African cities to which thousands of rural Africans were migrating in search of work. Evangelistic services would be held every evening by the light of swaying paraffin lamps tied to the tent poles. During the days, the evangelists would visit people in their homes. The lively singing and forthright preaching in the meetings awakened many people to their spiritual needs.

One such person was Shadrack Maloka, known then as *Mohanoe* (Sotho for Rejected). Knowing neither his father nor his mother, Mohanoe had become a feared gang leader. In December 1947 curiosity drew him into a Dorothea Mission tent that had been erected in Soweto for the free viewing of

---

62. Otto, *Rescue the Perishing*, 38.
63. Ibid., 50.

a film. For the first time in his life Maloka heard about a Father in heaven who gave his Son to die for sinners. The film depicted the crucifixion of Jesus, and Maloka was deeply impressed by the love of Christ. He sought counselling, and after confessing his sins, found forgiveness in Christ. That night he slept peacefully for the first time in years. Previously he had always slept fitfully, fearing the arrival of the police or of other gang leaders seeking his life.

Maloka made a break with his gangster friends and, desiring to give his life to Christian service, applied for admission to the Dorothea Mission Bible School. Although illiterate and penniless, he was accepted. Maloka quickly learned to read and write, and his remarkable mental abilities began to emerge. He spoke ten languages fluently. Maloka became a powerful preacher whose ministry bore remarkable fruit in many conversions. In 1970 he was invited to speak in Germany. Further invitations to Canada and Holland followed, where he also appeared on television. After twenty-five years of service as an evangelist in the Dorothea Mission, he accepted a call to a pastorate where he served until his death.

The Dorothea Mission gave special attention to communities that were often neglected by other Christian organizations, particularly those in poor, depressing and inhospitable areas where drink, drugs, poverty, ignorance, immorality, superstition and disease wreaked havoc. The work was hard and often unrewarding. Occasionally extraordinary incidents occurred, such as the following, reported in a worker's letter from Moroka (Soweto):

> The Lord has protected our evangelists in a remarkable way. As the men were unable to find accommodation in houses, they slept in the tent. A few days ago a woman asked them: "Weren't you afraid last night?" They replied: "No, why should we have been afraid? We committed ourselves into God's hands, as we do every evening, and slept peacefully all night." The woman explained: "A group of evil-doers had planned to burn down the tent over your heads. They approached with burning torches in the middle of the night. When they came near the tent, they fled in all directions. They had seen that it was surrounded by heavily armed soldiers. After some time the men approached again, hoping that the soldiers had left in the meantime. But they were still keeping watch right round the tent. The evil-doers fled panic-stricken, unable to understand who had summoned this army in the middle of the night!"

When the evangelists heard this story they realized that God had sent his angels to protect them.[64]

The Dorothea Mission drew its support chiefly from the more pious section of the Afrikaans community and to a large extent shared its conservative ethos, both spiritually and politically. The desire not to offend its loyal supporters or antagonize government officials, whose permission was necessary for evangelists to enter and work in black residential areas, meant that the mission adopted a conservative political stance. Workers were prohibited from engaging in any public political activity or comment. This meant, in practice, that no criticism was made of government institutions and policies. However, the mission was critical of Communists and the liberation forces engaged in the armed struggle against the white government. Outside observers found it hard to reconcile the Dorothea Mission's deep commitment to the salvation, blessing and welfare of the black people of Africa with its sympathetic support of the government engaged in oppressing those same people. Such apparent contradictions remain one of the enigmas of the complex story of the church in South Africa.

In some ways the Dorothea Mission was an extension of the zeal and vision of Hans von Staden. As he declined in his later years, so did the Mission. It survived his death, however, and continues its evangelistic work to this day.

---

64. Ibid., 73.

7

Towards a New South Africa

The Struggle Intensifies

One of the closing paragraphs of the Cottesloe Declaration stated:

> We give thanks to Almighty God for bringing us together for fellowship and prayer and consultation. We resolve to continue in this fellowship, and we have therefore made specific plans to enable us to join in common witness in our country.[1]

The fruit of these plans can be seen in at least two events: the launching of the Christian Institute (CI) by Beyers Naudé, and the reorganization of the Christian Council of South Africa (CCSA). Under the leadership of the Anglican bishop Bill Burnett, the CCSA was reorganized in 1968 and its name changed to the South African Council of Churches (SACC). Its new constitution declared the principal objects of the council to be:

> a. To foster that unity which is both God's Will and His gift to the Church, by discussions, conferences, ecumenical studies, joint endeavour and in such other ways as may from time to time seem expedient;
>
> b. To co-ordinate the work and witness of Churches and Missionary Societies and other Christian Organizations and Institutions in South Africa in order more effectively to carry out the Church's Mission in the World;

---

1. Hofmeyr, Millard and Froneman, *History of the Church*, 235.

c. To undertake on behalf of the Churches and Missionary Societies such joint action and service as may be possible and to encourage joint action and service among member Churches;

d. To do all such things and to encourage all such things as may best be calculated to reduce in scope the divisive factors, whether doctrinal or otherwise, presently existing among the Christian churches.[2]

The scope of the council's work rapidly widened. In the year of its reorganization, the SACC came into the limelight with the publication of its *Message to the People of South Africa*. Influential in preparing the text of the *Message* were Bill Burnett and Beyers Naudé who had attended the 1966 WCC Conference on Church and Society. In tones somewhat reminiscent of the Barmen Declaration of the Confessing Church in Nazi Germany, the *Message* declared apartheid to be incompatible with the gospel of the Jesus Christ. It affirmed that "in Christ God has broken down the walls of division between God and man, and therefore also between man and man." *The Message* claimed that "excluding barriers of ancestry, race, nationality, language and culture have no rightful place in the inclusive brotherhood of Christian disciples." With reference to the policy of apartheid it noted that

> there are alarming signs that this doctrine of separation has become, for many, a false faith, a novel gospel which offers happiness and peace for the community and for the individual. It holds out to men a security built not on Christ but on the theory of separation and the preservation of their racial identity. It presents separate development of our race-groups as a way for the people of South Africa to save themselves. Such a claim inevitably conflicts with the Christian Gospel, which offers salvation, both social and individual, through faith in Christ alone.[3]

The *Message* concluded with a forthright condemnation of the government policy as intrinsically un-Christian:

> Any scheme which is claimed to be Christian must also take account of the reconciliation already made for us in Christ. The

---

2. Ibid., 251.
3. Ibid., 244.

policy of separate development does not take proper account of these truths. It promises peace and harmony between the peoples of our country not by a faithful and obedient pursuit of the reconciliation wrought by Christ, but through separation, which, being precisely the opposite course, is a demonstration of unbelief and distrust in the power of the Gospel. Any demonstration of the reality of reconciliation would endanger this policy; therefore the advocates of this policy inevitably find themselves opposed to the Church if it seeks to live according to the Gospel and if it shows that God's grace has overcome our hostilities. A thorough policy of racial separation must ultimately require that the Church should cease to be the Church.[4]

Never before had the gauntlet been thrown down before the government with such boldness by representatives of the churches. The *Message* went far beyond the measured and moderate tones of the Cottesloe Declaration, and thus it bore witness to the growing rift and increasing animosity between the communities of South Africa. The text of the *Message* was sent to all English and Afrikaans-speaking clergy throughout the country, and was endorsed by six hundred of them. Predictably, the English-language churches affiliated with the SACC generally supported the document, while the Afrikaans-language churches were unhappy with it. The prime minister, John Vorster, in a speech a few weeks after the publication of the *Message* warned against people "who wish to disrupt the order in South Africa under the cloak of religion." In an open letter to him, a number of church leaders, including Bill Burnett and Beyers Naudé, defended their stance:

> With all due respect, though with the greatest firmness, we must assure you that as long as attempts are made to justify the policy of apartheid by appeal to God's Word, we will persist in denying their validity; and as long as it is alleged that the application of this policy conforms to the norms of Christian ethics, we will persist in denying its validity.[5]

Vorster wrote in response:

> It is your right, of course, to demean your pulpits into becoming political platforms to attack the Government and the National

---
4. Ibid., 245.
5. De Gruchy, *Church Struggle*, 119.

Party, but then you must not be touchy when I and others react to your political speeches in the way I have done. It does not surprise me that you attack separate development. All liberalists and leftists do likewise. It is with the utmost despisal, however, that I reject the insolence you display in attacking my Church as you do. This also applies to other Churches, ministers of the Gospel and confessing members of other Churches who do in fact, believe in separate development . . . I again want to make a serious appeal to you to return to the essence of your preaching and to proclaim to your congregations the Word of God and the Gospel of Christ.[6]

John Vorster's brother, Dr Koot Vorster, was an influential DRC minister who once served as moderator of the General Synod of the church. So the lines of division were clear: the DRC and other Afrikaans-language churches in support of government policy, the SACC against. There were, of course, exceptions on both sides. We have already noted prominent Afrikaans and DRC church leaders who were critical of apartheid.

Among the English-language churches, the Baptists were critical of the *Message* on theological grounds. While they condemned racism as contrary to the gospel, they felt that the *Message* confused eternal salvation with salvation relating to political issues. Separate development, they maintained, is not a rival gospel, even though it may be an unjust political policy. Salvation through grace cannot be made contingent upon supporting or rejecting a political philosophy: "The views and attitudes of an individual in racial matters do not enter into the realm of his being justified by faith."[7] The Baptist view was clearly open to debate, but in the highly polarized atmosphere of the time any kind of debate or dialogue between the churches was extremely difficult. The pressure to identify with clearly opposing camps was strong, and the Baptists themselves later withdrew their membership from the SACC.

Tensions were heightened even further when the WCC began to give financial support to liberation movements engaged in armed struggle against the South African government. In 1969 the WCC held a consultation on racism at Notting Hill near London. It was proposed that a Programme to Combat Racism be set up with the purpose of providing moral and practical support to organizations fighting racism. In 1970 an executive meeting of

---

6. Ibid.
7. Ibid., 121.

the WCC resolved to give financial aid to antiracist liberation movements fighting in southern Africa against white minority governments. News of these grants was greeted with outrage in the white community and put the SACC and its member churches into a very difficult position. They were perceived as being in league with Communist-inspired organizations seeking violent revolution in South Africa. Churches in membership of the SACC and the WCC felt considerable pressure, both from the government and from some of their members, to sever their ties with the WCC. As the various churches held their annual synods and assemblies towards the end of 1970 and resolutions concerning WCC membership were discussed, the atmosphere was tense. The Presbyterians came close to withdrawal, but the majority of their General Assembly delegates voted to retain their links with the WCC. The position taken by virtually all the SACC member churches was to retain their membership in the WCC, criticize WCC support of political movements employing violence, and protest against the racist policies of the South African government.

The position of the SACC, namely its rejection of apartheid and its decision to support violent means to overthrow the state, opened it up to criticism from all sides. It was argued that many Christian whites in South Africa were happy to enjoy the privileges of their ethnic status while drawing moral comfort from the fact that they rejected the policies that gave them those privileges. Some African Christian leaders, such as the general secretary of the All African Conference of Churches, Burgess Carr, justified the use of violence in the struggle for liberation, arguing that the 'selective violence' of the liberation movements stood in contrast to the "collective vengeance" of the regimes in South Africa, Rhodesia and Portugal.

It was against the background of these discussions that the SACC, during its 1974 annual national conference at Hammanskraal, north of Pretoria, raised the issue of conscientious objection. At the heart of the debate was the council's attitude to violence. If armed struggle against the state was rejected as an option for Christians, what was to be their attitude to the use of force by the state in order to maintain unjust policies? The preamble to the SACC Resolution on Conscientious Objection maintained that "the Republic of South Africa is at present a fundamentally unjust and discriminatory society." Therefore, since "the military forces of our country are being prepared to defend this unjust and discriminatory society," the question needs to be asked:

Can it be right for Christians to participate in the military?[8] The preamble went on to point out that Christian tradition, both Catholic and Reformed, "has regarded the taking up of arms as justifiable, if at all, only in order to fight a 'just war'", and this would exclude the "defence of a basically unjust and discriminatory society."[9]

The Hammanskraal Resolution provoked a storm of criticism within South Africa. The SACC was accused of deliberately undermining the country's ability to defend itself against Communist-supported revolutionary forces. The Minister of Defence, P. W. Botha, introduced legislation that made it illegal for anyone to attempt to persuade any person to avoid military service. Other than Jehovah's Witnesses, there were relatively few white South Africans who suffered imprisonment as a result of their refusal to do compulsory military service. Ironically, two of these were Baptists, members of a denomination that was equivocal in its response to the debate on conscientious objection.

In the highly polarized condition of the Christian community, Bill Burnett took a reconciliatory stance. After serving three years as general secretary of the SACC, he was elected Anglican bishop of Grahamstown in 1970. In 1972, as a result of being baptized in the Holy Spirit, he was drawn into the heart of the charismatic renewal, a movement which was having considerable impact on many churches at that time. Two years later he was elected archbishop of Cape Town, the first native-born South African to be appointed as head of the CPSA. Burnett was able to bring together in a powerful way the social concern of the ecumenical movement and the spiritual vitality of the Pentecostal/Charismatic movement. Pentecostal Christians in South Africa were generally suspicious of or hostile to the SACC and tended towards a conservative political stance. After his spiritual experience in 1972, Burnett also made a special effort to seek reconciliation with Afrikaans Christian leaders, apologizing that his attitude towards them had often been un-Christian. In his enthronement sermon in August 1974, preached before a large congregation which included the state president, Burnett called for a new Pentecost and expressed his support for the SACC Hammanskraal Resolution.

In some ways Bill Burnett can be compared to David du Plessis, the South African who became known internationally as "Mr Pentecost." Du

---

8. Ibid., 140.
9. Ibid.

Plessis grew up in a conservative Afrikaner Pentecostal context and through an ecumenical experience came to appreciate and cooperate with the broader Christian community, including the WCC and the Roman Catholic Church. Burnett was from a liberal English and Anglican background and through a Pentecostal experience came to appreciate the spiritual insights of conservatives and Pentecostals. Both confessed and repented of their prejudiced attitudes to certain fellow Christians and stressed the importance of reconciliation.

In the same year that the SACC produced its Hammanskraal Resolution (1974) the Dutch Reformed Church produced a report *Ras, Volk en Nasie* that reflected its own struggle to understand human relations in the light of Scripture. The report acknowledged,

> To an increasing degree the Christian church is aware of the danger of holding to certain attitudes in race relations which are not in accordance with the Word of God. For this reason the DRC is also concerned to listen anew to the teaching of God's Word on these matters in our contemporary situation.[10]

The report concluded:

> The DRC is deeply aware of the serious questions concerning human, social and racial relations in South Africa. It shares with other Christian churches the same ideals of social righteousness, human rights, and self determination of peoples, based on God's Word. It is also convinced of the calling of the church to fulfil a prophetic role, to develop a sympathetic understanding, to provide Scriptural guidance and to engage in intercession. Where the DRC differs from other churches is not in its fundamental concepts of moral principles or Christian ethics but rather in its analysis of the situation in South Africa and the requirements of God's Word for that situation. The difference in not over ideals and goals, but over the best methods to achieve them.[11]

But while the DRC was struggling to hear God's Word in the context of the times, political events were plunging the whole country into yet another crisis. In 1976 a student protest in Soweto against the use of Afrikaans in the teaching of certain high school subjects quickly escalated into widespread

---

10. Hofmeyr, Millard and Froneman, *History of the Church*, 268 (author's translation).
11. Ibid., 273 (author's translation).

and violent riots. Riot police were sent in, and soon there were reports of scores of students killed or injured by police action. The uprising rapidly spread throughout the country. Hundreds of political activists were arrested and detained. The Black Consciousness and student leader Steve Biko died in police custody. In the following month, October 1977, seventeen organizations were banned, including the CI of Beyers Naudé.

In response to these events the moderature of the General Synod of the DRC expressed itself as follows:

> To a great number of innocent people, White and Black, who suffered these losses, the Church expresses its sincere sympathy, and trusts that local church councils and other bodies charged with the task will make the necessary support and emergency aid available. Further, the Church calls its members to a worthy plan of action in which the example of the Lord can be followed, and the Christian demand of love of God in one's neighbour can be practised. The younger churches are assured of our Church's sympathy and prayer in these times of tension.[12]

Other churches also responded but were more willing to identify, in their view, the root cause of the troubles – apartheid – and to call for the scrapping of discriminatory laws. Meeting at Dar-es-Salaam in 1977, the Lutheran World Federation declared apartheid a sin and any theological justification thereof a heresy. This judgment was repeated by the Association of Black Reformed Christians in Southern Africa (ABRECSA), who declared that "apartheid is a sin, and that the moral and theological justification of it is a travesty of the Gospel, a betrayal of the Reformed tradition, and a heresy."[13] The following year the charge of heresy was repeated by the World Alliance of Reformed Churches at its meeting in Ottawa, when it also elected Alan Boesak as its president. Boesak was a minister of the Dutch Reformed Mission Church and a leading anti-apartheid theologian and activist in South Africa.

In 1978 Desmond Tutu became the first black person to be elected general secretary of the SACC, a position he held for seven years. With so many opponents of the government either banned or in prison, Tutu and the SACC felt that they had a moral obligation to speak out for those who had no voice or who had been silenced. So during this critical period the SACC

---

12. De Gruchy, *Church Struggle in South Africa*, 173.
13. Walshe, "Christianity and the Anti-Apartheid Struggle," 388.

became a leading vehicle of opposition to apartheid, and Tutu, along with Nelson Mandela who was in prison, the most famous symbols of resistance to it. As could be expected, the name Tutu aroused widely conflicting emotions within South Africa. To most blacks he was a courageous and prophetic spokesman willing to confront the government on issues of justice and righteousness. To many whites he was a politician posing as a clergyman, abusing his ecclesiastical status to attack the government. By any reckoning, his has been a remarkable career. Born in Klerksdorp in the Transvaal in 1931, he initially trained as a teacher and taught at schools in the Gauteng area for a few years. Befriended and encouraged by Trevor Huddleston, Tutu felt a call to Christian ministry and was ordained a priest in the Church of the Province in 1961. He then proceeded to England to complete postgraduate studies at Kings College, University of London. Returning to South Africa, he lectured in theology at various places for about seven years before being appointed dean of Johannesburg in 1975.

In 1976 Tutu was consecrated bishop of Lesotho, and two years later he took up the position of general secretary of the SACC. He received the Nobel Peace Prize in 1984.[14] Something of Tutu's commitment to peace can be gleaned from an open letter he wrote to then Prime Minister John Vorster in 1976, just one month before the Soweto riots:

> ... In short, I am writing to you as one human person to another human person, gloriously created in the image of the selfsame God, redeemed by the selfsame Son of God who for all our sakes died on the Cross and rose triumphant from the dead and reigns in glory now at the right hand of the Father; sanctified by the selfsame Holy Spirit who works inwardly in all of us to change our hearts of stone into hearts of flesh. I am, therefore, writing to you, Sir, as one Christian to another, for through our common baptism we have been made members of and are united in the Body of our dear Lord and Saviour, Jesus Christ. This Jesus Christ, whatever we may have done, has broken down all that separates us irrelevantly – such as race, sex, culture, status, etc. In this Jesus Christ we are forever bound together as one redeemed humanity, Black and White together.
>
> ... I write to you, Sir, because like you, I am deeply committed to a real reconciliation with justice for all, and to peaceful

---

14. Tlhagale and Mosala, *Hammering Swords into Ploughshares*, 5.

> change to a more just and open South African society in which the wonderful riches and wealth of our country will be shared more equitably.
>
> . . . We are ready to accept some meaningful signs which would demonstrate that you and your Government and all Whites really mean business when you say you want peaceful change. First, accept the urban Black as a permanent inhabitant of what is wrongly called White South Africa . . . repeal the pass laws . . . call a National Convention made up of genuine leaders . . . to work out an orderly evolution of South Africa into a non-racial, open and just society.[15]

As the violence escalated in the late 1970s and during the 1980s, Tutu continued to advocate a negotiated settlement. He himself played a considerable role in facilitating the meeting of government and ANC leaders.

Tutu was showered with many honours, including at least ten honorary doctorates, and has become the best-known South African Christian leader in the world. However, in the eyes of some critics, Tutu's desire to be a man for all people has undermined the clarity of his Christian profession. Conservative Christians have been dismayed by his advocacy of the ordination of practising homosexuals. Evangelicals have wondered whether his goodwill to people of other faiths has verged on syncretism. Tutu has expressed his views on religious pluralism as follows:

> For me, Jesus Christ is the revelation of God, but I am opposed to proselytisation. Our task as Christians is simply to live attractive lives that are transparent with the gospel. We take ourselves far too seriously when we think that God is relying on our evangelical campaigns to make everyone Christians, in order for them to enter into communion with God.
>
> . . . I have encountered holiness, spiritual insight and the presence of God in people of many different religions. I cannot be so arrogant as to insist that these people become Christians.[16]

In fact, Tutu's theological views are neither radical or unique and can be placed fairly squarely within the broad church tradition of Anglican theology.

---

15. Hofmeyr, Millard and Froneman, *History of the Church*, 278–282.
16. Hulley, Kretzschmar and Pato, *Archbishop Tutu*, 45.

The National Party government leaders drew considerable strength and comfort from the sympathy and support they received from the Afrikaans-language churches, particularly the DRC, the largest denomination in the country. It is therefore of interest to follow the evolution of thinking in that denomination as more and more of its leaders began to question their church's traditional support of apartheid.

In 1977 the Koinonia Declaration was issued by three DRC ministers in Cape Town in reaction to the government ruling that made public agitation against detention without trial unlawful. It warned against "any form of state absolutism or totalitarianism."[17]

On 31 October 1980 eight DRC academics issued their "Reformation Day Witness" in which they expressed "deep concern about the apparent powerlessness of the institutionalized church in South Africa to carry out its divine calling of reconciliation on a meaningful and credible basis in a situation of increasing tension and polarization between the various population groups in our country." The academics, including J. A. Heyns and W. D. Jonker, pleaded for greater unity and the reform of the present order "so that every individual can be given the scope to realize their potential as the bearer of the image of God."[18]

In 1981 the journal *Stormkompas* was published by a group of concerned Christians within the DRC. Attached to the first edition was a document containing forty-four theological statements regarding the role of the DRC in South Africa. These statements posed a bold and incisive challenge to the status quo, as evidenced in a small sample below:

> 3. The unity of the church is no superfluous luxury, but constitutes the being (*wese*) of the church. Mutual divisiveness must be deplored as a sin and be controlled.
>
> 5. A Christian may never unreservedly identify with his volk, group, class or culture. There must always be a certain distance. The highest loyalty of believers is exclusively to Jesus Christ as his Lord.
>
> 19. . . . Yet we fear that the DRC in the 1980s is fast becoming isolated from the mainstream of churches in and outside SA.

---

17. Hofmeyr, Millard and Froneman, *History of the Church*, 299.
18. Ibid., 303.

In the internal situation of SA the church runs the danger of becoming irrelevant and of losing its witness.

35. It is time that the DRC said clearly that the policy of apartheid in South Africa has many harmful consequences, in spite of the good intentions of the authorities about allowing population groups to develop separately. The church needs to state clearly that the Christian cannot support this policy without question.

38. The DRC must prepare its members for the fact that the white man clearly cannot forever exercise control in South Africa. Thus, it will have to teach them in a Christian way, how they should live and act as Christians in a minority situation.[19]

The following year 123 white ministers and theologians of the DRC family made a statement in the form of an open letter in which apartheid in politics and the church was categorically rejected on scriptural grounds.[20] Clearly a groundswell of protest was developing within the DRC itself. This was to bear fruit in the "Church and Society" report adopted by the 1986 General Synod of the DRC, which finally and formerly withdrew ecclesiastical support for the policy of apartheid. Only a few years after that the entire apartheid superstructure was dismantled.

In 1978 P. W. Botha became prime minister and initiated a set of reforms designed to give government policy a new and more acceptable face. Pass laws and the laws on mixed marriage were abolished. The right to belong to trade unions and to own property were acknowledged for urban blacks. In 1983 a referendum was held by which whites accepted a new constitution that granted limited political power to coloureds and Indians alongside whites in a tricameral parliament. This constitution granted no political power to blacks in "central" South Africa because, it was argued, they enjoyed full political rights in their homelands. In a pastoral letter dated 22 July 1983 the Roman Catholic Church criticized the proposed new constitution on the grounds that the rights of all citizens were not specified in the preamble, that two-thirds of the population had no democratic representation in parliament, that the unequal division of the chambers in parliament for coloureds, Indians and whites was a perpetuation of racial discrimination, and that the power of the state president was problematic. Most English-language churches responded

---

19. Ibid., 311–315.
20. Ibid., 319.

in a similar way. The DRC and the Hervormde Church decided not to advise their members with regard to participation in the referendum.[21]

Botha's reforms did not have the desired effect. When police opened fire on a crowd in Uitenhage in 1985, killing between eighteen and forty people, unrest flared up again and quickly spread throughout the country. In July Botha declared a state of emergency which was to remain in force for five years. As political tensions and conflict continued to escalate, so did the heat in the debate among Christians. In September 1985 *The Kairos Document* was released by the ecumenical Institute for Contextual Theology and signed by many Christians and church leaders. In a searing indictment it condemned the state and all who supported it and demanded that Christians take sides on behalf of the oppressed and those seeking to liberate them. It rejected as blasphemous the following reference to God in the preamble to P. W. Botha's new constitution: "In humble submission to Almighty God, who controls the destinies of nations and the history of peoples, who gathered our forebears together from many lands and gave them this their own." "This god," claimed *The Kairos Document*, "is an idol":

> It is as mischievous, sinister and evil as any of the idols that the prophets of Israel had to contend with. Here we have a god who is historically on the side of the white settlers, who dispossesses black people of their land and who gives the major part of the land to his "chosen people."
>
> ... From a theological point of view the opposite of the God of the Bible is the devil, Satan. The god of the South African State is not merely an idol or false god, it is the devil disguised as Almighty God – the antichrist.[22]

If the state was identified with the antichrist, then the DRC which legitimized it was a false prophet. Those who urged dialogue with the government and sought reconciliation between opposing points of view were also condemned.

> Nowhere in the Bible or in Christian tradition has it ever been suggested that we ought to try to reconcile good and evil, God and the devil. ... We are supposed to oppose, confront and reject the devil and not try to sup with the devil.[23]

---

21. Hofmeyr and Pillay, *History of Christianity*, 286.
22. *The Kairos Document*, 2nd ed., 8.
23. Ibid., 10.

For the framers of *The Kairos Document* the way forward was clear. Only when the apartheid regime repented, did away with injustice and transferred power to the people could there be talk of reconciliation and forgiveness.

A more conciliatory note was taken by the National Initiative for Reconciliation, launched in September 1985 under the auspices of Africa Enterprise (AE), one of the few South African organizations able to combine the social concern of the ecumenical movement and the evangelistic zeal of Evangelicals and Pentecostals. Michael Cassidy, who founded AE in 1962, had grown up in Lesotho and attended a private school in Natal. While at the University of Cambridge in 1955, a question posed by a friend concerning his relationship with Jesus Christ brought Cassidy to an experience of conversion and new birth in Christ. Hearing Billy Graham preach during a university mission in 1956 inspired Cassidy to devote his life to evangelism on the continent of Africa. He retained his Anglican affiliation and often worked closely with local Anglican parishes. This is a probable reason why Africa Enterprise, while retaining its primary evangelistic thrust of calling individuals to personal conversion to Christ, increasingly developed a vision to challenge the church to be an agent for righteousness and justice in the social and political realm. The National Initiative for Reconciliation was a meeting of church leaders representing forty-seven denominations. Philip Russel (Anglican archbishop), Desmond Tutu, Adrio König (DRC), David Bosch (DRC), Peter Storey (Methodist), Khoza Mgojo (Methodist), and Caesar Molebatsi were among those present. In a *Statement of Affirmation* they declared:

> We feel compelled as witnesses of Jesus Christ to share with the nation the hope that we have experienced together. For those who suffer under the pain and despair of the South African reality we feel bound by God to visible and obedient actions of hope. While not every participant in the conference could agree on the details of these actions, the clear majority of the Christian leaders gathered here in such remarkable denominational diversity resolved:
>
> > A. That on Wednesday October 9th, 1985 Christians, rather than attending the places of their usual employment (except so far as essential services are concerned), should give the day to repentance, mourning and prayer for those sinful

aspects of our national life which have led us to the present crisis. . . .

B. That a delegation representing this Assembly will visit the State President immediately to present the following initiatives:

1. End the state of emergency.

2. Remove the SADF and the Emergency Police forces from the townships.

3. Release all detainees and political prisoners, withdraw charges against the Treason trialists and allow exiles to return home.

4. Begin talks immediately with authentic leadership of the various population groups with a view toward equitable power sharing in South Africa.

5. Begin the process of introducing a common system of education.

6. Take the necessary steps towards the elimination of all forms of legislation discrimination.[24]

By the middle of the 1980s a growing chorus of voices was calling on the government for radical change. These voices emanated not only from the SACC and the international community but also from an increasing number of DRC ministers and other conservative churches not normally given to making political statements. The Baptist Union, for example, at its annual Assembly in 1985 agreed to send a letter to the state president in which, after assuring him that they were praying for him and for all those "who share with you the responsibility under God of directing the affairs of our land," requested that "the whole structure of apartheid be dismantled as a matter of extreme urgency." The letter then spelled out twelve specific areas of concern, and closed by pledging the prayers of Baptists "for you, and for all who will have a hand in establishing a truly righteous nation."[25]

With increasing pressure being exerted by international trade sanctions and the armed struggle of the liberation movements, it was clear that the National Party government would not survive much longer. Few in 1985,

---

24. Hofmeyr, Millard, and Froneman, *History of the Church*, 361.
25. Ibid., 354–356.

however, realized how quickly and totally change would come. Many Christians believe that prayer played a vital role in that change. But before we look at the final scenes of that drama, the story of some of the newest Christian groups to emerge in South Africa must be told.

The Newer Charismatic Churches

The rise of Pentecostalism at the dawn of the twentieth century released a spiritual dynamic that has continued to expand and evolve new forms which have increasingly influenced the church and the world. The first wave of this movement resulted in the formation of what are now called the classical Pentecostal churches (e.g. the Assemblies of God, the Apostolic Faith Mission, the Full Gospel Church of God). In the late 1950s and early 1960s a second wave of Pentecostal phenomena occurred in Episcopalian (Anglican), Lutheran, Presbyterian, Reformed, Baptist and Methodist churches. People testified to being baptized in the Holy Spirit, to speaking in tongues and to gifts of healing. This neo-Pentecostal or charismatic renewal gained even greater momentum after 1967 when it began to spread rapidly in the Roman Catholic Church. In an astonishingly short time, tens of millions of Christians from all over the world representing the entire spectrum of Christianity were identifying enthusiastically with charismatic renewal. Most of them were determined to remain in their denominations and saw the renewal as a potent force for the revitalization and expansion of historic Christianity.

Inevitably, there were cases where the old wineskins did not seem able to hold the new wine. Frustration and impatience with conservative church leaders and traditional structures and liturgies led some charismatic Christians to leave their churches and form new ecclesial communities which are here designated "newer charismatic churches." Terms such as "third wave" or "post-charismatic" churches have also been used for them. While they share with all other Pentecostal and charismatic Christians the emphasis on the special work of the Holy Spirit in empowering believers for service and imparting gifts for ministry, the prevailing ethos in the newer charismatic churches is quite different from that in the classical Pentecostal churches. The latter were heirs of the nineteenth-century Holiness movement and inherited from them strict prohibitions against activities such as drinking, smoking, dancing and attending cinemas. The former grew out of more liberal mainline churches and have carried with them a more tolerant view of such "worldly" activities. The older Pentecostal churches defined their doctrine more rigidly, usually insisting on the gift of tongues as a necessary evidence of the baptism of the Holy Spirit. The newer charismatic churches have been more flexible in their doctrinal definitions and interpretation of spiritual experiences. With such rapid expansion and the proliferation of many different movements and bodies, a wide variety of theological emphases has developed, too complex and nuanced to be explained here.

Some idea of the worldwide growth of all those designated Pentecostals and Charismatics can be seen in the following table compiled by David B. Barrett.[26]

	1900	1970	1975	1980	1985	1988	1990	2000
Pentecostal/ Charismatics	3.7m	75m	106m	169m	293m	361m	406m	619m
% of world's Christians	0.7	6.2	8.1	11.8	18.9	21.4	23.3	29.1

Barrett's definition of Pentecostal/charismatic is very wide and includes some groups with whom most regular Pentecostals would not wish to be associated. The figures nevertheless give some idea of the impact of this new expression of Christian faith on the world.

Reactions to the charismatic movement have varied from outright rejection to breathless praise. Some conservative Christians have denounced the entire movement as a demonic delusion, preparing the way for "the signs of antichrist by counterfeit fire (Rev 13:13, 14) and counterfeit miracles (Matt 7:22, 23)," as claimed by the International Council of Christian Churches.[27] Others have criticized the movement on the grounds of theological naiveté, spiritual pride, divisiveness, emotionalism, and social and political irrelevance. Still others, while admitting to weaknesses in all the aforementioned areas, have drawn attention to the positive gains of the charismatic renewal: radically changed lives, renewal of Christian faith and hope, deliverance from besetting sins, impressive church growth and evangelistic outreach, and dramatic ecumenical breakthroughs.

As the twentieth century wore on, an increasing number of internationally respected Christian leaders offered positive appraisals of the movement. In 1953 Lesslie Newbigin, renowned missionary, theologian and ecumenical leader, called the Pentecostal groups a "third stream" in Christianity and

---

26. Barrett, "Global Statistics," 812–813.
27. Rossouw, *Ecumenical Panorama*, 71.

pointed out that they should be drawn in as partners in the ecumenical discussion. Professor John Mackay, once president of Princeton Theological Seminary, made the following evaluation:

> What is known as the charismatic movement – a movement marked by spiritual enthusiasm and special gifts and which crosses all boundaries of culture, race, age and church tradition – is profoundly significant . . . Because "no heart is pure that is not passionate and no virtue is safe that is not enthusiastic," the charismatic movement of today is the chief hope of the ecumenical tomorrow.[28]

The Second Vatican Council acknowledged the vital importance of the gifts of the Holy Spirit, thus preparing the way for the Roman Catholic charismatic renewal. Pope John XXIII's prayer for "a new Pentecost in our times" was seen by many as prophetic. Popes Paul VI and John Paul II gave cautious but positive praise and encouragement to the movement.

In South Africa, the charismatic renewal has widely influenced most of the mainline churches and produced a cluster of new Christian groups and fellowships.

Edmund Roebert, for instance, became the pastor of the small Hatfield Baptist Church in Pretoria in 1963. Discouragement and lack of growth in the church led him to start praying early each morning for spiritual revival. News of the renewal movement in the USA encouraged him in this quest. Arguments with local Pentecostal pastors prejudiced Roebert against their doctrines, but the testimonies of a Methodist minister from Benoni and an Anglican priest from London, both advocates of the renewal, made a strong impression on him. Some of Roebert's church members visited the Methodist minister in Benoni and were baptized in the Holy Spirit, as they later testified. Soon the charismatic movement was flourishing in the Hatfield Baptist Church, despite the opposition of some of its deacons and members.

The rapidly growing congregation moved to a more spacious sanctuary in the Pretoria suburb of Brooklyn in 1976. Soon that was too small and yet another move to an even larger building in Pretoria East was required. By 1989 the congregation was nearly 5,000 strong. Roebert found the congregational form of church government, traditional in Baptist churches, unwieldy in the context of such a large membership. Further study led him to the conviction

---

28. Lederle, *Systematic Theology*, 3.

that it was also unbiblical. This brought him into conflict with the Baptist Union, which in its annual Assembly in 1984, passed a resolution insisting "that each individual member has the unalienable right and responsibility to participate fully in the life and government of the church, including the appointment of its leaders." Roebert led his church out of the Baptist Union, and it has subsequently been known as the Hatfield Christian Church.

Another independent charismatic congregation that was to grow even larger than the Hatfield Christian Church was the Rhema Bible Church, founded by Ray McCauley. McCauley had left school two years before matriculating to work as a hairdresser and to pursue his interest in bodybuilding. In a gymnasium a preacher befriended McCauley and led him to Christ. Soon McCauley was enthusiastically bearing testimony to his new-found faith in churches in Johannesburg. He regarded 1975 as a high point in his life for in that year he came third in the Mr Universe competition in London, met his future wife and was baptized with the Holy Spirit.

Feeling a call to the ministry, McCauley went to Tulsa, Oklahoma, in 1978 to study at the Rhema Bible Training Centre of Kenneth Hagin. Hagin, controversial advocate of the "Word of Faith" message, emphasized God's desire to bless all who do not doubt him in every area of life. After one year in Tulsa, McCauley returned to Johannesburg and began holding services in his parents' home. Within six weeks the growing congregation moved to a cinema building that could hold six hundred. Eighteen months later McCauley was holding three services every Sunday morning and attendance had grown to 2,500. In 1985 a large auditorium was built to accommodate over 5,000 people. By 1988 membership of the Rhema Bible Church had reached about 12,000.

Many other independent charismatic churches sprang up throughout South Africa. In 1985 Edmund Roebert called a meeting of the leaders of these churches to consider possible ways of cooperation. At this meeting in Durban it was decided to form the International Fellowship of Christian Churches (IFCC), "a united charismatic front . . . formed to provide spiritual covering, mutual support and open communication channels to non-denominational churches."[29] This body also gave its members an identity in their dealings with the government so that marriage officers and Defence Force chaplains could be appointed and tax concessions negotiated. Five leaders, including Edmund

---

29. Rossouw, *Ecumenical Panorama*, 264.

Roebert and Ray McCauley, were recognized as fulfilling an apostolic function within the fellowship. The leaders were determined that the IFCC should be

> not another denomination, but a fellowship of cross-denominational, non-racial churches and church leaders, endeavouring to recognise and release the fivefold ministry in our land, so that Christians in our country can come to unity. All churches and ministries in the IFCC remain autonomous, retain their individual identity and govern their own affairs.[30]

By November 1988, the IFCC claimed a membership of 493 congregations and ministries, representing a community of about 270,000 members. The close association of the IFCC, and especially the Rhema Bible Church, with the prosperity, or positive confession, theology of Kenneth Hagin, Kenneth Copeland and others in the USA, was the source of considerable controversy in the early years of the IFCC. According to this teaching, prosperity and health are God's will for all his children and can be attained and maintained by the right use of faith

Critics have pointed out that the principal teachers of positive confession theology do not properly distinguish between God and human beings. "You don't have a God in you. You are one," taught Copeland.[31] Word of Faith teachers have also been accused of holding erroneous doctrines concerning the person and work of Christ. There is no doubt that in his early ministry McCauley simply reproduced the doctrines of his teachers. But he was willing to learn and change, and quite soon he moved away from the extremes of the "faith" doctrine, which resulted in a reformation of his movement from within. In 1990 he made the following public statement:

The incarnation

> I believe that Jesus Christ alone is God-man, I believe that born again Christians are indwelled by God, but that they are not Gods incarnate. We have been redeemed by Christ but he does not deify us. I believe that we can be filled with all the fullness of God (Eph 3:19) and that "in him dwelleth all the fullness of Godhead bodily" and that "we are complete in him" (Col 2:9–10), but that does not make us gods incarnate. We are humans. We have the

---

30. Ibid.

31. Lovett, "Positive Confession Theology," in Burgess and McGee, *Dictionary of Pentecostal*, 719.

Lord Jesus living in us. We are indwelled by Christ. As such we are not "little gods," rather we are humans who are indwelled by the Holy Spirit.

The atonement

I believe that "Christ died for our sins" and that he totally redeemed us through "the blood of the New Testament which he shed for many for the remission of sins" (Matt 26:28). I believe that Jesus "bore in his own body our sins on the tree" (1 Pet 2:24).

I believe that when Jesus died on the cross and declared "it is finished" he had made total atonement for us. Through the sacrifice of himself on the cross he completely redeemed us, "for by one offering he has perfected forever them that are sanctified" (Heb 10:14). Jesus redeemed us through the offering of the sacrifice of his own body and the shedding of his precious blood. I believe that on the cross "Jesus who knew no sin became sin for us, that we might be made the righteousness of God in him" (2 Cor 5:21).

His redemption on the cross was complete and total. Man is redeemed by what Jesus did on the cross alone. Man can add nothing to it.

Repent and renounce

I acknowledge that I did in the past say that "while on the cross, he (Jesus) was going to have to take Satan as his stepfather." I have since come to a deeper understanding of what actually took place at the cross, have repented of that statement and have renounced that teaching. I have also withdrawn it from all our Rhema Bible Training Centre notes.

I believe that the Bible, the word of God, is the final authority for all that we believe. I believe that the Holy Spirit is leading us into all truth on the basis of the word.

This statement is fully supported by the leadership of the International Fellowship of Christian Churches and is dispatched to you from the IFCC office.[32]

---

32. Morphew, *Renewal Apologetics*, 8.

It was not only in matters of doctrine that McCauley was willing to acknowledge inadequacies and move on, but also in the areas of ecumenical relations and social ethics. In his desire to make a positive impact on the nation at a time when political strife was tearing it apart, McCauley began to make contact with Christian and national leaders outside Pentecostal and charismatic circles. This led the IFCC to apply for observer status in the SACC, a step that provoked some conservatives to leave the IFCC. But McCauley defended the step.

> You can't deal with major national issues unless you have an alliance . . . and deal with [the issues] collectively . . . It is imperative for us to realise – particularly the charismatics and Pentecostals – that we should be very much more tolerant, very much more understanding and respectful of other churches: that they do have some good things and so do we. Not all of us are perfect; not all of us have the answer to everything."[33]

McCauley played an important role in a conference held in Rustenburg in November 1990 which was was attended by delegates from eighty South African churches. This conference, described by McCauley as a "Damascus-type experience" for him personally, was pivotal in convincing him of the need for Christians to get involved in socio-political issues. McCauley came to define the four major aims of Rhema's ministry as "to be evangelistically potent, socially significant, morally relevant, and offer life in the Spirit."[34]

These developments in the life and ministry of the IFCC were not without internal tensions and conflict. Edmund Roebert was not happy with some of the developments, especially with the reorganization of the IFCC's structure in 1997. He felt that the fellowship was becoming a denomination. "Having come out of a denomination," he declared, "I don't want to go back into one."[35] He, together with about nine other churches, withdrew from the IFCC to form the South African Interchurch Network, which would be closer to the pattern of his original vision for the IFCC.

The IFCC is certainly not the only fellowship of independent charismatic churches in South Africa. Other smaller, cooperative groups of churches with a charismatic ethos have emerged: Christian Fellowships International, founded by Fred Roberts; Foundation Ministries, established by Derek

---

33. Gordon-Brown, "Impacting a Nation," 18.
34. Ibid., 16.
35. From a personal interview with the Rev Billy Marais.

Crumpton; and New Covenant Ministries, led by Dudley Daniels. A student Christian movement in Cape Town, His People, expanded to become a rapidly growing cluster of churches with extensions overseas. Still other associations have their origin outside South Africa. These include the Association of Vineyard Churches, originally established by John Wimber in the USA, and New Frontiers, a fellowship of churches with British links. Several of these groups have joined in a loose association called Christian Ministries Network. The names are not well known to the wider Christian public, yet these groups represent the growing edge of Christianity in South Africa and will play an increasingly important role in the twenty-first century.

Unlike the earlier generation of Pentecostal churches, some of these newer charismatic fellowships have leaders with a deeper depth of theological background. Scholars such as Derek Morphew, associated with the Vineyard churches, have made important contributions to theological discussions on contemporary issues.

The Collapse of Apartheid

From the time of Cottesloe in 1960, when Beyers Naudé and those of like thought were forced out of their leadership positions in the Dutch Reformed Church, the effective control of the DRC was in the hands of conservative, pro-apartheid men like Andries Treurnicht and John Vorster. There remained, however, those who challenged the church's support of apartheid, and their influence grew steadily in the 1970s and 1980s. One of them, Johan Heyns who had signed the 1980 "Reformation Day Witness," was elected moderator of the general synod of the DRC in Cape Town in 1986. During this synod the church adopted the "Church and Society" document in which the DRC finally and officially withdrew its support of apartheid. The relevant portion reads as follows:

> Following the reflection that has taken place through the years in church periodicals, conferences, committees and synods concerning the policy, which has become known as apartheid, the conviction has gradually grown that a forced separation and division of peoples cannot be considered a biblical imperative. The attempt to justify such an injunction as derived from the Bible must be recognized as an error and be rejected.
>
> The Dutch Reformed Church is convinced that the application of apartheid as a political and social system by which

human dignity is adversely affected, and whereby one particular group is detrimentally suppressed by another cannot be accepted on Christian ethical grounds because it contravenes the very essence of neighbourly love and righteousness and inevitably the human dignity of all involved.

The suffering of people for whom the church has concern must, however, not be attributed solely to the system of apartheid but to a variety of factors such as economic, social and political realities in which persons of different communities have not been accepted by one another. To the extent that the church and its members are involved in this, it confesses its participation with humility and sorrow.[36]

The document was immediately criticized on two fronts. Some felt it was too mild in its rejection of apartheid and that its confession of sin was only half-hearted. Conservatives in the DRC, however, criticized "Church and Society" for abandoning the historic position of the church. They issued a document titled "Faith and Protest" in which they especially condemned

- the rejection by the General Synod of amendments in which it was attempted to put aside this wrong confession of sin and this artificially created consciousness of guilt.
- the rejection by the General Synod of amendments in which it was attempted to do justice to the advantages of separate development.[37]

Clearly, there had been a great struggle in the synod between those for and those against apartheid, and equally clearly the former had lost. The group identifying with the "Faith and Protest" document eventually withdrew from the DRC to form the Afrikaanse Protestante Kerk (Afrikaans Protestant Church).

Although the DRC had turned an important corner, the country was wracked by ongoing violence and unrest which the government of P. W. Botha was unable to address adequately. In 1989 Botha suffered a minor stroke which necessitated his stepping down from his position as leader of the National Party although he remained state president. A power struggle ensued within the National Party and resulted in Botha's resignation. F. W. de Klerk emerged as the new state president, promising to scrap discriminatory legislation, end the state of emergency and negotiate a new constitution. In

---

36. General Synodical Commission, *Church and Society*, 47–48.
37. Hofmeyr, Millard and Froneman, *History of the Church*, 387.

his opening address to parliament in February 1990, De Klerk stunned the country and the world when he announced the unbanning of the African National Congress, the Pan Africanist Congress and the Communist Party. Nelson Mandela and many other leading political prisoners were released, and De Klerk pledged to work together with them towards a new constitution and a democratically elected government.

The major logjam had at last been broken, but the way ahead would not be at all smooth and there was no guarantee of a successful outcome. Some conservative whites were outraged by De Klerk's "betrayal," and there were fears of a right-wing military coup. Radicals on the left, especially among the black youth, did not trust De Klerk and demanded that the ANC should not enter into any talks with the white government but rather continue the armed struggle. To make things worse, the violence did not decrease with the new political initiatives, rather, it increased. Astute statesmanship by leaders on all sides kept the difficult process of negotiations on track until finally, on 27 April 1994, all the citizens of South Africa were able to vote in the first fully democratic elections in the history of the country. The relatively peaceful election and subsequent inauguration of an ANC-led government of national unity were heralded by many as nothing short of a miracle.

Various claims have been made concerning the role of the church in South Africa's "miracle" election and transition to a democratic, non-racial state. Much of the discussion around such claims involves subjective opinions not accessible to historical research. But one concrete event that certainly played an important part in the dramatic days between the release of Mandela and 27 April 1994 was the Rustenburg Conference mentioned above.

In his 1989 Christmas address to the nation, F. W. de Klerk appealed to the church in South Africa to formulate a strategy conducive to negotiation, reconciliation and change. The SACC felt that it was not appropriate for the state president to initiate such a conference, and it was only after De Klerk agreed to withdraw from further involvement that arrangements for such a conference could proceed. This was possibly the most representative gathering of Christian leaders ever to occur in South Africa. Member churches of the SACC, the Dutch Reformed Church, the Roman Catholic Church, African Instituted Churches, Classical Pentecostal churches, conservative evangelical churches and newer charismatic churches were all represented.

An unexpected motion from the SACC contingent calling on Louw Alberts to chair the meetings was followed by a proposal from a non-SACC member that Frank Chikane be his co-chairman. Alberts, a member of the

DRC, was an eminent physicist and a well-known evangelical leader. Chikane was president of the SACC and active in the Institute for Contextual Theology. Included on the steering committee were Michael Cassidy (Africa Enterprise), Justus du Plessis (AFM, brother of 'Mr Pentecost' David du Plessis), Johan Heyns (DRC), Ray McCauley (IFCC), Wilfrid Napier (Roman Catholic bishop), Temba Ntongana (Council of African Independent Churches) and Desmond Tutu (CPSA).

During an opening time of worship, Tutu had this to say:

> If anyone had predicted in September 1989 that in November 1990 virtually all the churches in South Africa would be gathered together in a national conference, most of us would have been convinced that that man was certifiably mad. . . .
>
> We come here not to engage in recrimination or accusation. Those who believe that they are right in their struggle for a new dispensation could so easily become self-righteous.[38]

Although there were recriminations and accusations at the conference, the dominant note was a spirit of painful reaching out to join hands in building a new South Africa. "We must exorcise and expel," urged Michael Cassidy, "from both church and nation the demon of division which has almost destroyed us all."[39] Khoza Mgojo of the Methodist Church expressed the hope that "at this Conference, competitive sectarianism will yield to cooperation. The vision I have for this Conference is that all streams of the Christian church will come together to form a 'permanent river' to bring Jesus Christ to a thirsty land."[40]

A dramatic moment of the conference was when Willie Jonker, DRC professor of theology at the University of Stellenbosch, made the following confession during his address to the conference:

> I confess before you and before the Lord, not only my own sin and guilt, and my personal responsibility for the political, social, economical and structural wrongs that have been done to many of you, and the results of which you and our whole country are still suffering from, but *vicariously* I dare also to do that in the name of the DRC of which I am a member, and for the Afrikaans

---

38. Alberts and Chikane, *Road to Rustenburg*, 21.
39. Ibid., 34.
40. Ibid., 39.

people as a whole. I have the liberty to do just that, because the DRC at its latest synod has declared apartheid a sin and confessed its own guilt of negligence in not warning against it and distancing itself from it long ago.[41]

In his response to Jonker's confession Tutu declared, "I believe that I certainly stand under pressure of God's Holy Spirit to say that, as I said in my sermon, when that confession is made, then those of us who have been wronged must say 'We forgive you,' so that together we may move to the reconstruction of our land."[42]

Jonker's confession was not the only one heard at the conference. Ellis André of the Baptist Union, speaking in his personal capacity, admitted,

> We [Baptists] have certainly felt the impoverishment of our self-imposed exile, and are much, much poorer for our foolish action of actually withdrawing even observer status from the SACC. Our resolutions have been impressive, but I have to confess that our actions have not measured up.[43]

Ray McCauley read the following formal confession on behalf of Rhema, the IFCC, the Christian Ministries Network, and Christian Fellowship International:

> Despite our short history, we recognise our guilt in that, for some of us, our opposition to apartheid did not go far enough... we were often silent when our sisters and brothers were suffering persecution.
>
> We confess that our silence in these areas was in fact a sin, and that our failure to act decisively against all forms of apartheid made us party to an inhuman political ideology.
>
> We therefore confess our failure and repent of our sin and declare our complete rejection of all forms of racism and the evil, unjust system of apartheid. Please forgive us.[44]

Manas Buthelezi, a bishop of the Evangelical Lutheran Church in South Africa, reminded the delegates:

---

41. Ibid., 92.
42. Ibid., 99.
43. Ibid., 196.
44. Ibid., 262.

> After apartheid has gone the struggle will continue. The liberation we seek should not be regarded as a final destination of all our aspirations, a type of crossover from an era of injustice to absolute justice, but rather a giant step forward on a long journey of life, until everything reaches the fullness of the image of God, when every knee shall bow and every tongue shall confess that Jesus Christ is Lord.[45]

Addressing the conference in the closing session of worship, the Methodist bishop Stanley Mogoba, a former political prisoner on Robben Island and future leader of the PAC, appealed to political leaders opposed to negotiations to change their mind.

> Any leader who ignores an appeal from a conference that represents so many South Africans must surely be inadequately briefed or ill-advised.[46]

To what extent national political leaders were influenced by appeals coming from the 230 church leaders from eighty denominations and forty parachurch organizations who met at Rustenburg is difficult to tell. But the conference was at least an important link in the extraordinary chain of events leading to the establishment of a new South Africa.

The New South Africa

Events occurring after 1994 are too close to the writing of this book to be seen in any historical perspective. However, a few general trends can be outlined.

The spirit of reconciliation manifested in gatherings such as that at Rustenburg and in the country as a whole has led to a growing movement of unity between some churches. The three "daughter" churches of the DRC (originally established for the coloured, black and Indian communities) joined together in 1994 as the Uniting Reformed Church. This new denomination engaged in unity discussions with the "mother" DRC in 1999. Despite some difficulties over the adoption of a new confession of faith, both bodies expressed a commitment to the goal of unity.

The various branches of the AFM, also ethnically based, came together in what was celebrated as the "the great Pentecostal reconciliation." The

---

45. Ibid., 209.
46. Ibid., 253.

predominantly white Baptist Union and the black Baptist Convention both pledged themselves in 1998 to engage in discussions towards a merger of the two bodies. The Presbyterian Church of Southern Africa and the Reformed Presbyterian Church in Southern Africa took formal decisions at their respective General Assemblies in 1998 to unite. At the close of the second millennium other groups of churches, too, were engaged in a process of unification.

However, any conclusion that the process of fragmentation within South African Christianity was now reversed would be premature, for the number of new and separate ecclesiastical bodies formed in 1999 exceeded the number of unions.

Another significant trend in the last few decades of the twentieth century was the steady decline in the membership of mainline churches as a percentage of the total population. In the Dutch Reformed, Methodist and Anglican churches, this decline has been seen since about 1970. The Roman Catholic Church was able to increase its membership percentage until 1980, but since then it too has been in decline. The black population is moving away from mainline churches into AICs, and in the white community the move is to new, independent and mainly charismatic churches. Since 1980 there has also been a sharp increase in the number of people describing themselves as "not religious."

The pride and joy felt by most South Africans on the formation of the new and free South Africa with its enlightened constitution protecting the dignity and rights of all people was tempered by anxiety and concern about grave problems facing the country. Escalating crime, economic stagnation, high unemployment, and a rampant HIV/AIDS epidemic were some of the most serious issues. In the period 1992–1997 there was a 30 percent increase in crime, but a 4 percent decrease in the number of convictions. *Time* magazine reported in May 1996 that South Africa had a murder rate six times that of the United States. The incentive to crime is high when employment is scarce. At the close of the twentieth century nearly half of the potential workers were unemployed or under-employed. Slow economic growth, hampered by world recession, gave little prospect of improving employment opportunities.

In 1996 Dr Ruben Sher of the University of the Witwatersrand in Johannesburg warned that "AIDS is spreading like wildfire." In that year it was estimated that 1.8 million were infected with the HIV virus and that

650 people were contracting the virus daily.[47] Only three years later it was reported in the national media that three million South Africans were HIV positive, and that the number becoming infected every day had risen to 1,500.

Clearly the challenges facing the church in its mission to the nation were, and still are, as serious as at any time during its history. Prophets of doom have more than enough material to predict dark scenarios for the future. But South Africa has surprised the world in the past in not fulfilling the gloomy expectations of experts. Desmond Tutu would ascribe this to the sheer grace of the "God of surprises":

> It was sheer grace, and that is how God always is – a God of grace. Thank you God, that you are that kind of God. How else would we have been saved, had it not been that God was a God biased in the favour of the weak and the poor and the helpless? Are we not fortunate that God is such a God and, as St Paul can rightly exult, while we were yet sinners, Christ died for us. If God had waited for us to be deserving of His grace, He would still be waiting! Our God is a God who takes the initiative on behalf of those who are undeserving, and so we see that God is the same yesterday, today and forever.[48]

---

47. Froise, *South African Christian Handbook*, 11.
48. Alberts and Chikane, *Road to Rustenburg*, 23.

8

The Last Twenty Years: A Brief Postscript

Events need to ripen over some years before they can become the proper subject of a history of anything. So as I write this brief postscript to the new edition of my book, I am acutely aware of the difficulty of commenting on the events of the last twenty years. I may well be overlooking some deeply significant movement, the importance of which will only become manifest in the future.

There is, however, one point that I can make with great certainty: the Christian scene in South Africa has followed the same pattern we have been discerning since it origins, in that it has become even more complex and diverse.

Let us look at what has been happening over the last twenty years in some of the Christian grouping within the country.

Mainline churches (i.e. the thirty-six member churches of the South African Council of Churches, including the Roman Catholic, Dutch Reformed, Anglican, Presbyterian, Methodist and Congregational churches) have generally experienced a decline, although it is difficult to quantify this as the last census to ask information about religious adherence was in 2001. However, a Win-Gallup poll conducted in 2012 indicated that the number of people in South Africa describing themselves as "religious" declined from 83 percent in 2005 to 64 percent in 2012.

One of the major issues dividing the mainline Protestant churches is the issue of homosexual relations and same-sex marriage. These discussions largely mirror the discussions in mainline Protestant churches in Europe and America. The controversy has landed individual churches and denominations in the law courts on a number of occasions, and will probably continue to do so. As in Europe and America, the traditional Protestant denominations are dividing over the legitimacy of same-sex relationships and marriage, with the observable trend being towards the acceptance of such relations.

Smaller and generally more conservative churches (Baptists, Reformed Evangelical Anglican Church, the Nazarenes, smaller Reformed churches) have generally held their own but without any significant growth. Many of them have protected themselves from the above controversies by inserting clauses defining their understanding of marriage in their confessional statements, although this has not entirely shielded them from heated discussions of gay rights and relationships. Issues relating to doctrine and structures of church leadership have, however, been contentious in these denominations.

Traditional or classic Pentecostal churches (Apostolic Faith Mission, Assemblies of God, Full Gospel Church of God, Pentecostal Protestant Church) have also held their numbers and seen some growth.

In 1996 the black and white sections of the AFM came together to become one operational unity, and the church's newly elected president, Isak Burger, apologized for the past treatment of non-whites. The AFM is now a growing church that has spread to all towns and villages in South Africa. It is claimed that more than 2,000 assemblies and branch assemblies have been established.

In 2002 the various AG groups found a formula for unity that drew them closer together. While still functioning separately, they were able to cooperate with greater unity and love than previously and the AG remains one of South Africa's largest classical Pentecostal denominations.

The Full Gospel Church of God also saw a process of unity. In March 1990 the United Assemblies of the Full Gospel Church of God was constituted, bringing together black, coloured and Indian churches, and some white churches. Seven years later, in 1997, the 242 Assemblies of the Irene Association were united with the 586 assemblies of the United Association, resulting in a total of 828 assemblies in the United Full Gospel Church of God, with a conservatively estimated membership of 350,000 members, excluding Namibia.

Newer charismatic churches and networks have seen some of the most dramatic growth in the last twenty years. Their rapid growth and changing patterns of networks makes it difficult to keep track of who they are. What follows is merely a list of some of the significant networks and churches.

- *The Christian Network* (popularly known as the Hatfield group) with the Hatfield Christian Church as a founding member.

- *The International Fellowship of Christian Churches* (IFCC) with the Rhema Church playing a leading role.
- *New Frontiers.* The church "God First" is linked with New Frontiers, but also with Advance, an international group of churches.
- *His People* has congregations in Cape Town and Gauteng.
- *Churches* connected with the *Hillsong Family*.
- *The Vineyard Churches.*
- *Christian Fellowship International.* The Durban Christian Centre with its 5,000 seat "Jesus Dome" is the flagship of this group.
- *Christian City.*

The growth of the charismatic churches has not been without controversy, and there is great diversity of doctrine and practice among them. An emphasis on health and wealth as a sign of divine favour plays a role in a significant number of churches, including the Universal Church of the Kingdom of God and Winners Chapel. It must be said, however, that many charismatic churches dissociate themselves from such groups.

It has been estimated that by the late 1990s Pentecostals comprised about 10 percent of the population, with the largest denominations being the Apostolic Faith, Assemblies of God and the Full Gospel Church of God. The mostly black Zionist and Apostolic churches, which constitute a majority of South Africa's AICs, account for an additional 30 percent or so of the population.

African Instituted or Zionist churches have continued to see significant growth in the last twenty years. Accurate statistics are not available, and the variety of religious teachings and practices are legion. The largest of these is undoubtedly the Zion Christian Church (ZCC). According to the 1996 census, the church had 3.87 million members. By the 2001 census, its membership had increased to 4.97 million. These numbers may be inflated, but there can be no doubt that the annual pilgrimage of ZCC people to Moria every Easter has become a major event in the South African calendar.

The Nazareth Baptist Church, popularly known as the Shembe Church, has not fared as well over the last twenty years. After the death of its founder, Johannes Galilee Shembe, in 1976 it divided into two groups. The larger group was led by Bishop Amos Shembe until his death in 1995, while the Right Reverend Londa Shembe led the smaller group of about 1,000 members. As of 2009 the Shembe Church was divided into four factions – three in KwaZulu-Natal and one in Gauteng.

These are only two of thousands of "Zionist" churches, all of them in a continual state of flux, division, growth or extinction, and with widely varying teachings and practices.

It must also be mentioned that renewal movements among some of the Zionist churches have resulted in a remarkable revival of gospel and biblical teachings in churches such as the NDJ Ethiopian Catholic Church of Zion in Africa. Such movements give hope for the future of Zionist phenomena.

The Truth and Reconciliation Commission

The previous pages of this history have shown the mercy of God in providing wise heads on both sides of the political conflict who had sufficient humility to persevere in the excruciatingly difficult talks that eventually led to a universal democratic election and a peaceful transition of power.

With the victory of the ANC in 1994, the question arose: How do we deal with the crimes and atrocities perpetrated during the many years of struggle and conflict? This is where the Truth and Reconciliation Commission came in. From the beginning it expressed the ideal of providing a forum in which the truth about the past could be openly expressed and reconciliation sought between former enemies.

> The Truth and Reconciliation Commission (TRC) was a court-like restorative justice body . . . Witnesses who were identified as victims of gross human rights violations were invited to give statements about their experiences, and some were selected for public hearings. Perpetrators of violence could also give testimony and request amnesty from both civil and criminal prosecution. . . .
>
> The commission was empowered to grant amnesty to those who committed abuses during the apartheid era, as long as the crimes were politically motivated, proportionate, and there was full disclosure by the person seeking amnesty. To avoid victor's justice, no side was exempt from appearing before the commission. The commission heard reports of human rights violations and considered amnesty applications from all sides,

from the apartheid state to the liberation forces, including the African National Congress.[1]

It is worth noting that the concepts of truth and reconciliation are themselves rooted in the Bible and the Christian gospel. The chairman and deputy chairman of the TRC were Desmond Tutu and Alex Boraine, both of whom deeply influenced by the Christian tradition. In his fascinating paper on the TRC, *"Ukubuyisa* and *Ukuhlanza,"* Piet Meiring describes how in the face of sceptical lawyers, jurists and politicians, Tutu defined reconciliation by opening his Bible and quoting the Apostle Paul on the reconciliation that Christ accomplished through the cross.[2]

Looking Ahead

Nearly thirty years after the first universal franchise democratic election, South Africans have much to be grateful for, and most especially for open doors and freedom to preach the gospel and worship God according to individual conscience.

On re-reading this story of the church in South Africa, I have been reminded of the tremendous storms the people and the church in South Africa have gone through. There have been titanic conflicts between Dutch and Khoikhoi; British, Xhosa, Zulu and Afrikaner; black and white. The fact that the country has survived these storms and conflicts at all is a marvellous thing, and surely any impartial observer must acknowledge that the influence of the message of Christ working in all peoples has played a role in bringing us to the present situation.

Is the battle over? The storms have subsided to a large degree, but honesty compels us to admit that there are still fracture lines in our divided society and that our country is still rent with potentially explosive tensions between black and white, industry and labour, and so on. Could these tensions explode into new and more terrible storms than in the past? It would be foolish to deny the possibility. But while such negative scenarios cannot be totally discounted, it would be great mistake to ignore the fruits of the gospel seen in many communities and churches throughout the land. Signs of the Spirit can

---

1. https://en.wikipedia.org/wiki/Truth_and_Reconciliation_Commission_(South_Africa).

2. Meiring, "Ukubuyisa and Ukuhlanza," http://hdl.handle.net/2263/37086.

be seen in an extraordinarily wide variety of churches belonging to different denominations and traditions.

The work of Christ in South Africa has been going on for more than three hundred years, in the midst of political, economic and military storms. It will surely continue through whatever storms and conflicts lie ahead. William Carey, the pioneering missionary to India endured many trials and difficulties, yet when asked how he saw his prospects for the future, his response was, "The future is as bright as the promises of God." South Africans are often asked, "How do you see the future of your country?" Perhaps we must answer in the words of that great man of God – the future is as bright as the promises of God.

Bibliography

Alberts, L., and F. Chikane. *The Road to Rustenburg*. Cape Town: Struik, 1991.
Anderson, A. "African Pentecostalism." *Studia Historia Ecclesiastica* 12, no. 2 (1996): 114–148.
———. *Bazalwane: African Pentecostals in South Africa*. Pretoria: UNISA, 1992.
Barrett, D. B. "Global Statistics." In *Dictionary of Pentecostal and Charismatic Movements*. Edited by S. M. Burgess and G. B. McGee. Grand Rapids, MI: Zondervan, 1993.
Brain, J. B. *Catholic Beginnings in Natal and Beyond*. Durban: Griggs, 1975.
———. "Moving from the Margins to the Mainstream: The Roman Catholic Church." In *Christianity in South Africa*. Edited by R. Elphick and R. Davenport. Cape Town: David Philip, 1997.
Briggs, D. R., and J. Wing. *The Harvest and the Hope: The Story of Congregationalism in Southern Africa*. Johannesburg: UCCSA, 1970.
Brown, W. E. *The Catholic Church in South Africa*. London: Burns and Oates, 1960.
Burgess, S. M., and G. B. McGee, eds. *Dictionary of Pentecostal and Charismatic Movements*. Grand Rapids, MI: Zondervan, 1993.
Cameron, T., ed. *A New Illustrated History of South Africa*. Cape Town: Human & Rousseau, 1991.
Casalis, E. *Mes Souvenirs*. Paris: Fischbacher, 1884.
Cassidy, M. *The Passing Summer: A South African Pilgrimage in the Politics of Love*. London: Hodder, 1989.
Church and Society. Bloemfontein: General Synodical Commission, 1987.
Crafford, D. *Trail-Blazers of the Gospel: Black Pioneers in the Missionary History of South Africa*. Pretoria: Institute for Missiological Research, 1991.
Cronje, J. M. *Born to Witness: A Concise History of the Churches Born out of the Mission Work of the Dutch Reformed Church*. Pretoria: NGK, 1982.
Daneel, M. L. *Quest for Belonging: Introduction to a Study of African Independent Churches*. Gweru: Mambo Press, 1987.
Daneel, M. L., et al. *Missiology: The Church in the Third World*. Pretoria: UNISA, 1985.
Davies, H. *Great South African Christians*. Cape Town: Oxford, 1951.
Davies, H., and R. H. Shepherd, eds. *South African Missions 1800–1950*. Edinburgh: Thomas Nelson and Son, 1954.
De Gruchy, J. *The Church Struggle in South Africa*. Cape Town, David Philip, 1979.
De Kock, W. J., ed. *Dictionary of South African Biography*. Pretoria: Tafelberg, 1976.
Du Plessis, I. G. L. *'n Pentekostalisties–Charismaties Beskouing oor Kerkregeering*. Paper read to the South African Church History Society, Potchefstroom, 1989.

Du Plessis, J. *Life of Andrew Murray of South Africa*. London, Marshall, 1919.
Elphick, R., and R. Davenport, eds. *Christianity in South Africa: A Political, Social and Cultural History*. Cape Town: David Philip, 1997.
Elwell, W. A., ed. *Evangelical Dictionary of Theology*. Grand Rapids, MI: Baker, 1984.
Florin, H. W. *Lutherans in South Africa: Revised Report*. Durban: Lutheran Publishing Co., 1967.
Froise, M., ed. *South African Christian Handbook 1996/7*. Welkom: Christian Info, 1996.
Garnett, M. *Take Your Glory Lord*. Roodepoort: Baptist Publishing House, 1981.
Gerdener, G. B. A. *Bouers van Weleer*. Cape Town: NG Kerkuitgewers, 1951.
Gordon-Brown, C. "Impacting a Nation." *Today* 88 (Dec–Jan 1999)
Hanekom, T. M. *Helperus Ritzema van Lier*. Cape Town: NG Kerkuitgewers, 1959.
Hewson, L. *An Introduction to South African Methodists*. Cape Town: Standard Press, 1952.
Hinchliff, P. B. *The Church in South Africa*. London: SPCK, 1968.
———. *The Anglican Church in South Africa*. London: Darton, Longman & Todd, 1963.
Hofmeyr, J. W. *Church History: Study Guide 2 for KGB 200-S*. Pretoria: UNISA, 1986.
Hofmeyr, J. W., and G. J. Pillay, eds. *A History of Christianity in South Africa, Vol. 1*. Pretoria: HAUM, 1994.
Hofmeyr, J. W., J. A. Millard, and C. J. J. Froneman. *History of the Church in South Africa: A Document and Source Book*. Pretoria: UNISA, 1991.
Hudson-Reed, S. *By Taking Heed . . . The History of Baptists in Southern Africa 1820–1977*. Roodepoort: Baptist Publishing, 1980.
———, ed. *Together for a Century. The History of the Baptist Union of South Africa 1877–1977*. Pietermaritzburg: S. A. Baptist Historical Society, 1977.
Hulley, L., L. Kretzschmar, and L. L. Pato, eds. *Archbishop Tutu: Prophetic Witness in South Africa*. Cape Town: Human and Rousseau, 1996.
Kinghorn, J. "Modernization and Apartheid: The Afrikaner Churches." In *Christianity in South Africa: A Political, Social and Cultural History*. Edited by R. Elphick and R. Davenport. Cape Town: David Philip, 1997.
Krüger, B. *The Pear Tree Blossoms: A History of the Moravian Mission Stations in South Africa 1737–1869*. Genadendal: Moravian Church, 1967.
Lederle, H. I. *Systematic Theology: Study Guide on Charismatic Theology*. Pretoria: UNISA, 1983.
Lossky, N., et al. *Dictionary of the Ecumenical Movement*. Geneva: WCC, 1991.
Lovett. L. "Positive Confession Theology." In *Dictionary of Pentecostal and Charismatic Movements*. Edited by S. M. Burgess and G. B. McGee. Grand Rapids: Zondervan, 1993.
Makhubu, P. *Who Are the Independent Churches?* Johannesburg: Skotaville, 1988.

Matthews, S. K. *Freedom for My People*. Compiled and edited by M. Wilson. Cape Town: David Philip, 1983.
McGee, G. "Nicholas Bhekinkosi Hepworth Bhengu." In *Dictionary of Pentecostal and Charismatic Movements*. Edited by S. M. Burgess and G. B. McGee. Grand Rapids: Zondervan, 1993.
Meiring, P. J. G. "Ukubuyisa and Ukuhlanza: Reconciliation and the Washing of the Spears. The Role of the Faith Communities in the Quest for Healing and Reconciliation." *Nederduitse Gereformeerde Teologiese Tydskrif* 54, no. 384 (2013). http://hdl.handle.net/2263/37086.
Moller, F. *Ons pinkstererfenis*. Johannesburg: Evangelie Uitgewers, 1955.
Morphew, D. *Renewal Apologetics*. Cape Town: Vineyard Christian Fellowship, 1995.
Murray, A. *The Spirit of Christ*. London: Marshall, Morgan & Scott, 1972.
Neil, S. *A History of Christian Missions*. Harmondsworth: Penguin, 1984.
Oosthuizen, G. C. *Pentecostal Penetration into the Indian Community in South Africa*. Durban: HSRC, 1975.
Oosthuizen, G. C. and I. Hexham, eds. *Empirical Studies of African Independent/Indigenous Churches*. New York: Edward Mellen Press, 1992.
Orr, J. E. *Evangelical Awakenings in Africa*. Minneapolis, MN: Bethany, 1975.
Otto, I. *Rescue the Perishing: The Story of the Dorothea Mission*. Pretoria: Dorothea Mission, 1984.
Pillay, G. J. "Community Service and Conversion: Christianity among Indian South Africans." In *Christianity in South Africa: A Political, Social and Cultural History*. Edited by R. Elphick and R. Davenport. Cape Town: David Philip, 1997.
Pillay, G. J., and J. W. Hofmeyr, eds. *Perspectives on Church History*. Pretoria: HAUM, 1991.
Pobee. J. "Zachariah Keodirelang Matthews." In *Dictionary of the Ecumenical Movement*. Edited by N. Lossky. Geneva: WCC, 1991.
Pretorius, H. and L. Jafta. "'A Branch Springs Out': African Instituted Churches." In *Christianity in South Africa: A Political, Social and Cultural History*. Edited by R. Elphick and R. Davenport. Cape Town: David Philip, 1997.
Rossouw, P. *Ecumenical Panorama*. Pretoria: Dr Pierre Rossouw, 1989.
Ryan, C. *Beyers Naudé: Pilgrimage of Faith*. Cape Town: David Philip, 1990.
Saayman, W. A. *A Man with a Shadow: The Life and Times of Professor Z. K. Matthews*. Pretoria: UNISA, 1996.
Saunders, C., ed. *Illustrated History of South Africa – the Real Story*. Cape Town: Readers Digest, 1992.
Scriba, G. and G. Lislerud, "Lutheran Missions and Churches in South Africa." In *Christianity in South Africa: A Political, Social and Cultural History*. Edited by R. Elphick and R. Davenport. Cape Town: David Philip, 1997.

Shaw, B. "Memorials." In *South African Missions 1800–1950*. Edited by H. Davies and R. H. Shepherd. Edinburgh: Thomas Nelson & Son, 1954.

Shaw, W. *The Story of My Mission among the Native Tribes in South Africa*. London: Wesleyan Mission, 1872.

Skevington-Wood, A. "John Wesley." In *The New International Dictionary of the Christian Church*. Edited by J. D. Douglas. Exeter: Paternoster, 1974.

Spittler, R. P. "David Johannes du Plessis." In *Dictionary of Pentecostal and Charismatic Movements*. Edited by S. M. Burgess and G. B. McGee. Grand Rapids: Zondervan, 1993.

Storey, P. *Our Methodist Roots*. Cape Town: Methodist Publishing, 1981.

Strassberger, E. *Ecumenism in South Africa 1936–1960*. Johannesburg: SACC, 1974.

Sundkler, B. G. M. *Bantu Prophets in South Africa*. London: Oxford University Press, 1961.

———. *Zulu Zion and Some Swazi Zionists*. London: Oxford University Press, 1976.

The Kairos Document. Second Edition. Johannesburg: Skotaville, 1986.

Tlhagale, B., and I. Mosala, eds. *Hammering Swords into Ploughshares. Essays in Honour of Archbishop Desmond Tutu*. Johannesburg: Skotaville, 1986.

Van der Watt, P. B. *Die Nederduitse Gereformeerde Kerk 1652–1824*. Pretoria: N. G. Kerkboekhandel, 1976.

Walshe, P. "Christianity and the Anti-Apartheid Struggle: The Prophetic Voice within Divided Churches." In *Christianity in South Africa: A Political, Social and Cultural History*. Edited by R. Elphick and R. Davenport. Cape Town: David Philip, 1997.

Watt, C. P. *The Assemblies of God: A Missiological Evaluation*. Unpublished MTh Thesis: UNISA, 1991.

Index

A
Africa Enterprise 200
Africa Evangelistic Band (AEB) 183
African Congregational Church 107
African Gospel Church 134
African Instituted (or Independent) Churches 131
African Methodist Episcopal Church (AMEC) 106
African National Congress 3, 146, 159, 211
African National Congress (ANC) 56, 58, 160, 164, 165, 167, 168, 174, 196, 211, 220
Afrikaans 28
Afrikaans Baptist church 64
Afrikaanse Protestante Kerk (Afrikaans Protestant Church) 210
Afrikaner, Jager 72
AIDS 215
Alberts, Louw 211
Allard, François 68
Ama-Nazaretha 138
AmaZioni 113, 119, 120, 141
André, Ellis 213
Anglicans 44
Anglo-Catholics 45
Apartheid 147, 188, 209
Apostolic Faith Mission (AFM) 119, 120, 123, 124, 130, 131, 133, 135, 137, 214, 218
Assemblies of God (AG) 127, 128, 129, 218, 219

B
Back to God Crusade 128
Baird, David 66
Baldeus, Philippus 13
Bantu Methodist Church 107
Bapedi Lutheran Church 120
Baptist Convention 215
Baptists 62
Baptist Union 63, 64, 159, 201, 205, 213, 215
Barrett, David B. 203
Baviaanskloof 19, 25, 26
Berlin Missionary Society (BMS) 109
Bethelsdorp 35
Bethesda Temple 124
Bhengu, Nicholas 128, 178
Biko, Steve 194
Bishopstowe 100
bittereinders 115, 170
Blourokkies 130
Boesak, Alan 194
Boraine, Alex 221
Bosch, David 174, 200
Botha, Louis 117
Botha, P. W. 192, 198, 199, 210
Bowie, George 123
Brain, J. B. 67
Brander, Samuel 107
Broederbond 170
Brownlee 40
Bryant, Daniel 118
Büchler, Johannes 118
Bulhoek Massacre 142
Buntingville 53
Burgers, T. F. 98, 99
Burnett, Bill 187, 188, 189, 192
Buthelezi, Manas 213
Butterworth 53

C
Cachet, Frans Lion 98
Cachet, Jan Lion 86
Carey, William 32, 64, 147, 222
Carr, Burgess 191
Casalis, Jean-Eugène 43
Cassidy, Michael 200, 212

Cattle Killing Tragedy 59
Cetshwayo 102
Charismatic churches 202
Charismatic movement 192, 203
Chawner, William 127
Chikane, Frank 211
Chiliza, Job 134
Christian Catholic Apostolic Holy Spirit Church in Zion 131
Christian Catholic Church in Zion (CCCZ) 118, 119
Christian City 219
Christian Council of South Africa (CCSA) 150, 151, 153, 158, 187
Christian Fellowship International 208, 213, 219
Christian Institute (CI) 173, 174, 187, 194
Christian Ministries Network 209
"Church and Society" 198, 209
Church of England in South Africa 47
Church of the Province of South Africa 47
Clarkebury 53
Coillard, François 150
Colenso, Bishop 47, 99
coloureds 28
Communist Party 211
concentration camps 115, 149
Congregationalists 32, 33, 37, 46, 62, 118, 164
Congregation of Missionaries of Mariannhill 70
conscientious objection 191
Cooper, Archibald 123, 134
Cottesloe 160, 164, 168, 171, 173, 187, 189
Council of Seventeen 16
Crumpton, Derek 209

D

da Costa, Isaac 86
Da Gama, Vasco 7
Daniels, Dudley 209
De Blank, Joost 161
Defiance Campaign 159, 168
De Klerk, F. W. 210, 211
Devereux, Aidan 67
De Vries, J. C. 93
Diaz, Bartholomew 7, 65
Dingaan 82, 83, 139, 140
Dlamini, Paulina 109
Doppers 86, 87
Dorothea Mission 182
Dowie, John Alexander 118, 120
Drakenstein 13
Duma, William 175
Du Plessis, Johannes 74
Du Plessis, David (Mr Pentecost) 122, 192, 212
Dutch East India Company (DEIC) 1, 7
Dutch Reformed 28
Dutch Reformed Church 1, 158
Dwane, James 106

E

Ecumenical Movement 122, 147, 192, 200
Ekukanyeni 100
Ekuphakameni 139
Ethiopian Catholic Church in Zion 107
Ethiopian Church 104
Ethiopianism 102
Eva 11
Evangelical Lutheran Church in Southern Africa 110, 213
Exorcism 177

F

"Faith and Protest" 210
Federal Mission Council (FMC) 153, 154, 155
Foundation Ministries 208
Francke, Hermann August 15
Franschoek 13
Fraser, Maria 130
Freedom Charter 168

Full Gospel Church (FGC) 123, 134, 218, 219

G
Gandhi 126
Genadendal 19, 27
General Missionary Conference (GMC) 150
Gerard, Father 68
Gereformeerde Kerk (GK) 86, 87
German Baptists 63, 64
Glasgow Missionary Society 56
Goodall, Norman 156
Govan, William 56
Gray, Robert 45, 67, 100, 101
Great Trek 79, 82, 85, 114, 149
Griffith, Raymond 66
Grout, Aldin 94
Gutsche, Hugo 63, 64, 65

H
Hagin, Kenneth 205, 206
Harms, Ludwig 109
Hatfield Baptist Church 204
Hatfield Christian Church 205, 218
Hermannsburg Mission Society (HMS) 109
Herrnhuters 15
Hewson, Leslie 168
Heyns, Johan A. 174, 197, 209, 212
Hezmalhalch, Thomas 119
Hillsong 219
Hinchliff, Peter 41, 117
His People 209, 219
Hofmeyr, J. W. xii, xiii
Hofmeyr, N. J. 94
Holiness Movement 117, 202
Hottentot xii, 14
Huddleston, Trevor 195
Huguenots 13
Huguenot Seminary 90

I
Institute for Contextual Theology 199, 212

International Fellowship of Christian Churches (IFCC) 205, 206, 207, 208, 213, 219

J
Jolivet, Charles 68, 69
Jonker, W. D. (Willie) 197, 212

K
Kairos Document 199
Keet, B. B. (Bennie) 159, 171, 174
Kendrick, Sergeant 49
KhoiKhoi 10
Koinonia Declaration 197
Kolver, Andreas 21
Kotzé, J. J. 99
Kruger, Paul 115
Kühnel 26
Kuruman 72
Kwena 76

L
Lake, John G. 119
Langalibalele 102
Latter Rain Assemblies 130
Leaves of Healing 118
Lekganyane, Engenas 134, 135
Leliefontein 50
Lena 26
Le Roux, Pieter L. 118, 119, 120, 131, 135, 137
Letwaba, Elias 120, 121, 122
Lindley, Daniel 82, 85
Livingstone, David 56, 75, 76
lobola 84, 97
London Missionary Society 33, 71
Lovedale 56
Lutherans 20, 108
Luther, Martin 108
Luthuli, Albert 159, 160, 164

M
Mackenzie, John 76
Mahlangu, Elias 131
Mahon, Edgar 118
Makhubu, Paul 135, 146

Malan, D. F. 154, 156
Maloka, Shadrack 184
Mandela, Nelson 3, 61, 160, 195, 211
Marais, Ben 159, 170, 171, 174
Mariannhill 68
Marie-Gertrude 67
Maritz, Gert 82
Marsveld 26
Masango, Petros 137
Matthews, Z. K. 161, 164, 166
Maurice, F. D. 99, 101
McCauley, Ray 205, 212
Melck, Martin 21
Message to the People of South Africa 188
Methodists 46
Mgijima, Enoch 142
Mgojo, Khoza 200, 212
Mgwali 57
Mhlakaza 59
Miller, William 62
Moffat, Robert 71
Mogoba, Stanley 214
Mokone, Mangena 106
Moravians 14, 20, 25
Moriah 136
Morley 53
Morphew, Derek 209
Moshoeshoe 68
Motaung, Edward 122, 133, 135, 137
Mott, John R. 148, 151
Mount Coke 53
Murray, Andrew 85, 87, 89, 93, 94, 99, 118, 122, 183
Murray du Toit, J. 152
Murray, John 88
Mvuyana, Gardiner 107
Mzilikazi 74, 75, 82, 83
Mzimba, P.J. 107

N
Namaquas 49
Napier, Wilfrid 212
National Initiative for Reconciliation 200
National Party (NP) 131, 149, 154, 156, 158, 163, 170, 172, 197, 201, 210
National Thembu Church 104
Naudé, Beyers 160, 169, 187, 188, 189, 194, 209
Ndebele 75, 83
Nederduitsch Hervormde Kerk (NHK) 85, 87
Newbigin, Lesslie 203
New Covenant Ministries 209
New Frontiers 209, 219
Ngqika 34, 39, 57
Nicol, W. 152, 153
Nkonyane, Daniel 131
Nkosi, Sikelel' iAfrika 96
Nku, Ma Christina 137
Nongquase 59
Norwegian Mission Society 109
Ntabelanga 143
Ntsikana 35, 38

O
Odendaal, J. D. 64
Oncken, Johan 62, 63
Order of Ethiopia 106
Ordinance Fifty 42
Oxford Movement 45

P
Paarl 13
Pamla, Charles 55, 95, 96
Pan Africanist Congress 160, 211
Pape, Carl 64
Parham, Charles 119
Paris Evangelical Missionary Society 43, 68, 102
Pentecostal Protestant Church 131
Pentecostals 131
Pfanner, Franz 68
Philip, John 41
Plütschau 16
Postma, Dirk 86
Presbyterian Church of Southern Africa 215
Presbyterians 55

Programme to Combat Racism 190
Pro Veritate 172

R

Rangiah, John 65
Ras, Volk en Nasie 193
Read, James 35
Reformation Day Witness 197
Reformed Presbyterian Church in
 Southern Africa 215
Reichel, Johann 26
Retief, Piet 81, 83
Revival 92
Rhema Bible Church 205, 206, 219
Rhenish Missionary Society
 (RMS) 108
Rhodes, Cecil John 115
Roberts, Fred 208
Roebert, Edmund 204, 205, 208
Roman Catholics 13, 32, 65
Rowlands, John Francis 124
Rustenburg Conference 211

S

Saint John Apostolic Faith 137
Sargent, William 95
Schmelen 49
Schmidt, George 14
Schreuder, H. P. S. 109
Schwinn 26
Sechele 76
Second Anglo-Boer War 113, 114, 119, 149, 169
Senzangakhona 140
Settlers, 1820 51
Shaka 74, 140
Sharpeville 158, 160, 164, 165, 168, 171
Shaw, Barnabas 49
Shaw, William 51
Shembe Church 219
Shembe, Isaiah 138
Shembe, Johannes Galilee 140
slaves 11, 23, 28, 78
Smit, Erasmus 82
Smuts, Jan 117, 144, 170, 184

Smyth, John 62
Snyman, J. H. 131
Sobukwe, Robert 160, 165
Soga, Tiyo 57
South African Council of Churches
 (SACC) 114, 153, 174, 187, 189, 190, 191, 193, 194, 195, 201, 208, 211, 213
South African Interchurch
 Network 208
South African Republic (SAR) 85, 89, 109, 114
Spener, Philip 15
Stellenbosch 14
Stewart, James 56, 107, 150
Stormkompas 197
Sundkler, Bengt 131, 132, 133, 134, 138, 140, 141, 143, 145
Synod of Dort 8, 12

T

Taylor, J. Dexter 151
Taylor, William 95, 96
Thom, George 41, 55
t'Hooft, Visser 168
Tile, Nehemiah 104
Tlhaping 74
Tractarians 45
Trappists 69
Treurnicht, Andries P. 173, 209
Turney, R. M. 127
Tutu, Desmond 194, 200, 212, 213, 216, 221

U

Umgeni Road Baptist Church 177, 179, 181, 182
United Congregational Church 33
Uniting Reformed Church 214

V

Van Arckel, Johan 12
Van der Hoff, Dirk 85, 86
Van Lier, Helperus Ritzema 21
Van Riebeeck, Jan 8
Verwoerd, Hendrik 161, 163, 170, 172

Vineyard Churches 209, 219
Von Staden, Hans 182
Vorster, John 170, 189, 195, 209
Vorster, Koot 190
Vos, Michael Christiaan 24

W

Wakkerstroom 118
Waterboer 74
Wellington Missionary Training
    Institute 90
Wesley, John 15, 20, 48, 117
Wesleyville 53
Wessels, G. R. 130
Williams 39
World Council of Churches (WCC)
    122, 148, 163, 168, 169, 172, 188,
    190, 193
Wylant, William 10

Z

Ziegenbalg 16
Zinzendorf 15
Zion Apostolic Church of South
    Africa 131
Zion Apostolic Faith Mission
    (ZAFM) 133
Zion Christian Church (ZCC) 135, 219
Zionists 117, 118, 119, 120, 131, 132,
    134, 136, 145, 147, 219, 220
Zule, Alphaeus 161
Zulu Congregational Church 107

Langham Literature and its imprints are a ministry of Langham Partnership.

Langham Partnership is a global fellowship working in pursuit of the vision God entrusted to its founder John Stott –

> *to facilitate the growth of the church in maturity and Christ-likeness through raising the standards of biblical preaching and teaching.*

Our vision is to see churches in the majority world equipped for mission and growing to maturity in Christ through the ministry of pastors and leaders who believe, teach and live by the Word of God.

Our mission is to strengthen the ministry of the Word of God through:
- nurturing national movements for biblical preaching
- fostering the creation and distribution of evangelical literature
- enhancing evangelical theological education

especially in countries where churches are under-resourced.

Our ministry

Langham Preaching partners with national leaders to nurture indigenous biblical preaching movements for pastors and lay preachers all around the world. With the support of a team of trainers from many countries, a multi-level programme of seminars provides practical training, and is followed by a programme for training local facilitators. Local preachers' groups and national and regional networks ensure continuity and ongoing development, seeking to build vigorous movements committed to Bible exposition.

Langham Literature provides majority world preachers, scholars and seminary libraries with evangelical books and electronic resources through publishing and distribution, grants and discounts. The programme also fosters the creation of indigenous evangelical books in many languages, through writer's grants, strengthening local evangelical publishing houses, and investment in major regional literature projects, such as one volume Bible commentaries like *The Africa Bible Commentary* and *The South Asia Bible Commentary*.

Langham Scholars provides financial support for evangelical doctoral students from the majority world so that, when they return home, they may train pastors and other Christian leaders with sound, biblical and theological teaching. This programme equips those who equip others. Langham Scholars also works in partnership with majority world seminaries in strengthening evangelical theological education. A growing number of Langham Scholars study in high quality doctoral programmes in the majority world itself. As well as teaching the next generation of pastors, graduated Langham Scholars exercise significant influence through their writing and leadership.

To learn more about Langham Partnership and the work we do visit **langham.org**

www.ingramcontent.com/pod-product-compliance
Lightning Source LLC
Chambersburg PA
CBHW071228170426
43191CB00032B/1092